Closed Circuit Television

Closed Circuit Television

Second edition

Joe Cieszynski
IEng MIEE (elec) Cert. Ed. CGI

ELSEVIER

AMSTERDAM • BOSTON • HEIDELBERG • LONDON • NEW YORK •OXFORD
PARIS • SAN DIEGO • SAN FRANCISCO • SINGAPORE • SYDNEY • TOKYO

Newnes is an imprint of Elsevier

Newnes

Newnes
An imprint of Elsevier
Linacre House, Jordan Hill, Oxford OX2 8DP
200 Wheeler Road, Burlington, MA 01803

First published 2001
Reprinted 2002
Second edition 2004

British Library Cataloguing in Publication Data
A catalogue record for this book is available from the British Library

ISBN 0 7506 5728 6

For more information on all Newnes publications
visit our website at www.newnespress.com

Typeset by Replika Press Pvt Ltd, India
Printed and bound in Great Britain

Contents

Preface

In the preface to the first edition I wrote that closed circuit television (CCTV) was a growth industry, and that the growth was very much a result of the impact of new technology. As I write this preface to the second edition of *Closed Circuit Television*, this situation has not changed. Technology has continued to advance, bringing with it the possibility of much clearer images even in conditions where a few years ago it would have been impossible to film. Add to this the advances in digital recording, high speed data transmission and biometric recognition and alarm systems, and we have the ability to design and install CCTV systems that just a few years ago were the stuff of science fiction.

However, like any high tech installation, these systems will only function correctly if they are properly specified, installed and maintained. Consequently a CCTV engineer needs to be conversant with modern electrical, electronics, digital and microprocessor principles, electrical installation practice, health and safety issues and telecommunications and broadband technology, in addition to having an in-depth knowledge of CCTV principles and technology.

This book has been written to provide the latter in the above list – a knowledge of CCTV principles and technology. Like the first edition, it uses the City & Guilds/SITO Knowledge of Security and Emergency Alarm Systems syllabus (course 1851) as its basis, making it suitable reading for trainees studying towards this qualification or for those who are working towards an NVQ level II or III in CCTV installation and maintenance. However, to cater for those who are already practising in the industry but who wish to further their technical knowledge and understanding, this second edition includes discussion of such topics as digital video signal compression, digital tape and hard disk recording, and CAT5 structured cabling.

This second edition includes two completely new chapters covering lighting and ancillary equipment. Furthermore, where the first edition was devoted primarily to the UK PAL television system, having noted that the book was being purchased in somewhat large numbers across the Atlantic in the USA, it was felt only right that this new edition should incorporate NTSC television standards.

It is my hope and wish that trainees and engineers alike will find this a useful handbook and aid towards their personal development.

Joe Cieszynski

Acknowledgements

I would personally wish to thank all of those who have helped in the production of this book by providing information and/or support. I should mention Andrew Holmes of Data Compliance Ltd, David Grant of ACT Meters, Gar Ning of NG Systems, Martin Kane, Simon Nash of Pelco UK Ltd and Simon Liddy and Steve Pilling of PAC International Ltd.

There are some people who I would like to thank in particular: Ian Fowler of Norbain SD Ltd for his patient proofreading of parts of the book, and for the many times that he made himself available to discuss aspects of theory and technology; David, Hannah, John and Ruth my four (grown-up) children for their patience with me during what, at times, appeared to be the endless writing stage; and Linda my wife for her much-appreciated support.

1 The CCTV industry

The term 'closed circuit' refers to the fact that the system is self-contained, the signals only being accessible by equipment within the system. This is in contrast to 'broadcast television', where the signals may be accessed by anyone with the correct receiving equipment.

The initial development of television took place during the 1930s, and a number of test transmissions were carried out in Europe and America. In the UK these were from the Crystal Palace transmitter in London. The outbreak of the Second World War brought an abrupt end to much of the television development, although interestingly transmissions continued to be made from occupied Paris using an experimental system operating from the Eiffel Tower; the German propaganda machine was very interested in this new form of media.

Ironically, the war was to give television the boost it needed in terms of technology development because in the UK it seemed like every scientist who knew anything about radio transmission and signals was pressed into the accelerated development programme for radar and radio. Following the war many of these men found themselves in great demand from companies eager to renew the development of television.

Early black and white pictures were of poor resolution, however the success of the medium meant that the money became available to develop new and better equipment, and to experiment with new ideas. At the same time the idea of using cameras and monitors as a means of monitoring an area began to take a hold. However, owing to the high cost of equipment, these early CCTV systems were restricted to specialized activity, and to organizations that had the money to invest in such security. These systems were of limited use because an operator had to be watching the screen constantly; there was no means of recording video images in the 1950s, and motion detection connected to some form of alarm was the stuff of James Bond (only even he did not arrive until the 1960s!).

Throughout the 1960s and 1970s CCTV technology progressed slowly, following in the footsteps of the broadcast industry which had the money to finance new developments. The main stumbling block lay in the camera technology which depended completely on vacuum tubes as a pick-up device. Tubes are large, require high voltages to operate, are generally useless in low light conditions (although special types were developed – for a price), and are expensive. Furthermore, an early colour camera required three of these tubes. For this reason throughout these years CCTV remained on the whole a low resolution, monochrome system which was very expensive.

By the 1980s camera technology was improving, and the cost of a reasonable colour camera fell to a sum that was affordable to smaller businesses and organizations. Also, VHS had arrived. This had quite an impact on the industry because for the first time it was possible to record CCTV images on equipment that cost well below £1000. Prior to this, CCTV could be recorded on monochrome reel-to-reel machines, however these were expensive and were not exactly user-friendly.

From the mid 1980s onwards television technology advanced in quantum leaps. New developments such as the CMOS microchip and charge coupled device (CCD) chip brought about an increase in equipment capability and greatly improved picture quality, whilst at the same time equipment prices plummeted. Manufacturers such as Panasonic and Sony developed digital video recording machines, and although these were intended primarily for use in the broadcast industry (at £50000 for a basic model the CCTV industry was not in a hurry to include one with every installation!), they paved the way for digital video signal processing in lower resolution CCTV and domestic video products.

Up until recently, CCTV has had to rely on its big brother the broadcast industry to develop new technologies, and then wait for these technologies to be downgraded so that they become affordable to customers who cannot afford to pay £30000 per camera and £1000 per monitor. However, the technology explosion that we are currently seeing is changing this. PC technology is rapidly changing our traditional ideas of viewing and recording video and sound, and much of this hardware is inexpensive. Also, whereas in the early years the CCTV industry relied largely on the traditional broadcast and domestic television equipment manufacturers to design the equipment, there are now a number of established manufacturers that are dedicated to CCTV equipment design and production. These manufacturers are already taking both hardware and concepts from other electronics industries and integrating them to develop CCTV equipment that not only produces high quality pictures but is versatile, designed to allow easy system expansion, user-friendly, and can be controlled from anywhere on the planet without having to sacrifice one of its most valuable assets – which is that it is a closed circuit system.

The role of CCTV

So often CCTV is seen as a security tool. Well of course it is, however it also plays equally important roles in the areas of monitoring and control. For example, motorway camera systems are invaluable for monitoring the flow of traffic, enabling police, motoring organizations and local radio to be used to warn drivers of problems, and thus control situations. And in the case of a police chase, control room operators can assist the police in directing their resources. The same of course applies to town centre CCTV systems.

CCTV has become an invaluable tool for organizations involved in anything to do with security, crowd control, traffic control, etc. Yet on the other hand the proliferation of cameras in every public place is ringing alarm bells among those who are mindful of George Orwell's book *Nineteen Eighty-Four*. Indeed, in the wrong hands, or in the hands of the sort of police state depicted in that book, CCTV could be used for all manner of subversive activity. In fact the latest technology has gone beyond the predictions of Mr Orwell. Face recognition systems which generate an alarm as soon as it appears in a camera view have been developed, as have systems that track a person automatically once they have been detected. Other equipment which can see through a disguise by using parameters that make up a human, such as scull dimensions and relative positions of extreme features (nose, ears, etc.), or the way that a person walks, is likewise under development. At the time of writing all such systems are still somewhat experimental and are by no means perfected, however with the current rate of technological advancement we can only be a few years away from this equipment being installed as standard in systems in town centres, department stores, night clubs and anywhere else where the authorities would like early recognition of 'undesirables'.

To help control the use of CCTV in the UK the changes made to the Data Protection Act in 1998 meant that images from CCTV systems were now included. Unlike the earlier 1984 Act, this has serious implications for the *owners* of CCTV systems as it makes them legally responsible for the management, operation and control of the system and, perhaps more importantly, the recorded material or 'data' produced by their system. The Data Protection Act 1998 requires that all non-domestic CCTV systems are registered with the Information Commissioner. Clear signs must be erected in areas covered by CCTV warning people that they are being monitored and/or recorded. The signs must state the name of the 'data controller' of the system and have contact details. When registering a system, the data controller must state its specific uses and the length of time that material will be retained. Recorded material must be stored in a secure fashion and must not be passed into the public domain unless it is deemed to be in the public interest or in the interests of criminal investigations (i.e. the display of images on police-orientated programmes).

On 2 October 1998 the Human Rights Act became effective in the UK. The emphasis on the rights to privacy (among other things) has strong implications for CCTV used by 'public authorities' as defined by the Act, and system designers and installers should take note of these implications. Cameras that are capable of targeting private dwellings or grounds (even if that is not their real intention) may be found to be in contravention of the rights of the people living there. As such, those people may take legal action to have the cameras disabled or removed – an expensive undertaking for the owner or, perhaps, the installing company who specified the camera system and/or locations.

In relation to CCTV, the intention of both the Data Protection and Human Rights Acts is to ensure that CCTV is itself properly managed, monitored and policed, thus protecting against it becoming a law unto itself in the future.

The arguments surrounding the uses and abuses of CCTV will no doubt continue, however it is a well-proven fact that CCTV has made a huge positive impact on the lives of people who live under its watchful eye. It has been proven time and again that both people and their possessions are more secure where CCTV is in operation, that people are much safer in crowded public places because the crowd can be better monitored and controlled, and possessions and premises are more secure because they can be watched 24 hours per day.

The CCTV industry

Despite what we have said about CCTV being used for operations other than security, it can never fully escape its potential for security applications because, whatever its intended use, if the police or any other public security organization suspect that vital evidence may have been captured on a system, they will inspect the recorded material. This applies all the way down to a member of the public who, whilst innocently using a camcorder, captures either an incident or something relating to an incident. For this reason it is perhaps not surprising to hear that the CCTV industry is largely regulated and monitored by the same people and organizations that monitor the security industry as a whole.

The British Security Industry Association (BSIA) Ltd is the only UK trade association for the security industry that requires its members to undergo independent inspection to ensure they meet relevant standards. The association has over 500 members and represents thirteen different sectors of the industry. There are 50 CCTV companies in membership, representing approximately 75% of the UK turnover for this sector. The BSIA's primary role is to promote and encourage high standards of products and services throughout the industry for the benefit of customers. This includes working with its members to produce codes of practice, which regularly go on to become full British/European standards. The BSIA also lobbies government on legislation that may impact on the industry and actively liaises with other relevant organizations, for example the Office of the Information Commissioner (in relation to the Data Protection Act) and the Police Scientific Development Branch. The BSIA also provides an invaluable service in producing technical literature and training materials for its members and their customers.

Inspectorate bodies are charged with the role of policing the installation companies, making sure that they are conforming to the Codes of Practice. Of course, a company has to agree to place itself under the canopy of an Inspectorate, but in doing so it is able to advertise this fact and gives it immediate recognition with insurance companies and police authorities.

To become an approved installer a company must submit to a rigorous inspection by its elected Inspectorate. This inspection includes not only the quality of the physical installation, but every part of the organization. Typically, the inspector will wish to see how documentation relating to every stage of an installation is processed and stored, how maintenance and service records are kept, how material and equipment is ordered, etc. In addition the inspector will wish to see evidence that the organization has sufficient personnel, vehicles and equipment to meet maintenance requirements and breakdown response times.

In some cases the organization is expected to obtain BS EN ISO 9002 quality assurance (QA) accreditation within two years of becoming an approved installer. At the time of writing there is no specific requirement that engineers working for an approved installation company hold a National Vocational Qualification (NVQ) in security and emergency systems engineering, however this may well become the case in the future.

Another significant body is the Security Industry Training Organization (SITO Ltd). SITO is responsible for the development of training standards for the security industry, and is recognized and approved by the DfES for this function. During recent years SITO has worked to develop NVQs as well as other awards for all sectors of the security industry, and in relation to CCTV engineering have developed awards to NVQ levels II and III. These awards are jointly accredited by SITO and City & Guilds.

City & Guilds are an established and recognized examinations body. With regard to the security industry, apart from awarding certificates to successful NVQ candidates, the City & Guilds appoint the external verifiers whose role it is to check that NVQ assessment centres, be these colleges, training organizations or installing companies, are carrying out the assessments to the recognized standards.

The City & Guilds also offer the Underpinning Knowledge test papers (course 1851) for the four disciplines relating to security and emergency system engineering; these being CCTV, intruder alarm, access control and fire alarm systems. These awards are intended to contribute towards the underpinning knowledge testing for the NVQ level III award, although a candidate may elect to sit these tests without pursuing an NVQ. It must be stressed, however, that the 1851 award is not an alternative qualification to an NVQ, and a person holding only the 1851 certificates would not be deemed to be qualified until they have proven their competence in security system engineering.

The Home Office department of the Police Scientific Development Branch (PSDB) play a most significant role in CCTV. For many years the CCTV industry had no set means of measuring the performance of its systems in terms of picture quality, resolution and the size of images as they appear on a monitor screen. This meant that in the absence of any benchmarks to work to, each surveyor or installer would simply do what they considered best. This situation was not only unsatisfactory for the industry, potential customers were in a position where they had no way of knowing what they could expect from a system and, once installed, had no real redress if they were unhappy, because there was nothing for them to measure the system performance against.

The PSDB set about devising practical methods of defining and measuring such things as picture resolution and image size and, for example, in 1989 introduced the Rotakin method of testing the resolution and size of displayed images (see Chapter 12). They have also developed methods of analysing and documenting the needs of customers prior to designing a CCTV system. This is known as an Operational Requirement (OR).

CCTV is currently a growth industry. It has proven its effectiveness beyond all doubt, and the availability of high quality, versatile equipment at a relatively low cost has resulted in a huge demand for systems of all sizes. Within the industry there is a genuine need for engineers who truly understand the technology they are dealing with, and who have the level of underpinning knowledge in both CCTV and electronics principles that will enable them to learn and understand new technologies as they appear.

2 Signal transmission

A CCTV video signal contains a wide range of a.c. components with frequencies between 0–5.5 MHz, in addition to a d.c. component, and problems occur when engineers consider a video signal in the same terms as a low voltage d.c. or low frequency mains supply. However, when you consider that domestic medium wave radio is transmitted around 1 MHz, then it becomes clear that the 0–5.5 MHz video signal is going to behave in a similar manner to radio signals.

In this chapter we shall examine the peculiar way in which radio frequency signals behave when they are passed along cables, and therefore explain the need for special cables when transmitting video signals.

CCTV signals

An electronically produced square wave signal is actually built up from a sinusoidal wave (known as the fundamental) and an infinite number of odd harmonics (odd multiples of the fundamental frequency). This basic idea is illustrated in Figure 2.1 where it can be seen that the addition of

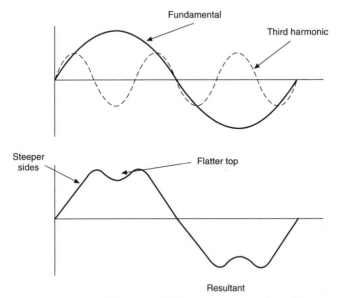

Figure 2.1 *Effect of the addition of odd harmonics to a sinusoidal waveshape*

just one odd harmonic component changes the appearance of the fundamental sine wave, moving it towards a square shape.

If we reverse this process, i.e. begin with a square wave and remove some of the harmonic components using filters, then the corners of the square wave become rounded, and the rise time becomes longer. This effect is illustrated in Figure 2.2.

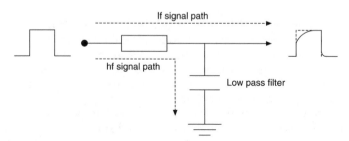

Figure 2.2 *Removal of high frequency harmonic components reduces the rise time and rounds the corners*

In Chapter 5 we shall be looking at the make-up of the video signal (Figure 5.18), and we will see that it contains square wave components. It is the sharp rise times and right-angled corners in the video signal waveform which produce the high definition edges and high resolution areas of the picture. If for any reason the signal is subjected to a filtering action resulting in the loss of harmonics, the reproduced picture will be of poor resolution and may have a smeary appearance. Now one may wonder how a video signal could be 'accidentally' filtered, and yet it is actually quite possible because all cables contain elements of resistance, capacitance and inductance; the three most commonly used components in the construction of electronic filter circuits. When a signal is passed along a length of cable it is exposed to the effects of these R, C, L components.

The actual effect the cable has on a signal is dependent on a number of factors, which include the type and construction of cable, the cable length, the way in which bends have been formed, the type and quality of connectors and the range of frequencies (bandwidth) contained within the signal. This means that, with respect to CCTV installations, it is important that correct cable types are used, that the correct connectors are used for a given cable type, that the cable is installed in the correct specified manner and that maximum run lengths are not exceeded without suitable means of compensation for signal loss.

Different cable types are used for the transmission of CCTV video signals and, indeed, methods other than copper cable transmission are employed. Both the surveyor and the installing engineer need to be aware of the performance and limitations of the various transmission media, as well as the installation methods that must be employed for each medium.

Co-axial cable

The behaviour of high frequency signals in a copper conductor is not the same as that of d.c. or low frequencies such as 50/60 Hz mains or audio, and specially constructed cables are required to ensure constant impedance across a range of frequencies. Furthermore, radio frequency signals have a tendency to see every copper conductor as a potential receiving aerial, meaning that a conductor carrying an RF signal is prone to picking up stray RF from any number of sources, for example emissions from such things as electric motors, fluorescent lights, etc., or even legitimate radio transmissions. Co-axial cable is designed to meet the unique propagation requirements of radio frequency signals, offering constant impedance over a range of frequencies and some protection against unwanted noise pick-up.

There are many types of co-axial cable, all manifesting different figures for signal loss, impedance, screening capability and cost. The construction of a co-axial cable determines the characteristics for a particular cable type, the basic physical construction being illustrated in Figure 2.3.

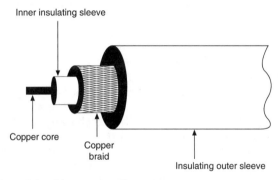

Figure 2.3 *Co-axial cable construction*

The signal-carrying conductor is the copper central core, which may be a solid copper conductor or stranded wire. The signal return path could be considered to be along the braided screen, however, as this is connected to the earth of a system, the signal may in practice return to its source via any number of paths. However, the screen plays a far more important role than simply to serve as a signal return path. It provides protection against *radio frequency interference* (RFI). The way that it achieves this is illustrated in Figure 2.4, where it can be seen that external RF sources in close proximity of the cable are attracted to the copper braided screen, from where they pass to earth via the equipment at either end of the cable. Provided that the integrity of the screen is maintained at every point along the cable run from the camera to the monitor, there is no way that unwanted RF signals can enter either the inner core of the co-axial cable or the signal processing circuits in the equipment, which will themselves be screened, usually by the metal equipment casing.

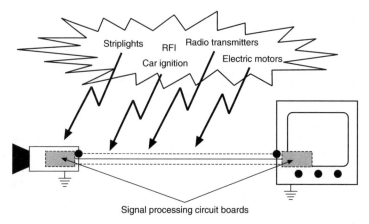

Signal processing circuit boards

Figure 2.4 *RFI is contained by the copper screen, preventing it entering the signal processing circuits*

Integrity of the screen is maintained by ensuring that there are no breaks in the screen at any point along the cable length, and that all connectors are of the correct type for the cable and have been fitted correctly. We shall consider connectors later in this chapter, but the issue of breaks in the screen is one which we need to consider. Co-axial cable is more than a simple piece of wire, and only functions correctly when certain criteria have been met in relation to terminations and joints. Under no circumstances should a joint be made by simply twisting a pair of cores together and taping them up before twisting and taping the two screens. Although this might appear to be electrically correct, it breaks all the rules of RF theory and, among other things, exposes the inner core to RFI. All joins should be made using a correctly fitted connector (usually BNC) on each cable end, with a coupling piece inserted in between.

Where RFI is present in a video signal, it usually manifests itself as a faint, moving, patterning effect superimposed onto the picture. The size and speed of movement of the pattern depends on the frequency of the interfering signal.

The inner sleeve of the co-axial cable performs a much more important function than simply insulation between the two conductors; it forms a dielectric between the conductors which introduces a capacitive element into the cable. This cable capacitance works in conjunction with the natural d.c. resistance and inductance to produce a *characteristic impedance* (Z_o) for the cable. One of the factors which governs the value of a capacitor is the type of dielectric (insulator) used between the plates, and co-axial cables of differing impedances are produced by using different materials for the inner core. This is why not all co-axial cables are suitable for CCTV applications, and why a connector designed for one cable type will not fit onto certain other types; the cable diameter varies depending upon the dielectric. The equivalent circuit of a co-axial cable is shown in Figure 2.5.

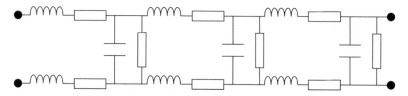

Figure 2.5 *Equivalent circuit of a co-axial cable, also known as a transmission line*

The characteristic impedance for a cable of infinite length can be found from the equation $Z_0 = \sqrt{L/C}$. However, this concept is somewhat theoretical as we do not have cables of infinite length. On the other hand, for a co-axial cable to function as a transmission line with minimum signal loss and reflection (we will look at this in a moment), the termination impedance at both ends must equal the calculated characteristic impedance for an infinite length. Thus, if the characteristic impedance, Z_0, for a cable is quoted as being 75Ω, then the equipment at both ends of the cable must have a termination impedance of 75Ω.

If this is not the case a number of problems can occur. First of all signal loss may be apparent because of power losses in the transfer both to and from the cable. It can be shown that for maximum power transfer to occur between two electrical circuits, the output impedance of the first circuit must be equal to the input impedance of the second (Figure 2.6). If this is not the case, some power loss will occur. In our case the co-axial cable can be considered to be an electrical circuit, and this is why all equipment connected to the cable must have a matching impedance.

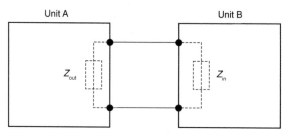

Figure 2.6 *Maximum power transfer only occurs when Z_{out} in Unit A is equal to Z_{in} in Unit B. (Assume that the connecting cables have zero impedance)*

Another problem associated with incorrect termination is one of *reflected waves*. Where a cable is not terminated at its characteristic impedance, not all of the energy sent down the line is absorbed by the load and, because the unabsorbed energy must go somewhere, it travels back along the line towards its source. We now have a situation where there are two signals in the cable, the forward wave and the reflected wave. In CCTV, reflected waves can cause ghosting, picture roll, and loss of telemetry signals. However, these symptoms may not be consistent and may alter sporadically, leaving the unsuspecting service engineer chasing from one end of the installation to the other looking for what appears to be a number of shifting faults; and perhaps for no other reason than because a careless installation engineer has made a Sellotape style cable connection in a roof space!

CCTV equipment is designed to have 75Ω input and output impedances. This means that 75Ω co-axial cable must always be used. Here again the installing engineer must be aware that not all co-axial cable has 75Ω impedance, and 50Ω and 300Ω versions are common. For example, cable type RG-59 is a common 75Ω co-axial cable used in CCTV installations. Cable type RG-58 looks very similar, but it is designed for different applications and has a characteristic impedance of 50Ω. A CCTV installation using this cable would never perform to its optimum capability, if indeed it were able to perform at all.

The subject of termination and termination switches will be discussed again in Chapter 7.

Up to now we have not taken into consideration the length of the co-axial cable. Over short distances the effects of C and R on the signal are small and can be ignored. However, as the cable length is increased these components have an effect on the signal which is similar to a voltage drop along a d.c. supply cable, the main difference being that the filtering action of the cable results in greater losses at the higher signal frequencies. Figure 2.7 illustrates a typical co-axial cable frequency response. Cable losses are usually quoted in terms of dB per 100m, at a given frequency. Manufacturers may quote figures for a range of frequencies, however those quoted for around 5MHz are the most significant to the CCTV engineer because, as seen from Figure 2.7, it is at the top end of the video signal frequency response where the most significant losses occur.

Every cable employed in CCTV signal transmission has a specified maximum length, beyond which optimum system performance will only

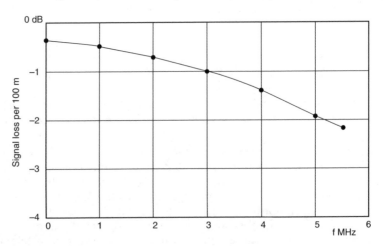

Figure 2.7 *Frequency losses in a typical co-axial cable*

be maintained if additional equipment is installed. Typical specifications for the three most common co-axial cables employed in the CCTV industry are given in Table 2.1. The figures quoted for the maximum cable run length are those quoted in the BSIA Code Of Practice for Planning, Installation and Maintenance of CCTV Systems, October 1991, and some variance with these figures may be noted when comparing different manufacturers' data, however the installer will do well to heed the guidelines laid down in the BSIA document.

Table 2.1

Cable type	Max run length	Impedance	Loss/100m at 5MHz
URM-70	250m	75Ω	3.31dB
RG-59	350m	75Ω	2.25dB
RG-11	700m	75Ω	1.4dB

As a rule, monochrome signals tend to cope better with long cable runs than do colour signals. This is because a PAL colour signal contains a high frequency 4.43MHz colour subcarrier which is affected by the filtering action of the cable. However, even a monochrome signal contains hf components and, bearing in mind the effects of hf filtering on a square wave (Figure 2.2), will therefore suffer some loss of resolution where the cable run length is excessive.

To illustrate the problem of signal loss, consider the cable illustrated in Figure 2.7. At 3MHz the loss per 100m is approximately –1dB. Thus, over a distance of 350m the loss will be in the order of –3.5dB. In terms of voltage, assuming that a standard 1Vpp video signal was injected into the cable, –3.5dB represents an output voltage at the end of the cable of around 0.7Vpp; a signal loss of 0.3V. At 5MHz the loss is in the order of –1.75dB per 100m, therefore over 350m the loss in dBs will be approximately –6dB. Thus, it can be shown that at 5MHz the signal output will be approximately 0.5V. Now consider what would happen if an installer were to ignore these figures and fit a 700m length of this cable. The output figures become 0.45V at 3MHz, and 0.25V at 5MHz. At best such a signal will produce a low contrast picture, quite possibly with loss of colour, and perhaps with picture roll due to the loss of sync pulses.

Where runs in excess of the maximum specified length for a particular cable are unavoidable, launch amplifiers and/or cable equalizers can be installed. The use of these can at least double the length of a cable run.

A launch amplifier is usually installed at the camera end of the cable where there is an available source of power, although there is a sound argument for installing it half way along a length of cable if a means of supplying power can be found. A typical launch amplifier response is shown in Figure 2.8, where it can be seen that the level of amplification is not uniform across the 0–5.5MHz video signal bandwidth. The amplifier is designed to give extra lift to the higher frequencies where the greater losses occur.

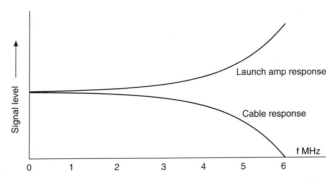

Figure 2.8 *A launch amplifier compensates for the filter action of the cable*

The amplifier usually has an adjustment to allow the gain to be set to suit the length of cable; the longer the cable the higher the gain setting. The idea is to set the output voltage level such that, after losses, a uniform 1 Vpp signal appears at the other end. In some cases the gain control is calibrated in cable lengths, and it is therefore necessary to have an approximate idea of the length of the run. Do not simply turn the control until a 'good, strong picture' appears on the monitor. This practice can lead to problems in relation to vertical hold stability where switchers or multiplexers are involved, and possibly a loss of picture resolution.

A cable equalizer is a form of amplifier, however it is designed to be installed at the output end of the cable. The problem with this is that the unit is having to process the signal once the losses have been incurred, and in boosting the signal levels it will also boost the background noise level which will have arisen in the absence of a strong signal. The advantage of using a cable equalizer is that it can be installed in the control room, which can be a real plus in cases where the camera is inaccessible (Figure 2.9). If the installer has a choice of which to use, a launch amplifier is preferable as it lifts the signal before losses occur, thus maintaining a better signal to noise ratio.

It is possible to employ more than one amplifier in cases where very lengthy cable runs are required. The idea is that these are placed at even distances along the cable such that, just as the signal would begin to deteriorate, another amplifier lifts it once again. This principle is shown in Figure 2.10 where it can be seen that the total cable loss is −33.75 dB, which is compensated for by the overall gain in the system of 36 dB.

All this sounds well and good, however it takes a highly experienced engineer with the correct equipment to be able to adjust the gain and response of all of these units to a point where a perfect, uniform 1 Vpp, 0–5.5 MHz video signal is obtained at the other end without any increase in noise level. And remember, once noise has been introduced into the

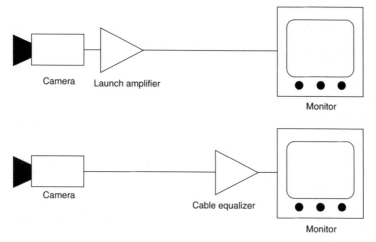

Figure 2.9 *Use of launch amplifiers and cable equalizers*

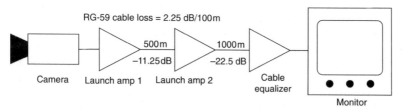

Figure 2.10 *Launch amp 1 gain = 12dB. This compensates for the first 500 m of cable; Launch amp 2 gain = 12dB. This compensates for 50% of the losses in the following 1km of cable; Cable equalizer gain = 12dB correcting for losses in the 1km cable run*

signal, it will simply be boosted along with the signal in each subsequent amplifier.

Still on the subject of losses, it should be noted that every BNC (or other type) connector introduces an element of signal attenuation and reflection, and it is good practice to keep the number of joins in a cable to a minimum.

All CCTV signal cable installation should comply with current codes of practice as laid down in BS 7671: Requirements for Electrical Installations, especially in relation to electrical segregation of low and high voltage cables. However, apart from the electrical safety issues surrounding segregation, installers should pay particular attention to the proximity of co-axial cables with mains power cables, in particular those carrying a high current, or supplying large numbers of fluorescent lights, heavy machinery, etc. Any current-carrying conductor produces an electromagnetic field around its length. Furthermore, high frequency spikes passing along a cable can produce large electric fields. Therefore it follows that both of these energy fields must surround all mains supply cables, because they are carrying high frequency noise spikes in addition to the high current 50Hz mains supply. Where co-axial cables are laid parallel to mains cables, there is a good chance of the *electromagnetic interference* (EMI) penetrating the screen and superimposing a noise signal onto the video signal. Where this occurs, the displayed or recorded picture will suffer such effects as horizontal ripples rolling up or down, or random flashes when lights are switched or machinery operated.

Naturally the co-axial screen provides much protection against such noise ingression, however at best the screen will be no more than 95% effective, and some 'budget' cables may have a much lower figure. To prevent noise ingression it is good practice to avoid long, close-proximity, parallel co-axial/mains supply cable runs where ever possible, maintaining at least 30cm (12″) between cables. This may rule out using plastic segregated trunking because, although it offers electrical segregation, it does nothing to prevent the problems we have just outlined. Metal trunking provides screening against interference, and in cases where co-axial video cable must run through areas of high electrical noise, it is good practice to use steel trunking or conduit to minimize the chances of EMI compromising system performance.

Having looked at the construction of co-axial cable we know that the characteristic impedance depends, among other things, upon the capacitance of the cable, which is determined by the type and thickness of the inner insulating material. Therefore, should the inner sleeve become damaged by the cable being crushed, kinked or filled with water, the characteristic impedance will alter, opening the system up to the inherent problems of signal loss and reflected waves. Putting this another way, installers should take care not to damage the cable during installation, and should not lay cables in places where they may easily be damaged at a later time. BNC connectors are not waterproof and were never intended for external use. Therefore, where external connections are necessary, they should always be enclosed in a weatherproof housing. Once water enters a co-axial cable the capillary action may allow it to travel many metres along the cable, introducing all manner of undesirable picture effects, and very often these can be intermittent.

In order to prevent damage to the inner sleeve, co-axial cable should not have any severe bends. A rule of thumb is to ensure that *the radius of all bends is no tighter than five times the diameter of the cable*. For example, if the cable diameter is 6.5mm, the radius of a bend should be at least 32.5mm.

Ground loops

These occur when the earth (voltage) potential differs across the site. Because every item of mains powered equipment must be connected to earth, where the earth potentials differ, an a.c. 50Hz current will flow through the low impedance screen. The problem is illustrated in Figure

2.11 where a length of co-axial cable has a potential difference of +40V between its ends. It naturally follows that a current will flow through the low impedance co-axial screen which is by-passing the much higher impedance of the ground, which was the cause of the potential difference in the first place.

Differing ground potentials are very common, especially over long distances, and the problem can be further compounded when equipment at one end of a cable is connected to a different phase of the mains supply than that at the other end. The example in Figure 2.11 indicates a potential difference of 40V, however a difference of just 2–3V is sufficient to cause problems.

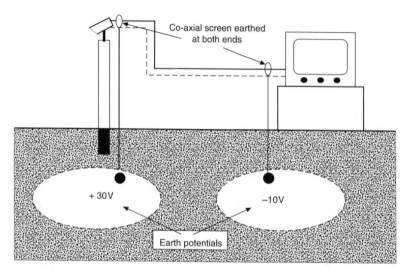

Figure 2.11a *A CCTV system where earth potentials differ*

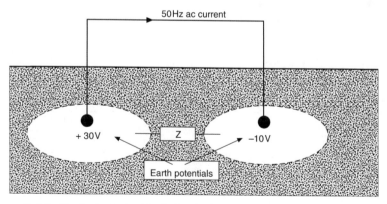

Figure 2.11b *Equivalent electrical circuit. The high impedance earth path (Z) is bypassed by the low impedance of the co-axial screen*

When a ground loop current flows along a co-axial cable screen, because the centre core is referenced to the screen, a 50 Hz ripple is superimposed onto the video signal. This means that the brightness levels in the signal information are constantly moving at a rate of 50 Hz, and the effect on the monitor display is either a dark shadow or a ripple rolling vertically through the picture. This effect, often known as a *hum bar*, can also upset the synchronizing pulses, resulting in vertical picture roll.

It is possible to test for an earth potential problem during installation by taking an a.c. voltage measurement between the co-axial screen and the earth of the equipment to which it is to be connected. Under perfect earthing conditions, the reading should be 0 V. In practice it is usual to obtain a reading of at least a few hundred millivolts, however in severe conditions potentials of 50 V or even greater are possible. In such cases it is not safe to assume that the problem is simply caused by differences in earth potential as there might actually be a serious fault in the earth circuit of the electrical supply, and if the CCTV installer himself is not a qualified electrician, he should report the potential fault to the appropriate authorities, in writing, in order that a full inspection of the supply can be carried out.

There are various ways of avoiding or overcoming the problem of ground loops in a CCTV system. Avoidance is always the best policy, but is not always practical. Remember that ground loops occur because the system has more than one earth point, and these are at differing potentials. Therefore if 12 V d.c. or 24 V a.c. cameras can be used, the only earth connection to the co-axial cable is at the control room end, and ground loops will not occur. This principle is illustrated in Figure 2.12. Other methods of avoidance are to employ twisted pair or fibre-optic cables,

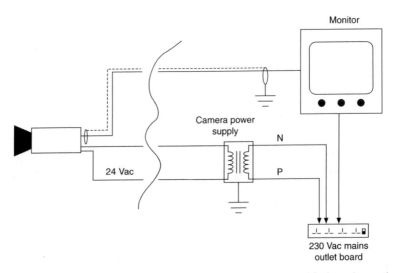

Figure 2.12 *In a low voltage camera supply, the co-axial cable is only earthed at the monitor end*

which we shall be looking at later in this chapter. However, fibre-optic cables are more expensive to install, and besides, the problem may not be identified until after co-axial cables have already been installed.

Ground loop correction equipment is available. There are two types: transformer and optical. Transformer types are usually contained in a sealed metal enclosure which acts as screening. In order to provide ideal coupling of the broadband video signal, the internal circuits may contain more than just a transformer. Nevertheless, the principle behind these units is to break the co-axial cable earth circuit but still provide video signal transmission without affecting the integrity of the cable screen. The basic circuit operation is shown in Figure 2.13. In practice a single unit may contain two transformers, allowing two separate video circuits to be corrected. The unit can be fixed at either end of the cable, although it is usually more convenient to locate it at the control room end.

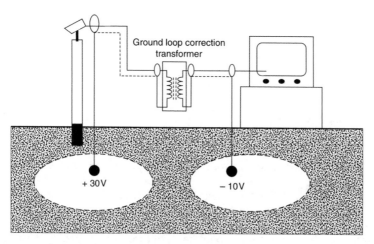

Figure 2.13 *Inclusion of a transformer breaks the 50Hz current path through the co-axial screen*

It is worth noting that not all correction transformers perform to the same standard when it comes to broadband video signal coupling, and sometimes a loss of resolution may be evident. Furthermore, where a transformer is not capable of coupling high frequencies, this can pose problems for certain types of telemetry control signal, resulting in a loss of telemetry to cameras which have a ground loop correction transformer included. As with any type of CCTV equipment, careful selection is important, and when you have found a product which performs satisfactorily, stay with it.

Optical correctors rely on opto-couplers to break the co-axial screen. The video signal is applied to a light emitting diode which converts the varying voltage levels in the video signal into variations in light level. These in turn are picked up by a photodiode which converts the light signal back into a variable voltage (Figure 2.14). Units containing a number of individual inputs (typically 8 or 16) are available, and can be included with the control room equipment, acting as a buffer for each camera input. These are ideal for installations where it is anticipated at the planning stage that ground loops may pose a problem because it is known that cameras will either be connected across different phases of the mains supply, or will span a large geographical area. A multiple input ground loop corrector can be included in the initial quotation, thereby removing the problems of additional costs once the installation is underway.

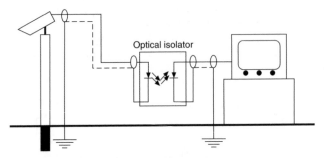

Figure 2.14 *Principle of a single channel opto-isolator*

Twisted pair cable

As the name implies, this cable comprises two cores which are wrapped around each other. The number of twists per metre varies depending upon the quality of the cable, however a minimum of ten turns per metre is recommended; the more turns there are the better the quality of the cable in terms of noise rejection.

This type of cable provides *balanced signal transmission* (as opposed to *unbalanced*, which is how co-axial cable works). As illustrated in Figure 2.15, in a balanced transmission system, because the two conductors are

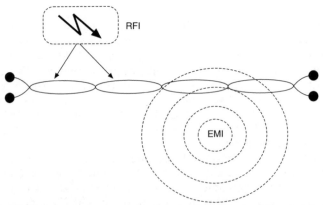

Figure 2.15 *Noise is induced equally into both conductors in a twisted pair*

twisted together, they are evenly exposed to any sources of electrical or magnetic interference present. Furthermore, the induced noise signals travel in the same direction along both conductors, whereas the video signal is travelling in opposite directions along each conductor (signal send and return).

The signal output from the BNC connector on the camera is fed immediately to a twisted pair transmitter which both isolates the twisted pair from earth, and places the video signal across the two wires. The transmitter also provides impedance matching between the 75Ω co-axial cable and the 100–150Ω twisted pair cable.

At the control room end a twisted pair receiver picks up the video signal and places it back onto a co-axial output for transmission to whatever equipment it is to be coupled. The receiver contains an *operational amplifier* (Op-amp) circuit which has two inputs: one wire of the pair is connected to each input. Because the noise signals are travelling in the same direction on both wires, they are effectively applied to both op-amp inputs where they are added in antiphase, thus cancelling them out. The video signal, on the other hand, is only present on the 'send' cable and is therefore only applied to one op-amp input, allowing it to be amplified in the normal way. This noise cancelling action is illustrated in Figure 2.16.

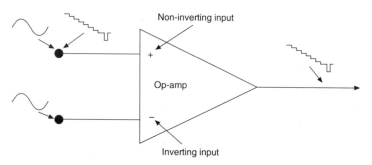

Figure 2.16 *Noise at the inverting input is added to that at the non-inverting input, resulting in cancellation*

In theory a twisted pair cable need not be screened; this type of cable is commonly referred to as *unshielded twisted pair* (UTP). However, in some instances a screen is recommended as it gives added protection against induced noise; this cable type is known as *shielded twisted pair* (STP). Note that because of the action of the twisted pair, mains hum introduced by ground loops is cancelled in the same manner as any other noise signal and thus the inclusion of the screen poses no problems in this area.

The equipment arrangement for a twisted pair installation is shown in Figure 2.17. The main drawback with using twisted pair is the need for a transmitter and receiver at each end of every cable run, which inevitably increases the cost of the installation. Multiple channel receiver units are available which reduce both the installation cost and the number of separate boxes scattered behind the control console.

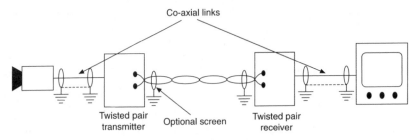

Figure 2.17 *Twisted pair transmission arrangement*

The primary advantage of using twisted pair video signal transmission in CCTV is the much longer cable runs possible owing to the much lower attenuation of the cable. Thus, 1000m for a colour signal transmission is easily possible, and manufacturers frequently quote figures in excess of 2000m for a monochrome signal.

There is no reason why twisted pair and co-axial cabling cannot co-exist in a CCTV installation, where shorter cable runs are made using co-axial cable and longer runs where signal loss and ground loops might prove problematic are made using twisted pair cable.

In some CCTV telemetry control systems a twisted pair cable is run alongside the co-axial video signal cable to carry the telemetry data to the pan/tilt/zoom (PTZ) units. Where the installer has chosen to use twisted pair for both video and telemetry signals, either two cables can be run, or alternatively a single four-core cable containing two separate twisted pairs is available.

Category 5 (Cat 5) cable

Category 5 cable is not specific to CCTV, rather it is a UTP data communications cable and cabling system that has been adopted by the industry for CCTV applications.

The ANSI/EIA (American National Standards Institute/Electronics Industries Association) have devised a number of standards that specify categories of twisted pair cable systems for commercial buildings. An outline of the six current categories can be seen in Table 2.2 and, at the time of writing, a seventh category is under consideration. The specifications for each category encompass not just the cable but the complete data transmission system including data transmission rates, system topologies, cable specifications, maximum cable and patch lead lengths, termination impedance and installation practice.

ANSI/EIA Standard 568-A covers Category 5 cabling systems. In Europe these same standards can be found in BS EN 50173:1995. Cat 5 (as it is

Table 2.2

Category	No. of twisted pairs	No. of wires	Max data rate (bps)
1	2	4	voice only – not used for data
2	4	8	4M
3	4	8	10M
4	4	8	16M
5	4	8	100M
6	4	8	1G

commonly referred to) is currently the system which is of most interest to the CCTV industry because its high data rate makes it ideal for the transmission of video signals. During recent years Cat5 data systems have been installed into many buildings to support IT needs and in all modern buildings a structured data cable installation is as much a requirement as power and lighting cables. The communication used over the Cat5 system is the *Ethernet 100BaseT* where '100' indicates a 100 Mbit per second (bps) data rate, 'Base' means that it is baseband signalling and 'T' indicates that it uses twisted pair cable. The earlier 10BaseT was capable of only 10 Mbps and does not really have sufficient bandwidth to support the transmission of high definition digital video signals.

Connection to the Cat5 system is via a *RJ-45* (Registered Jack) plug/socket. The idea behind the system is that any Ethernet-compatible device may be connected to any socket and quickly set up to establish communications. This is commonly achieved by assigning an IP address to the device which, in the context of this book, would be a CCTV camera. The address may be dynamic, meaning that it is automatically requested by the camera when connected and the administrator computer automatically assigns an address, but more commonly the address is static. This means that an available address must be found and then manually assigned to each camera, a task that is normally performed with the assistance of the IT technician responsible for the computing and IT system.

The implications for CCTV (and indeed security alarm and access control systems) are enormous because, if cameras and pan/tilt units are made to be Ethernet/Internet Protocol (IP) ready, then installation is greatly simplified because there is no requirement for any cable installation. Furthermore, by using this interface, the system can be operated remotely from any point on the globe! Well, that is the theory. There are some practical considerations that should be made. First of all we must remember that digital video signals require a lot of bandwidth, even when compression is used (see Chapter 5), so there must be sufficient bandwidth in the system to handle the data. Then there is the issue of *available* bandwidth because, if the IT system is already working almost to capacity, then the addition of just one camera may well take it over the top, resulting in some devices on the network becoming excluded; and it may not be the camera that goes off-line, but perhaps other devices on the network such as printers, scanners, or even things like air conditioning if the building management system is also reliant on the Ethernet network. However, all too often it is seen as the task of the CCTV engineer to resolve such problems because, when all is said and done, everything worked until the cameras were brought on-line!

As a general rule, when considering using IP cameras the specifier or engineer must first ascertain the limitations of the existing Cat5 system. How much *available* bandwidth is there? How many cameras will be required? What is the bandwidth requirement of each camera? And finally, how well has the Cat5/Ethernet system performed to date? Before connecting your CCTV system to an existing CAT5 network, it is prudent to find out if there has been a history of recurrent communications problems, otherwise you may find yourself attempting to resolve problems that have nothing at all to do with the CCTV installation. There are many systems that have been installed claiming to be Category 5 which, for one reason or another, do not comply with the ANSI specifications and thus fail to function correctly or reliably. The reasons for this may be that the cabling is incorrectly installed, equipment does not meet Category 5 standard, or IT protocols may be unsuitable for the application. In the latter case it is usual to confer with the system administrator to confirm system protocols.

On the other hand, where an IP CCTV camera is failing to function on a structured cable system which should be capable of supporting it, the engineer should check that an IP address has been given to the camera, that the socket is actually connected into the network, that the patch cable between the camera and RJ-45 socket is both correctly wired and is Cat5 compliant, and that the IP address being used by the camera has not already been assigned to another item of equipment. For this last check, the *PING command* is very helpful because a computer connected to the network will tell you immediately if the IP address is already in use. To execute the PING command you must first open the DOS screen, which is usually done from the START button on the bottom toolbar (assuming the operating system is Microsoft Windows™ 95 or later). Select the RUN option, type either CMD or COMMAND and the DOS screen should open with the flashing cursor at the CMD prompt. At this prompt, type PING followed by the IP address for the device you are looking for – in this case the camera in question. A typical PING command will look like:

PING 100.100.5.10

A few seconds after pressing the RETURN key, a response will be obtained. If a device is present, the response on the screen will look something like 'Reply from 100.100.5.10: bytes = 32 time = 10 ms TTL = 128' and will be repeated four times. If no device is present, the response 'Request timed out' will appear. Bearing in mind that you are trying to ascertain whether or not there are two devices sharing an IP address, before executing the PING command, disconnect the CCTV camera in question. Thus, if a device is found you will know that you have been given an address that is already in use and the system administrator will have to provide you with another. If no device is found, connect the camera and execute PING again. A device should now be found. If it is, then you know that at least the camera is on the network and that the reason for a lack of signal from it must lay somewhere else. If no device is found then, as previously stated, check the connections, cables, etc. and that the IP address is a valid one.

Another point to be aware of is that Cat3 and Cat5 cables physically look very similar; however Cat3 cable is only certified for 10Mbps (10BaseT) performance. For a UTP cable to meet Cat5 specifications, it should have a cable capacitance of not more than 17 pF/ft (55 pF/m) and a characteristic impedance of 100Ω. Also look out for excessive bending, stretching or crushing of the cable as all of these will alter the cable properties and can result in excessive data errors and subsequent system failure.

Where it is felt that an existing Cat5 network would be inadequate to support an IP CCTV system, the installer could consider having a dedicated Cat5 installed solely for the use of the CCTV system (and possibly other security systems such as intruder and access control). In these circumstances it once again becomes necessary to install cables whether they be co-axial, twisted pair or Cat5, but by employing Cat5, the CCTV system will have all of the advantages of an IP addressable system. A word of warning; if you have never installed Category 5 cable before, it would be inadvisable to take on the responsibility for installing a system without having prior training or at least working through one of a number of distance learning structured cabling courses. Remember, a Category 5 system will only perform to its design specifications when certain rules (which are beyond the scope of this textbook) are adhered to.

Many manufacturers now have a range of cameras that have no composite video output, but simply an RJ-45 connector. Such cameras are ready to hook up to an Ethernet system and, when used with supporting IP ready controllers and switchers, greatly simplify the installation of powerful, yet versatile CCTV systems.

Ribbon cable

Also known as 'Flat Twin' cable, this has two parallel conductors and functions on the balanced transmission principle we have just been discussing. Because the conductors are not twisted it cannot be guaranteed that they will both be subjected to identical amounts of noise energy, although in practice over short distances this will usually be the case. A typical ribbon cable construction is shown in Figure 2.18.

This type of cable is useful for interconnection between equipment in a control room, especially for desk mounted units where a larger, more rigid cable type can prove cumbersome.

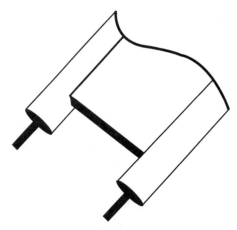

Figure 2.18 *Ribbon cable construction*

Fibre-optic cable

Fibre-optic signal transmission was largely pioneered by the telecommunications industry, and for many years it remained very much within that industry. Perhaps this was because of the specialized skills and equipment required to install fibre-optic cables, particularly in relation to joining (splicing) and terminating. Or perhaps it was due to the relatively higher cost of the cable compared with co-axial or other copper transmission media. Whatever the reason, the CCTV industry was slow to pick up on what is by far the most effective method of sending CCTV signals over any distance.

Because the signal travelling through a fibre-optic cable is in the form of light, the medium is not prone to any of the problems associated with copper transmission systems such as RFI, EMI, lightning, etc. Yet fibre-optic transmission has a much wider bandwidth and much lower signal attenuation figures, which means that signals can be sent over far greater distances without the need for any line correction equipment. Fibre-optic cable also provides complete electrical isolation between equipment so there is never any chance of a ground loop, and from a security point of view it is almost impossible to tap into without it being obvious at the receiving end.

One of the greatest problems associated with signal transmission through optical cable is that of *modal distortion* which is caused by the light energy finding a number of different paths through the cable. Because the path lengths are not all the same, a single light pulse with a duration of, say, 1ns applied at the input arrives at the output over a period of around 2ns. In other words the information becomes distorted. The longer the cable run, the more acute the problem.

The degree of modal distortion per unit length is determined by the construction of the fibre-optic material, and there are a number of cable types available, each having differing characteristics. In order to minimize modal distortion, specially engineered cable must be used, however the manufacturing of these cables is very expensive. For CCTV systems the cable runs are relatively short (compared with something like a transatlantic undersea telephone cable!), and therefore the effects of modal distortion are minimal and cheaper cable designs are adequate.

Three forms of fibre-optic transmission are illustrated in Figure 2.19. *Mono mode cable* is the most expensive of the three owing to its very small core diameter (typically 5µm) but it offers the greatest transmission distances with minimal distortion. *Step index multimode cable* employs

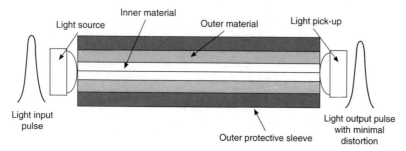

Figure 2.19a *Mono mode cable. Light travels in a straight line through the inner material*

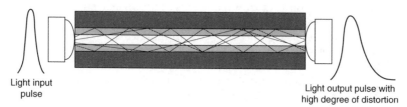

Figure 2.19b *Step index multimode cable. Refraction between two different materials results in multiple light paths*

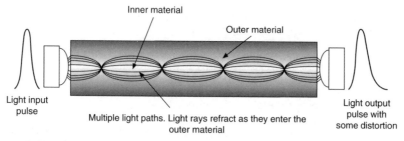

Figure 2.19c *Graded index multimode cable. The constantly changing refractive index results in numerous light paths*

two different materials in the core, each having a different refractive index. This results in multiple light paths of differing path lengths which are added at the output to produce a resultant signal. This cable is relatively inexpensive, however it offers the greatest degree of signal distortion. *Graded index multimode cable* also employs two different core materials, however in this case they are diffused into each other, resulting in a multitude of refractive indexes which causes the light to effectively 'bounce' from side to side as it passes along the cable. Graded index (GI) cable offers much better distortion figures than step index cable and is much less expensive than mono mode cable, making it the prime choice for CCTV applications. For both step and graded index cables the core diameter is much larger than for mono mode cable (typically 50μm).

With this particular type of fibre-optic cable, runs can easily reach 2km and, depending on the frequency of the light source, may extend much further without the need of any signal booster equipment.

The light source may be either a light emitting diode (LED) or a laser diode. Of the two, the LED is far less expensive, however it has a much lower operating frequency. Having said this, an LED can respond at frequencies of up to 100MHz which is more than adequate for CCTV applications. The frequency of light emitted by the LED/laser diode varies between devices, however some frequencies suffer less attenuation than others, therefore offering much longer transmission distances, a factor which manufacturers cannot afford to ignore. The video signal is applied to the light source which translates the variations in signal voltage into brightness variations.

The light pick-up is a *photodiode* which is a device that converts light levels into corresponding voltage levels. This forms part of a receiver unit containing the necessary electronic signal processing to produce a 1Vpp standard video signal on a 75Ω impedance co-axial output.

There are a number of ways of multiplexing CCTV analogue video signals so that more than one can be transmitted through a single fibre-optic cable. The actual multiplexing techniques are complex and beyond the scope of this textbook, however it is useful for the CCTV installer who is considering fibre-optic video transmission to be aware that these multiplexers are available. The alternative to using a multiplexer is to use multicore fibre-optic cables, although these may prove to be a more expensive option.

Fitting connectors and making terminations requires special tools and jigs, although the equipment itself makes the process very simple. However, because of the specialisms associated with fibre-optic cable installation, the majority of CCTV installers sub-contract this part of the installation out to companies who specialize in this type of work. However, as the advantages of fibre-optic become clear, this situation might change as the number of fibre-optic installations increase.

It is important to point out the safety issues surrounding fibre-optic cable. Although the cable is quite substantial, the optical fibre itself is thinner than a human hair and particles of fibre can present an almost invisible health hazard to engineers. Small fragments can easily puncture the skin and break off, causing irritation and even infection which can be difficult to deal with medically. Furthermore, broken particles can be inhaled under certain conditions and could remain lodged in the lung indefinitely. Even for engineers who do not deal with fibre-optic cable directly, where their work is following fibre-optic installation, they should check that the area has been properly cleaned, and should avoid allowing their skin to come into direct contact with the floor or other surface areas where they suspect that fibres may still be present.

Infra-red beam

In essence this is a variation of fibre-optic signal transmission. An infra-red light source is modulated by a video signal, and the light is focused by an optical assembly onto a receiver unit which may be a kilometre or more distant. Both the transmitter and receiver must be able to 'see' each other in a straight line of sight.

As with fibre-optic, there are two types of light source: LED and laser diode. Comparing the two, the LED transmitter is far less expensive, and it produces a wide, diverging beam in the order of 10–20°. However, the diverging beam limits the range to, generally, a few hundred metres. Naturally the limited range can be a problem, however the wide beam makes for fairly simple system alignment, and the structures to which the transmitter and receiver units are mounted do not have to be completely stable. The laser diode transmitter, on the other hand, produces a very tight beam of light (around 0.2°) which can travel much greater distances. However, the tight beam requires very accurate alignment, and equipment really needs to be mounted onto solid structures such as buildings to avoid signal loss caused by movement. Also beware of the effects of direct sunlight which can cause movement of the metal mountings, throwing the light beam off target.

When locating these units it must be remembered that any break in the light path will result in immediate loss of signal, and although infra-red light can penetrate fog and rain to some extent, the range of the equipment will be reduced and severe weather conditions may result in a loss of signal. Therefore beware of operating these at their specified limits; always allow for some amount of signal loss. Also be aware of other changes which may occur, such as leaves appearing on trees during spring, trees that may grow after the equipment has been installed, structures which might be erected, etc.

Infra-red links can be very useful for bridging gaps in a CCTV system which would otherwise prove difficult to deal with. For example, it might be decided that an additional camera is required in a town centre system, however its sighting would mean a lot of expensive civil work and much inconvenience to traffic. In these circumstances an infra-red link could prove to be a much more cost effective and desirable solution. A typical application is shown in Figure 2.20.

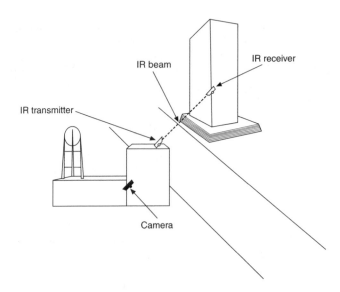

Figure 2.20 *A wide beam infra-red link across a main road*

The equipment usually resembles a pair of small camera housings, and a good quality product will include many of the essential 'extras' which come with camera housings such as wash/wipe, heater, and in some cases an optional fan to cool the equipment during the summer, remembering that extreme heat could cause temporary misalignment of the optics.

Microwave link

The term 'microwave' refers to a band of frequencies in the radio spectrum which extends from 3 GHz to 30 GHz (G = Giga which is 10^9, or 1 000 000 000). These frequencies are above the domestic UHF television channel frequencies and incorporate many of the domestic satellite TV transmissions and mobile phone signals.

In order to prevent interference between signals, the air waves are regulated and no-one is permitted to operate a radio signal transmitter without proper authority, unless it is on one of the frequency bands that have been allocated for free, unlicensed use, and even then the equipment must comply with certain regulations regarding its transmission power and bandwidth. A typical example of one of these 'free for all' channels is the CB radio band. These restrictions mean that CCTV signal transmitting equipment must operate within certain bands, and must not exceed certain power output levels. In the UK, microwave CCTV equipment operates on frequencies located around either 3 GHz or 10 GHz.

Directional (dish) aerials are normally used (Figure 2.21). There are two advantages in this: firstly the transmission range is greatly increased if the power is channelled in one direction, and secondly the signal is more secure against interception by someone operating receiving equipment tuned to the same frequency. However, dish aerials require careful alignment, as just a few degrees of error can result in a loss of signal. This also means that the dishes must be stable. Note that if the dish alignment is only approximate, the signal may produce a perfect

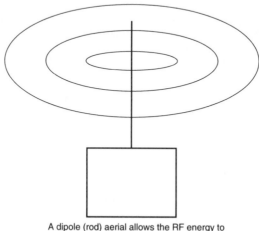

A dipole (rod) aerial allows the RF energy to spread in all directions.

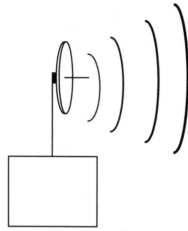

A dish aerial directs the RF energy in one direction, increasing the transmission range.

Figure 2.21 *Comparison of non-directional and directional radio transmission*

picture in good weather conditions, however as soon as rain or snow settles on the dishes the signal attenuation causes the picture to degrade, with the familiar 'sparklies' appearing. The technology is identical to satellite TV, and this phenomenon is familiar to anyone who has a mis-aligned or incorrectly sized dish on their home!

Microwave energy does not penetrate solid objects, and thus there must be a clear line of sight between the transmitter and the receiver. This factor tends to limit the use of microwave to short range, unless it is possible to locate the equipment at both ends of the system on top of high structures. Alternatively the signal would propagate well across flat expanses, however there are not many of these in the UK!

In a CCTV application, the transmitter is located close to the camera, connected by a co-axial link. The receiver is located somewhere within line of sight, but in a place where the signal can be sent via cable to the control room, ideally as close to the control room as possible.

Two-way versions are available. These allow transmission of video in one direction, and transmission of telemetry in the other. The advantage of this can be seen, however the equipment cost somewhat restricts the use of this technology. Some transmitters also include a sound channel.

UHF RF transmission

In recent years a number of domestic DIY CCTV kits have become available, however many DIY householders are unhappy at having to run cables around their homes, and when you see the way some of these have been installed it is not difficult to understand why! Thus the proposition of a wireless CCTV system can be very appealing to the householder.

These wireless systems have been adapted from a technology that was originally developed for domestic TV and VCRs. The idea is to connect the composite video output from a VCR into a local UHF transmitter. Because UHF will penetrate solid objects to a limited degree, the signal can be picked up in every room in the house. However, it must be noted that in many cases the signal may be picked up by the neighbours. This same equipment has been adopted for local CCTV signal transmission, but it must be noted that the range is very poor, and there is no security of the signal whatsoever. On the other hand there are circumstances where a UHF video transmitter designed for domestic VCR use can prove to be a cost-effective solution to a difficult problem.

CCTV via the telephone network

This idea is not new, it has been around for a few decades, however the problem for many years was the very narrow bandwidth of the *PSTN* (Public Switched Telephone Network), which is in the order of 4kHz. The idea of sending a 5.5MHz video signal along such a cable might at first appear impossible to achieve, however this was successfully done for many years with specially developed *slow scan* equipment.

The principle behind slow scan is to grab a single TV picture frame, digitize it, send it along the PSTN line in the form of a dual tone audible signal, and then decode this signal at the receiving end. The problem is the time that it takes to send the digital information for just one frame, which is in the order of 32 seconds, not including dialling time.

Developments in digital video signal compression brought about an increase in the transmission rate, and *fast scan* was born. There are a number of variations on this theme, however the principle is to remove unnecessary information, and one of the ways in which this is achieved is by only transmitting changes in picture information once the first frame has been sent. This is known as *conditional refresh*. The drawback with this is that the picture begins to break up (pixelate) when a lot of sudden movement occurs, such as when the camera is panning. This can be overcome by using other compression tools such as prediction, where picture elements that are seen to be moving in a certain direction are not transmitted, but instead a mathematical algorithm is used to move these elements progressively to where the control chip 'expects' them to be. The subject of video signal compression will be discussed in more detail in Chapter 5.

These reductions in the amount of data, coupled with increased modem speeds for PSTN lines, have led to picture transmission rates of up to one TV picture frame per second. The picture quality can be very good, however the engineer should be aware that there is some trade-off between picture quality and transmission rate, and that the refresh rate for monochrome transmissions is much faster. Basically, the faster the transmission rate the lower the picture quality, and before selecting the equipment for an installation it is wise to determine the requirements of the customer. Do they want a lower resolution picture with a fast refresh rate, or a high resolution picture with a lower refresh rate, and is colour really necessary?

On PSTN the bit rate is in the order of 14 kilobits per second (kb/s). This figure is dwarfed by the more recent innovation in telecommunications; *ISDN* (Integrated Services Digital Network). Developed during the 1970s, this was brought in to cope with the rapidly increasing demand on the telephone network. As the name implies, it is a digital system and therefore offers much higher data rates; 64kb/s. This can be increased by paralleling lines up to offer $2 \times 64 = 128$kb/s.

ISDN lines are installed to order by British Telecom, and a customer wishing to use this for CCTV fast scan must be prepared to pay for the installation and use of this facility. However, this is a very effective medium for CCTV signalling, and the size of the telephone network enables signals to be delivered over very long distances without the need for complex and expensive cable installation. Furthermore, it is possible to send telemetry back to the camera and pan/tilt unit using this medium.

Reductions in the costs of using ISDN links, coupled with the development of sophisticated control equipment has led to an increase in remote monitoring of CCTV installations. External passive infra-red detectors or Video Motion Detection (VMD) can be used to generate a warning at the central monitoring station of potential intrusion. The operator can then take control of the system, switching and/or steering cameras to carry out a patrol of the area.

Such control equipment tends to be PC-based, and very often engineers require specific training by manufacturers or suppliers before they are able to program, adjust and fault-find on such systems.

Connectors

The most common co-axial cable connectors in CCTV are the BNC (Bayonet–Neil–Concelman), phono (also known as RCA) and SCART (Syndicat des Constructeurs d'Appareils Radio Recepteurs et Televiseurs). Another type of connector that is very effective and robust is the UHF (PL259) type, however this has never really been adopted extensively in CCTV, and tends to be looked upon as something of a nuisance when it does appear because often engineers do not carry replacements, couplers or converters. A range of connectors is shown in Figure 2.22.

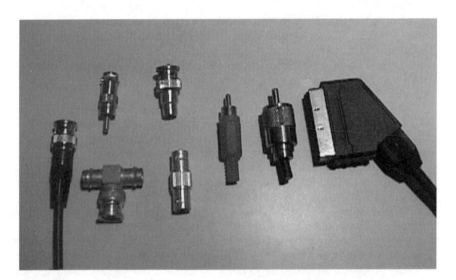

Figure 2.22 *Range of connectors. From left to right: BNC crimp, BNC T coupler, BNC straight coupler, two variations of BNC/phono adapter (top), Phono, UHF, SCART*

Of the other three types, BNC is by far the most robust, and the locking action of the bayonet fitting means that it does not easily come adrift. Furthermore, its construction and method of termination of the screen and core means that it maintains the characteristic impedance of the cable and does not introduce a significant amount of signal attenuation, provided that good quality connectors are used. The best types have a gold-plated inner pin; or gold-plated inner ferrule in the case of the female connector.

BNC connectors for cable mounting are available as crimp, twist-on and solder fitting. Crimp types are by far the most suitable for CCTV applications, as long as the correct crimping tool is used. Flattening the flanges with pliers, wire cutters, hammers, etc., does not produce a low impedance or robust fixing, and where this practice is carried out installers can expect to have problems such as intermittent signal loss, ghosting, poor contrast, noisy picture, and loss of telemetry, to name just a few. Twist-on types are very quick and simple to fit, and no special tools are required, however care must be taken to make certain that the screen is compressed tight against the metal body. If this is not the case, then a high impedance connection exists, if not immediately, then perhaps some time afterwards if the copper screen is exposed to a damp or corrosive atmosphere. Soldered types make a very strong, low impedance connection, however they can be extremely messy to fit and the operation is not one which an engineer would wish to perform on site, especially whilst working from the top of a ladder!

Phono connectors were not originally intended to be used with video signal cables, however some equipment uses phono sockets for input/ output connections because it keeps the cost down. Where this is the case, the installer has no choice but to either fit a phono plug to the co-axial cable, which can prove very difficult, or fit a BNC-to-phono adapter, which introduces another set of contacts, thus increasing the signal attenuation. Having said this, where these sockets are used on a monitor or VCR, the chances are that the connecting leads will only be short, interconnecting cables between items of equipment, and in this case ready made phono–phono leads using simple screened cable will generally perform satisfactorily.

The SCART connector was originally designed for domestic TV and video equipment. During the 1980s it became clear that the television receiver of the future was going to have to be able to accept more than one input source. Furthermore, it was ridiculous to employ UHF RF coupling when equipment such as VCRs were capable of sending a much cleaner composite video signal. Thus a number of leading manufacturers worked to develop a multi-pin connector which would facilitate VCRs, a satellite receiver, stereo audio and RGB input and output links, all on separate screened cables contained within a multicore cable. As can be imagined, initially there were a number of variations, but thankfully an international standard was agreed. SCART was never intended for use in industrial applications, but nevertheless they are found on some VCRs and monitors. The assigned pin connections for a SCART connector are given in Figure 2.23.

Another common connector type is the 4-pin miniature Din specially developed for S-VHS applications (see Figure 5.19). We shall look at these in more detail in Chapter 5.

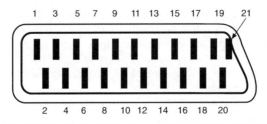

1   3   5   7   9   11 13 15 17 19   21

2   4   6   8   10 12 14 16 18 20

1	= Audio out, right	12	= Data
2	= Audio in, right	13	= Red ground
3	= Audio out, left	14	= Data ground
4	= Audio common (ground)	15	= Red in
5	= Blue ground	16	= Fast RGB blanking
6	= Audio in, left	17	= Composite video ground
7	= Blue in	18	= Fast blanking ground
8	= Function switching	19	= Composite video out
9	= Green ground	20	= Composite video in
10	= Data	21	= Socket ground
11	= Green in		

Figure 2.23 *SCART connector configuration*

When fitting co-axial connectors, care must be taken to ensure that there are no short circuits between the screen and core. A single strand of wire between the two conductors and the signal is lost. Careful and accurate stripping of the outer and inner insulators is the key to avoiding short circuits, and although a sharp pair of wire cutters may be used for this purpose, wire strippers specially designed for RG-59 cable make the task much faster and reliable.

Cable test equipment

Perhaps the simplest method for testing co-axial cable is to use a multimeter and test for an open circuit between the core and screen when the cable is open at both ends, and 75Ω when one end is terminated. This, however, will only tell us that there are no short or open circuits in the cable, it tells us nothing about the signal (picture) quality, and the whereabouts of a fault, should one exist.

One method of testing the signal quality capability is to pass a specific test signal along the cable and measure it at the other end. The test signal could be a sync pulse and black and white test bar pattern derived from a video signal generator. Alternatively a 'pulse and bar' generator may be used. This piece of equipment generates a continuous black, white and grey pattern without any sync pulses or vertical blanking period, and is ideal for signal analysis because of its square waveshape –

remembering that a square wave is made up from an infinite number of odd harmonics, so if the cable is introducing any high frequency attenuation the pulses will appear to have rounded edges (refer to the filtering action illustrated in Figure 2.2). The measuring equipment at the output end of the cable on which the waveform is monitored would be an oscilloscope (for instruction on how to set up an oscilloscope to observe a video signal, see Chapter 12).

When the pulse and bar test indicates that a cable is introducing hf attenuation, the engineer has to decide what to do about it. If the cable run is only a few tens of metres in length, there is no reason why attenuation should occur, and the cable itself must be suspect, unless it was damaged during installation. Either way, it would have to be replaced. If the cable length is a few hundred metres, then it is clear that some form of correction equipment should be installed, e.g. a launch amplifier. When these have been installed, the pulse and bar generator may be used to check that the signal is correct. In many cases it is necessary to adjust the launch amplifier response to obtain a correct waveshape, and it is not only rounded edges that are a problem, in some cases there is excessive hf gain and the waveshape appears to have spikes (called overshoots) on it.

The problem with oscilloscopes is that they are rather bulky to carry around, and although there are some hand-held units available, the LCD

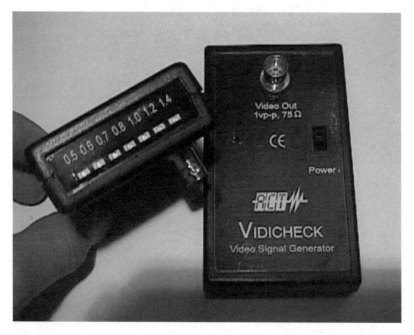

Figure 2.24 *A typical hand-held test instrument for testing co-axial cables, checking video signal levels, verifying camera output, etc. (Courtesy of ACT Meters Ltd)*

display makes them expensive and it would be something of a luxury for every engineer in a larger company to be equipped with one. However, it is not always necessary to actually see the video signal, the engineer may only wish to know that it is present, and that it is of the correct amplitude. To provide this information without the need to set up an oscilloscope there are a number of video signal strength indicators on the market. A typical example is illustrated in Figure 2.24, where a signal generator is connected to one end of the cable under test and a strength meter with an LED display is connected to the other. Alternatively, the meter can be substituted with a monitor and the black and white bar display can be viewed, although with this arrangement the engineer would not know whether or not the amplitude is correct.

Another item of test equipment for use with co-axial cables is the *Time*

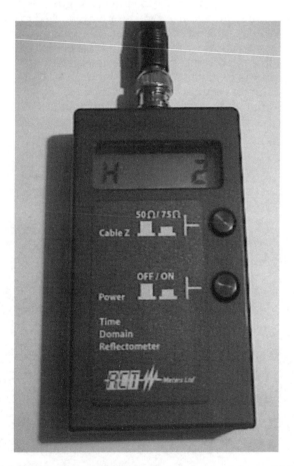

Figure 2.25 *A Time Domain Reflectometer is an extremely useful item of test equipment for installation and service engineers alike. (Courtesy of ACT Meters Ltd)*

Domain Reflectometer (TDR). This takes advantage of the reflected waves that occur in a co-axial cable when it is either incorrectly terminated or is not terminated at all. Both ends of the cable are disconnected, and the TDR is connected to one end. When switched on, the unit sends a succession of short and long duration pulses which travel along the cable until they come to the unterminated end, whereupon they reflect back down the cable and are picked up by a receiving circuit in the TDR. Because the speed at which the signal travels along a co-axial cable is known (approximately 200 Mm/sec), the TDR is able to calculate the cable length by analysing the time it takes for a pulse to return once it has been sent.

The TDR is used primarily to detect the *position* of a fault in a cable, which is a very useful thing to know when faced with a cable length of a few hundred metres, installed in a building, and all you know from your multimeter is that 'somewhere' along the cable there is a short or open circuit. Upon reaching the fault in the cable the pulses reflect, and the TDR calculates the distance to the fault, usually indicating this on a digital display (see Figure 2.25). The TDR is remarkably accurate, and even over a distance of a few hundred metres it can be accurate to within just two metres.

Apart from detecting cable faults, the TDR can be very useful for determining the length of cable left on a roll, rather than having to reel it all out and measure it. The TDR can also indicate the location of an excessive bend in the cable which is impairing its performance.

An optical TDR is available for use with fibre-optic cables and, like the co-axial version, it is an essential part of a service kit for anyone dealing with fibre-optic cables regularly. Although the optical unit is somewhat more expensive, it can very soon pay for itself by making savings in both time and materials.

3 Light and lighting

Although the majority of the equipment in a CCTV system is in the business of processing electronic images in some form or another, the lens has the task of processing the light that is reflected off the surface of the target. The importance of this task cannot be stressed enough because, if the lens fails to focus a true image onto the camera pick-up device, then the rest of the system will have no chance of producing faithful and useful images. But before we can look at the operation of the lens we need to be clear on the nature of the quantity that it is processing, so in this chapter we will look at those aspects of light and lighting that appertain to CCTV system design and operation.

The world's leading physicists are still uncertain about the true nature of light, however they are generally of the opinion that it is made up from minute particles called photons. But this photon energy is electromagnetic in nature – just like radio waves – and as such propagates sinusoidally, therefore having a *frequency* and thus *wavelength* (the higher the frequency, the shorter the wavelength). The frequency of a light wave determines the colour.

The spectral distribution for visible light, as well as the infra-red and ultra-violet regions, is shown in Figure 3.1. As you can see, the human eye begins to respond to light in the red region at wavelengths around 700 nm (nanometres), and loses its response around 350 nm. However, we must remember that the camera pick-up device can have a much wider response, particularly in the infra-red region, making it capable of producing a picture in what would appear to us to be total darkness.

Light and the human eye

The eye reacts to light, converting the incoming electromagnetic radiation into small electrical signals which are sent to the brain. The brain converts these signals into an image.

The eye contains four sets of cells; one set have a cylindrical structure and are known as rods. The other three sets are conical in shape and are known as cones. The cones are sensitive to different frequencies of light, and it is these which enable the eye to differentiate between colours.

One set of cones responds to the range of frequencies with corresponding wavelengths in the order of 600–700 nm. Upon receiving signals from

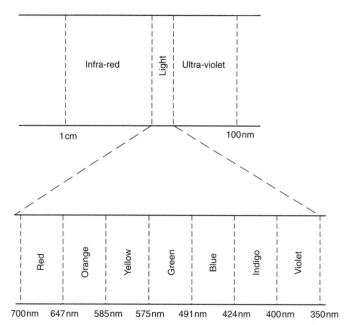

Figure 3.1 *Spectral distribution of light, with associated wavelengths*

these cones the brain acknowledges that it has seen red light. The second set of cones responds to wavelengths around 500–600 nm, that is, green light, and the third set responds to 400–500 nm, blue light.

The eye does not respond equally to all frequencies, nor is the response equal for all people. As Figure 3.2 illustrates, the response is best at wavelengths around 550 nm, that is, green light.

What we perceive to be white light is actually red, green and blue light emanating simultaneously from a source. Red, green and blue are known

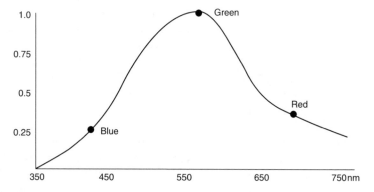

Figure 3.2 *Response of the eye to different wavelengths of light*

as *primary colours*, and from these all of the colours in the visible light spectrum are produced. Mixing any two primary colours together produces a *secondary colour*, these being yellow, magenta and cyan. This process, known as *additive mixing*, is illustrated in Figure 3.3.

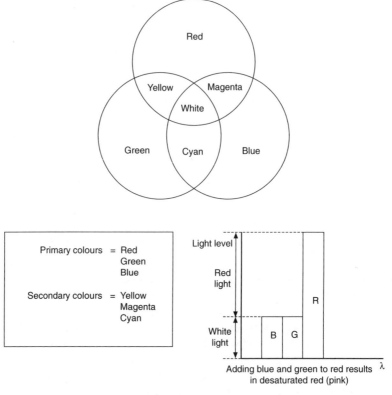

Figure 3.3 *Principle of additive mixing*

We use the term 'colour' in everyday language to distinguish between, say, red and blue. But in practice this term actually encompasses two aspects which describe the colour; the *hue* and the *saturation*. Hue describes the frequency of the light, i.e. red, blue, etc. Saturation describes the intensity or strength of the colour. For example, desaturated red is the correct term for pink, because it defines the hue as being red, but because of the addition of small amounts of green and blue, there is an element of white which desaturates it.

The rods are not frequency (and therefore colour) conscious. These cells measure the intensity of the total amount of incoming radiation. Thus they determine if the scene is very bright, very dark, or somewhere in between. If the eye were to contain only rods we would see everything in black and white.

Summarizing, the rods determine the black and white content of an image, and the cones determine the colour content. The brain constantly processes the information coming from the four sets of cells to determine the brightness, hue and saturation of the image.

In a CCTV system, the camera performs the function of the human eye, converting the incoming light into red, green and blue electronic signals. At the other end of the system, the monitor (or other type of display device) has to take these signals and convert them back into red, green and blue light outputs.

Measuring light

In reality this is a complex science, but it is not necessary for the CCTV engineer to have an in-depth understanding of the subject. However, it is important for them to have a basic understanding of the quantities and units used for light measurement as these are frequently referred to in both system and manufacturers' specifications. The unit of light most commonly encountered is the *lux* (lx), so let's see how this unit is derived and in the process we shall also define a few other units that engineers may well come across.

From the point of view of the eye (and therefore the CCTV camera) there are two sources of light: primary sources such as lamps, display devices, etc., and secondary sources, which are surfaces or objects from which light is reflected.

The light radiated from a primary source is known as the *luminous intensity*. This is measured in *candelas* (cd), which is the amount of light that is radiated in all directions from a black body that has been heated to a temperature equal to that at which platinum changes from a solid to a liquid state.

The *lumen* (lm) is a measure of *luminous flux*, which is the light contained within an area of one radian of a solid angle. One lumen is equal to a luminous intensity of 1 cd within that given area. If this all sounds a bit much, just imagine one lumen as being 1 cd of light within a given area! Because the light is constantly diverging as it moves away from the source, the intensity, when measured at different points away from the source, will reduce. The divergent light reduces by an amount equal to the square of the distance from the source. This effect is illustrated in Figure 3.4

When one lumen of light falls onto an area of one square metre, the surface intensity will be 1 lux (see Figure 3.5).

Another measure of surface intensity is the *foot-candle* (or *foot-candela*). This unit, which is the common unit used in America, is derived in the same manner as the lux, however imperial units of feet are used in place of metres. Conversion between lux and foot-candles is not difficult because

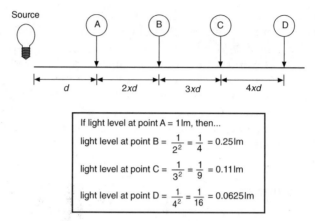

Figure 3.4 *Light illumination reduces by an amount equal to the square of the distance from source*

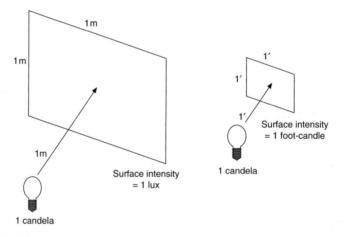

Figure 3.5 *As an approximation, we can say that one lux = ten foot-candles*

three feet approximates to one metre and therefore, as a rule of thumb, we can say that one foot-candle = one tenth of one lux or, conversely, one lux = ten foot-candles.

Illumination refers to the amount of light coming from a secondary surface or object, the unit of measurement being in lux or foot-candles. The material covering or making up a surface will determine the amount of light reflected off that surface, so even if the primary light source has a high intensity, if the reflective quality of a surface is poor the level of illumination will be low. As a typical example, a white projector screen may reflect 90% of the incident light and will itself serve to illuminate other objects in the area, however a dark-coloured coat may reflect only 5% of the incident light, resulting in low illumination.

Thus we can see that the level of illumination is dependent on both the source lighting and the reflective properties of the surface areas. As a guide, some typical levels of illumination are given in Figure 3.6.

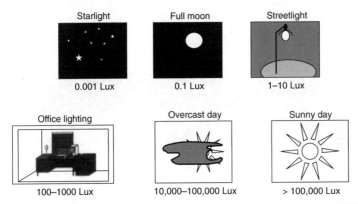

Figure 3.6 *Typical illumination levels for conditions encountered in CCTV installations*

Light characteristics

As far as we are concerned, we can assume that light travels in a straight line through a vacuum. It also travels in straight lines through a medium, however the speed at which it travels is different and depends on the density of the medium. For example, when a ray of light passes from air into a solid such as glass, the change in velocity causes the ray to bend. As the ray emerges from the glass back into the air once again, its velocity increases and it bends back towards its original angle of incidence. This effect, known as *refraction*, is illustrated in Figure 3.7.

The amount by which a ray is refracted depends upon the change of velocity, which in turn is governed by the density of the solid. Each solid has its own *refractive index* which is found by dividing the velocity of light in a vacuum by the velocity of light within that solid. Air and clear gases are taken as having a refractive index of 1.

However, it is not only the refractive index which governs the angle of refraction. The frequency (i.e. the colour) of the light ray also has a bearing. Experimentation proves that for any given solid, the blue end of the light spectrum will always be refracted more than the red. This is why when we pass white light through a prism, we observe a 'rainbow' effect. Although this effect might look striking on a table ornament, it causes considerable headaches for lens manufacturers, as we shall see in the next chapter.

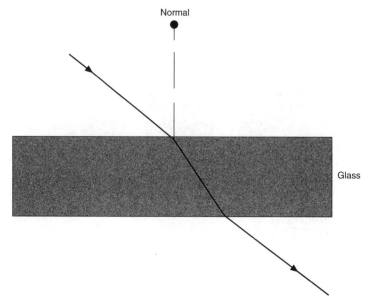

Figure 3.7a *Effect of a solid on the path of a light ray*

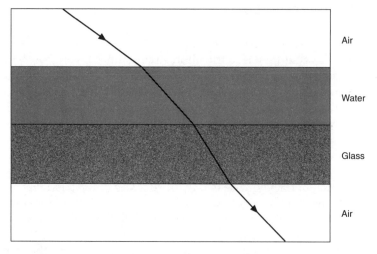

Figure 3.7b *Effect of differing media on a light ray*

Artificial lighting

All too frequently lighting is the one factor that the CCTV system designer, installer and end user has little control over. To guarantee clear, true colour images from a video camera, the scene should be illuminated with a high level of evenly distributed white light. To illustrate this point, consider this scenario. A television production company wish to film a scene in a street. Apart from the film crew, sound engineers, production people, electricians, actors, catering van, etc., there will be a dedicated lighting crew who will erect as much lighting and reflective surfaces as they deem necessary to ensure a high quality picture. Now the crew have gone away, and all that is left is the CCTV camera covering that same street, which is expected to produce the same quality images in all weather and lighting conditions, with the only form of artificial lighting at night being the sodium street lights.

Bearing in mind that visible white light actually comprises of the three primary colours red, green and blue, then it follows that the only way (using current technology) of achieving true colour reproduction with either video or photographic cameras is to illuminate the subject area with white light. This point is illustrated in Figure 3.8 where, for the sake of this illustration, we shall assume that the person's jacket is pure blue. The pigment in the jacket is such that the red and green light energy is absorbed, however the blue light energy is reflected off the surface. Therefore the eye (and thus the brain) discerns only blue light in that part of the image. Now consider the same image if it is illuminated with a pure red light. All of the light would be absorbed, so the eye would perceive the jacket as being black. This leads us to a very important point regarding CCTV installation; colour cameras are only effective where the area is illuminated with white light. There is no point in installing a colour camera where infra-red (IR) lighting is to be used although, as we shall see in Chapter 6, there are some colour cameras that will automatically switch to black and white operation when it is dark or when IR lighting is present.

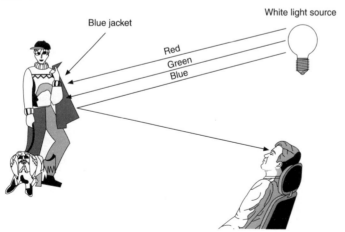

Figure 3.8 *Pigment in the blue jacket absorbs red and green frequency radiation, reflecting only blue frequencies*

Of course the truth is that there are a number of sources of 'white' light and most are not true white, but nevertheless when used with CCTV equipment many of these will provide adequate illumination. The type of light produced by a source is determined by the *colour temperature*, which is a scientific measure of the wavelengths of light and is stated in degrees Kelvin. For example, the light from a fluorescent tube is known to be about equivalent to that of an overcast day because in both cases their colour temperature is around 6000–6500K.

The spectral output range for a number of common sources of artificial lighting is given in Figure 3.9. Bearing in mind that monochrome cameras respond well to IR light (unless they have been manufactured with IR filters), then we can see that for monochrome CCTV installations almost any of the common artificial light sources will provide adequate illumination. However, for colour operation we must be more selective. As a general rule, colour cameras work best with tungsten or tungsten halogen lighting. Although Figure 3.9 would indicate that high pressure sodium lighting covers the visible spectrum, in practice this type of lighting produces mainly yellow illumination with only small amounts of blue and red. Fluorescent lighting produces a reasonably even output across the visible spectrum, however where the tubes are operating at the 50 Hz (60 Hz) mains frequency, this can result in an undesirable flickering effect on the picture. Note the very narrow response of low pressure sodium lamps. These produce mainly a yellow/orange light, making them unsuitable for both colour and monochrome cameras – however until

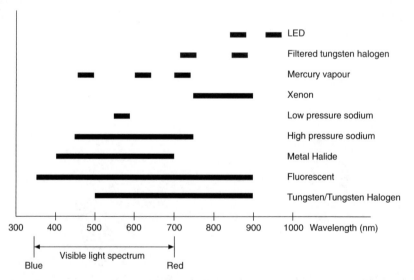

Figure 3.9 *Spectral output range for common sources of artificial lighting*

recent years this type of lighting has been used as the main form of street lighting in the UK and much of it is still in use in urban areas.

Another problem associated with gas discharge lamps (i.e. low and high pressure sodium) is the time that it takes for them to strike and then reach their optimum light output performance. The time from strike to maximum light output can be a few minutes and, furthermore, if they are turned off, it is not safe to strike them again until they have cooled, which can also take a few minutes. For this reason, these types of lighting are unsuitable for use where switched security lighting is required. On the other hand, although tungsten halogen lamps reach their optimum light output almost immediately, where they are being constantly switched on and off it is generally found that the lamp life is relatively short.

Infra-red lighting units are usually tungsten halogen lamps with a filter mounted in front. There are two common types in use, one producing illumination around 730 nm, the other having a longer wavelength in the order of 830–860 nm. 730 nm units tend to produce a small amount of visible red light which makes them visible to the naked eye – although the area that they are illuminating appears dark. These units are ideal for use in locations where white lighting is undesirable (perhaps because the local residents do not want their bedrooms illuminating like a theatre stage!) but where overt CCTV is required to serve as a deterrent. Where the CCTV system is required to be covert, employment of IR lamps in the 830 nm region will result in a high infra-red illumination of the cover area, but the lamps will be invisible to the eye.

Because infra-red lamps are often located in places that are not easily accessible, the problem of lamp unreliability is made more acute. For this reason LED (light emitting diode) IR lamps comprising of an array of infra-red LEDs are becoming increasingly popular for applications of up to around 100 W. The idea is illustrated in Figure 3.10. In general these lamps are covert, operating at around either 850–880 nm or 950 nm.

Figure 3.10 *The drawing illustrates the principle of the LED array. The photograph shows a typical lamp unit. Note the heat sink fins at the rear of the lamp which provide convection cooling*

When we think about the intensity of CCTV lighting, too often we are only concerned about the area being too dark, however too much lighting can also pose problems. Just as the human eye does not cope well with excessive bright light, neither does a CCTV camera. Consider the situation where a fully functional camera (i.e. one mounted on a pan/tilt unit and having full operator control) with artificial lamps is required to cover a large car parking area. In order for the operator to be able to discern activity anywhere in the area it may well be necessary to install two 500 W flood lamps – either white or infra-red. However, problems will arise when the camera is tilted downwards to view a target in close proximity because the target will appear completely overexposed. This problem may be overcome by having more than one type of lamp available to the operator, each being independently switched. For example, in the case of the car park, a high wattage flood lamp could be used when viewing the general area and a low wattage spot lamp could be switched on when the camera is being used to monitor the area close by.

In general there are three types security lamps available: flood, wide angle, or spot coverage (Figure 3.11). The choice of distribution type is important. A 500 W flood lamp will cover a wide area, but it may not provide sufficient illumination in any particular part of the area. At the other extreme, a 500 W spot lamp will leave large areas with no illumination and might well result in over-exposure of the target area. From this we should appreciate that, when installing lighting for CCTV, consideration should be given to such factors as the areas to be covered, the amount of illumination required, and the types of lighting, i.e. white, infra-red, overt or covert.

Consideration should also be given to the angle of the lighting. In

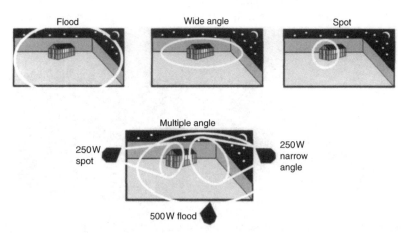

Figure 3.11 *In some situations a mixture of lighting distributions is required to provide adequate illumination*

general, security lights have to be mounted high up both to ensure their safety and to place them in the proximity of the camera (where the power source and telemetry control will be available). However, if the only lighting source is from above then facial features may be lost due to the heavy shadowing effects around the eyes and mouth. For example, the shadow cast by the nose could well be misinterpreted as a moustache. Also beware of low-level downlighting used to illuminate some paths and walkways. Whilst this level of illumination can be more than adequate to satisfy the needs of the CCTV camera, this type of lighting tends only to provide illumination of the waist down, therefore making it impossible to identify the persons in the shot.

We have already seen that light levels are measured in lux. The instrument used for taking these measurements is a light-level meter, or lux meter. From the point of view of CCTV camera installation, where it is felt necessary to test the light level in an area, the most practical point to take the measurement is at the camera lens because this will give an indication of the actual amount of reflected light entering the lens from the secondary surfaces and objects (see Figure 3.12). When using a light meter, take note that the photo sensor deteriorates with exposure to light. Manufacturers provide a black cover for the sensor and, to ensure accurate readings and preserve the life of the meter, this should only be removed whilst taking a reading.

Figure 3.12 *When using a light level meter, take the reading at the camera location*

4 Lenses

The performance of a CCTV system is very much reliant on the quality and type of lens fitted to the camera. Many installations offer poor picture performance because the installer did not specify the correct lens during the initial survey. And correct lens does not simply mean choosing a lens which will offer the correct field of view, although this is one important factor. The quality of the lens, the format size and the spectral response are all important factors relating to lens performance and thus image quality. For example, there is no point in fitting a lens with an infra-red filter when the system is expected to perform in the dark with the assistance of artificial infra-red lighting! And this has been known to occur.

In this chapter we shall be looking at the principle of operation of optical lenses, before moving on to discuss the lenses employed in the CCTV industry.

Lens theory

An optical lens is a device which makes use of the refractive effect on light paths. There are two types of lens, *convex* and *concave*.

A simple convex lens is shown in Figure 4.1a. The light rays entering the lens are refracted, however, because the lens surface is curved, the angle of emergence at each point on the lens is different. If the lens is ground accurately then all of the rays of light will converge at a single point somewhere behind the lens. This point is called the *focal point*.

The concave lens is shown in Figure 4.1b. This is known as a diverging lens because the light rays are bent outwards. In this case the focal point is said to be at a point on the entry side of the lens from where the light appears to have originated.

One problem encountered with a simple lens is *chromatic aberration*. Remember that different colours of the spectrum have a different refractive index, so for the lens in Figure 4.1a, the red end of the spectrum will not be bent as far inwards as the blue end. This means that there are a number of focal points, i.e. one for each wavelength in the light spectrum, resulting in an image that appears to have a number of coloured halos around it. In effect, the lens is behaving rather like a prism. The problem of chromatic aberration can be overcome by using a lens assembly comprising of a series of converging and diverging lenses, each made from glass with a differing refractive index.

The efficiency of a lens is reduced if the glass is highly reflective because a considerable amount of light simply bounces off the front face. Lenses

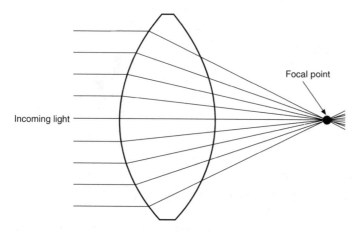

Figure 4.1a *Convex lens. Light converges onto a focal point*

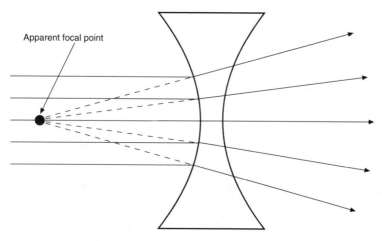

Figure 4.1b *Concave lens. Light diverges from an apparent focal point behind the lens*

often have a bluish tinge because they have been coated with a filter material to reduce this effect.

Looking again at Figure 4.1a we can see another important characteristic of the convex lens. Because the light paths cross over at the focal point, *the image is inverted*. Of course, this inversion is cancelled if the light is passed through another convex lens.

A practical *lens assembly* incorporates more than one optical lens, which means that the light paths may cross a number of times as they pass through. This is illustrated in Figure 4.2.

The image will only appear in correct focus on the pick-up device when all of the lenses within the assembly are at the correct distance from each other. We shall see later that some lenses are made adjustable

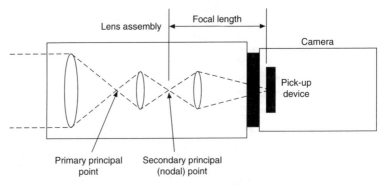

Figure 4.2 *Light paths through a lens assembly*

to offer *zoom effects*, however this means that the focus must be readjusted which is done by moving the position of the lens assembly using an adjustment called the *focus ring*.

Lens parameters

Having looked at the basic operating principle of a lens, we can now give a more detailed consideration to the subject. A sound understanding of the meaning of, and the principles behind, the terms *lens format, focal length, angle of view, field of view, aperture, F-number* and *depth of field* is essential for anyone who wishes to effectively specify and/or install CCTV systems.

Let's begin with *lens format*. This is directly related to *camera format*, which refers to the size of pick-up device employed by any particular camera. Pick-up devices come in a range of formats (sizes). CCTV cameras originally employed vacuum tube pick-up devices, and the 1" tube was a common choice, offering reasonable performance at an affordable price. However, tubes have largely been superseded by the Charge Coupled Device (CCD). We shall look at these in Chapter 6.

CCDs do not require the same pick-up size as their tube counterparts to produce a picture of matching resolution, which is why $\frac{1}{4}''$, $\frac{1}{3}''$ and $\frac{1}{2}''$ format cameras are common in the CCTV industry. Continuing developments in CCD chip technology have enabled smaller chips to achieve even greater resolution, which to some extent has led to the phasing out of the $\frac{2}{3}''$ chips which require a larger and thus more costly lens. $\frac{2}{3}''$ and 1" format CCDs are available, offering very high resolution and excellent low light level performance, but at a very much higher cost.

Five formats are shown in Figure 4.3, along with the corresponding horizontal and vertical chip dimensions. The chip size complies with the industry standard ratio (aspect ratio) of 4:3, and these horizontal and vertical dimensions are standard for all pick-up devices. Imperial units are used to denote the camera and lens format to prevent confusion between the lens format and focal length figures. For example, it is much less confusing to talk about a $\frac{1}{2}''$ 12mm lens than it is to refer to a 12mm 12mm lens, even though these are more or less the same.

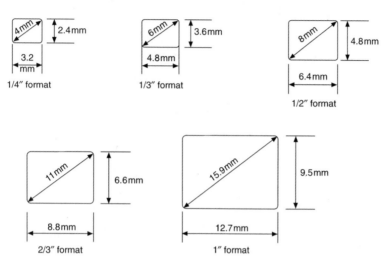

Figure 4.3 *Dimensions of image size for each CCD chip format*

Format		Height	Width
Imperial X″	Metric X mm	X mm	X mm
$\frac{1}{4}''$	4	2.4	3.2
$\frac{1}{3}''$	6	3.6	4.8
$\frac{1}{2}''$	8	4.8	6.4
$\frac{2}{3}''$	11	6.6	8.8
1″	15.9	9.5	12.7

It is important to note that the actual dimensions of the CCD device are smaller than the format size. Take for example the $\frac{1}{2}''$ format CCD. You might expect the diagonal dimension to be a $\frac{1}{2}''$ (12.5mm), however it is only 8 mm. The same rule applies to the other three image devices; their diagonal dimensions are all smaller than their quoted format sizes. The reason for this is that we do not use the light output from the lens at the outer edges of the image, as this is where maximum optical distortion occurs. The relationship between lens and camera is illustrated in Figure 4.4.

Let's now look at what happens when the lens/camera formats have

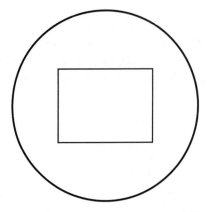

Figure 4.4 *Proportional dimensions of a 1/2" format CCD when compared with a 1/2" diameter circle, illustrating the relationship between lens and camera formats*

not been correctly matched. In Figure 4.5a the lens format is *smaller* than the camera format, and so the image does not fill the display. When viewed on a monitor, it would appear as if we were looking through a porthole! In Figure 4.5b the lens format is *larger* than the camera format, so in this case the image fills the monitor screen – however not all of the image produced by the lens is being used. This is not necessarily a bad thing, because by only using the centre area of the lens there will be minimal optical distortion, however the operator must be able to view the area specified in the operational requirement.

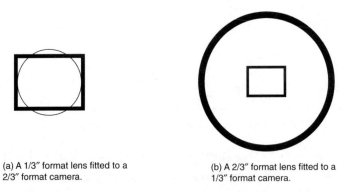

(a) A 1/3" format lens fitted to a 2/3" format camera.

(b) A 2/3" format lens fitted to a 1/3" format camera.

Figure 4.5 *Two examples of mixed lens and camera formats, drawn to scale*

Moving on to *focal length*, looking again at Figure 4.2 we see that the focal length is the distance, measured in millimetres, from the secondary principal point to the final focal point. The secondary principal (or nodal) point is the last occasion where the light paths cross in the assembly, and the camera pick-up device is located at the focal point. For small, wide-angle lenses that have a very short focal length, it would not be possible to fit the lens to the camera because the rear lens assembly would be forced against the pick-up device. In these cases it is necessary to fit additional optical devices to compensate for this, moving the final focal point further away from the rear lens assembly, without altering the effective focal length of the lens.

The focal length has considerable effect on the performance of the lens. The effect of changing the focal length (that is, moving the nodal point) is shown in Figure 4.6, where it can be seen that the *angle of view* changes.

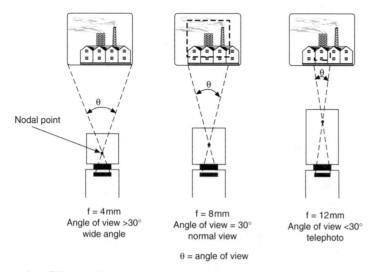

Nodal point

f = 4mm	f = 8mm	f = 12mm
Angle of view >30°	Angle of view = 30°	Angle of view <30°
wide angle	normal view	telephoto

θ = angle of view

Figure 4.6 *Effect of focal length on the angle of view*

But moving the nodal point not only changes the angle of view, it also affects the *magnification* (M). All people with normal eyesight have more or less the same angle of view (which is approximately 30°) and magnification. Taking this value as a magnification of $M = 1$, it can be shown that a $\frac{1}{3}''$ format CCTV camera fitted with an 8mm lens has a magnification of approximately 1, thus producing an image close to that perceived by the human eye. Table 4.1 shows the focal lengths for other lens formats having a magnification of $M = 1$.

Table 4.1 *Lens sizes having a magnification M = 1. In each case the angle of view is approximately 30°*

Format size	1″	$\frac{2}{3}''$	$\frac{1}{2}''$	$\frac{1}{3}''$	$\frac{1}{4}''$
Focal length	25mm	16mm	12mm	8mm	6mm

Increasing the magnification increases the apparent size of an object, and lenses with a long focal length are known as *telephoto lenses* because they have a narrow angle of view, but objects far away appear much larger than they would when viewed with the naked eye. Lenses with focal lengths that produce an angle of view wider than 30° are known as *wide-angle lenses* because they cover a broader area than the eye: however the magnification is less.

It can be shown that the magnification of a lens is determined by the expression

$$M = \frac{\text{focal length } (f)}{\text{format size}}$$

where M = magnification factor
              format size = the size of the lens

For example, for a $\frac{1}{2}''$ format camera fitted with a 12.5 mm $\left(\frac{1}{2}''\right)$ format, 25 mm focal length lens, the magnification will be

$$M = \frac{25}{12.5} = 2 \text{ times}$$

However, if a 100 mm focal length lens is fitted to the same camera, the magnification becomes

$$M = \frac{100}{12.5} = 8 \text{ times}$$

So we see that *increasing the focal length increases the magnification*. However, the increase in focal length gives a corresponding reduction in the angle of view and thus the image size, known as the *field of view*, is reduced. Putting this another way, increasing the magnification (zooming in) reduces the area that can be viewed.

Field of view is one of the more critical factors in CCTV system specification and design because it determines how large an image will appear on the monitor screen for a given distance from the camera. When we talk about the field of view we need to define whether we are referring to the vertical or horizontal dimension (Figure 4.7).

But field of view is not only affected by the focal length, it is also a function of the format size and the distance from the camera to the object in focus. This relationship is expressed as

$$\frac{w}{W} = \frac{h}{H} = \frac{f}{D}$$

where w = width of format
             W = width of scene or object
             h = height of format
             H = height of scene or object
             f = focal length of lens
             D = object distance from camera

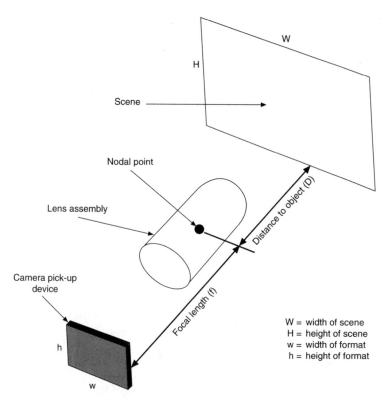

W

H

Scene

Nodal point

Lens assembly

Distance to object (D)

Camera pick-up device

Focal length (f)

h

w

W = width of scene
H = height of scene
w = width of format
h = height of format

Figure 4.7

Note that in some instances the letters 'V' and 'H' are used to denote the Vertical height and the Horizontal width. This is particularly the case with some lens calculators (see later in the chapter).

Example

It is required that an object of 2.5m in height fills the monitor screen when observed at a distance of 15m. The camera format is $\frac{1}{2}''$. Calculate the lens size required.

Solution

From the table of imager sizes (Figure 4.3), a $\frac{1}{2}''$ format pick-up has a vertical size of 4.8mm. Thus

from $\dfrac{h}{H} = \dfrac{f}{D}$

$$f = \frac{h}{H} \times D = \frac{4.8}{2500} \times 15000$$

$$= 28.8\text{mm focal length}$$

Naturally this is not an ideal size, and the nearest available size, e.g. 32mm, would have to be employed.

Example

For the example above, what would be the horizontal field of view (*W*)?

Solution

From the table of imager sizes (Figure 4.3), a $\frac{1}{2}''$ format pick-up has a horizontal size of 6.4mm. Thus

$$\text{from} \quad \frac{w}{W} = \frac{f}{D}$$

$$W = \frac{w \times D}{f} = \frac{6.4 \times 15\,000}{28.8}$$

$$= 3333\,\text{mm or } 3.333\,\text{m wide}$$

The above examples site the maximum height and width of the field of view, but in some cases we have to calculate the lens size from the point of view of the size of an image on the screen. For example, it may have been decided that in order to be able to recognize a person of average height at a range of 15m, the image of the person must fill at least 67% ($\frac{2}{3}$) of the vertical size of monitor screen. Faced with such a situation, the specifying engineer must ensure that the lens fitted to the camera will perform to this specification. This problem may be approached in the following manner.

- Assume that a $\frac{1}{3}''$ format camera is to be employed, then (from Figure 4.3) *h* = 3.6mm.
- Assume it has been decided that a person of height 1.6 m will be the minimum height of person we wish to target. For this image to fill 67% of the screen, the full field of view height will be 1.6m × 1.5 = 2.4m, or 2400mm = *H*.
- *D* = 15000mm.

$$\text{Thus,} \quad f = \frac{3.6}{2400} \times 15\,000 = 22.5\,\text{mm}$$

In this example it was simple to find the full field of view height because it was a convenient number, $\frac{2}{3}$. An alternative method of calculating this figure when the percentage screen height is not so straightforward is

$$H = \frac{100\%}{\text{target height (\%)}} \times \text{target height (metres)}$$

To prove this equation, let's insert the figures from the last example

$$H = \frac{100\%}{67\%} \times 1.6 = 2.39 \text{ metres}$$

As a general rule, for any format size, *doubling the focal length halves the field of view, and doubles the magnification*. In other words, we only see half as much, but it appears twice as large. This is a useful rule of thumb when working on site.

Calculating the lens size for a particular application is very important. Failure to get this right at the specifying stage can prove expensive in the long run when a customer refuses to pay the bill because the images produced on the screen are nothing like those laid down in the specification, or *Operational Requirement* (OR). Given the cost of some lenses it could prove expensive to go around changing them afterwards. The calculations in the previous examples are based on simple geometry, however there are those people who simply don't like having to perform mathematical calculations. For these people there is some good news. Various lens calculators, look-up tables and lens finders have been developed which for most applications do away with the need for any calculations. We shall look at these at the end of this chapter.

For many fixed cameras, an alternative to precision lens calculation is to use a *varifocal lens*. This offers a crude 2:1 adjustment ranging between either 4–8 mm or 6–12 mm. Many installers employ these lenses because they allow for a margin of error and/or a change of mind on the part of the customer once the installation has been completed. On the other hand, these lenses are more expensive than an equivalent quality and size fixed lens and, if the lens is never going to be adjusted after the initial installation, a fixed lens is far more cost effective and can make a quote for a system much more competitive.

Another important consideration for a CCTV camera is the amount of light falling onto the pick-up sensor. Insufficient light results not only in a dark picture, but it will also be lacking in contrast. Excessive light will result in what is known as picture burn-out. This is where lighter areas of the picture become overexposed resulting in bright white patches with no detail whatsoever. In general, as long as the image is not allowed to burn out, the picture quality will be better where there is a high level of light input. The contrast ratio will be high, and the depth of field (we shall look at this later in the chapter) will be greatest.

Because a camera is expected to function effectively across a wide range of lighting levels, the lens must have some means of controlling the amount of light falling onto the camera pick-up. This is done by means of a mechanical iris. The iris is a delicate mechanism comprising of a number of plates which slide as they are rotated. The principle is illustrated in Figure 4.8.

The size of the hole created by the iris is known as the *aperture*. As the diameter of the aperture changes, the change in the amount of light passing through follows a mathematical rule known as the inverse square law. If this sounds a bit of a mouthful, then consider it this way: doubling the diameter of the aperture results in an increase in light throughput of 4 times (2^2); tripling the diameter of the aperture gives an increase of 9 times (3^3), and so on. Similarly, halving the diameter of the aperture results in a light reduction factor of four, etc.

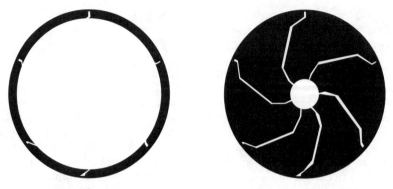

Figure 4.8 *Sliding plates are used to perform the function of an iris*

The light-gathering ability of a lens is known as its *optical speed*. The greater the amount of light falling onto the camera pick-up, the faster the CCDs will charge. Hence a lens with a high light throughput is said to have a fast speed. Larger aperture lenses will obviously be capable of gathering more light than smaller ones, and so in general they have a faster optical speed than smaller lenses. The optical speed is stated as an *F-number*.

The F-number is determined from

$$F = \frac{\text{focal length}}{\text{lens/aperture diameter}}$$

If you look at the F-numbers on the side of a manual iris lens, you will see that they appear to have somewhat peculiar values. This is because each position, known as an *F-stop,* is designed to give either a halving or doubling of light throughput, and the reason why the numbers are at first glance unusual is down to simple geometry. To double the light throughput, the aperture *area* is doubled; however to double the area of a circle, the diameter is not doubled, rather it is increased by a factor of 1.4142. Likewise, to halve the area of a circle, the diameter is divided by a factor of 1.4142. Look at the following example.

For a 50 mm diameter lens with a focal length (FL) of 50 mm, the F-number would be 50 ÷ 50 = 1.

- In order to reduce the light gathering area of this lens, the aperture area will be 50 ÷ 1.4142 = 36 mm.
- This gives an F-number of 50 ÷ 36 = 1.4.

Repeating these calculations for the 36 mm aperture area would give us a 25 mm aperture size, and an F-number of 2.0. So it can be seen that moving the aperture setting from the 1.4 position to the 2.0 position, i.e. one F-stop, reduces the light throughput by a factor of 50%. *Each and every F-number represents a halving or doubling of light throughput.* Table 4.2 shows the effect of each F-stop on the aperture diameter and the light attenuation for a total of 13 stops on a 36 mm diameter, 50 mm focal length lens. Thus F1.4 indicates that the aperture is fully open, and it has been assumed that when the aperture is open a light level of 2 lux is passing through the lens. 2 lux represents a very low light level, and one in which the average camera is just beginning to produce an acceptable clear image.

Table 4.2 *Effect of F-stops on aperture diameter and amount of light cut. It is assumed that the light landing onto the pick-up device is 2 lux when the aperture setting is 1.4*

Aperture diameter	Area ÷ 2 (÷ 1.4142)	F-number	Light input (lux)
36 mm	–	1.4	2
36 mm	25 mm	2.0	4
25 mm	18 mm	2.8	8
18 mm	12.5 mm	4.0	16
12.5 mm	8.8 mm	5.6	32
8.8 mm	6.25 mm	8.0	64
6.25 mm	4.4 mm	11	128
4.4 mm	3.1 mm	16	256
3.1 mm	2.2 mm	22	512
2.2 mm	1.6 mm	32	1024
1.6 mm	1.1 mm	44	2 k
1.1 mm	0.8 mm	64	4 k
0.8 mm	0.6 mm	88	8 k

On a manual iris (MI) lens the aperture is adjusted by rotating a ring or collar which has the F-numbers indicated beside it, the letter 'C' marking the point where the aperture is completely closed.

From Table 4.2 notice that when the light level increases from 2 lux to 8000 lux, the aperture diameter changes from 36 mm to 0.6 mm, a total of 13 stops, in order to maintain a constant level of light at the pick-up. 8000 lux is what might be expected on a dark, overcast day. For this same lens to deliver 2 lux at the pick-up on a bright sunny day where the light level is typically 500000 lux, the aperture would have to close down another six stops, and the diameter would become just 0.1 mm. Such a small diameter is simply not possible to control, either manually or automatically, because an error of just 0.05 mm would result in a light difference of 25%, and in the case of an automatic iris lens the control circuit would 'hunt' causing the iris mechanism to oscillate (see 'Electrical connections'). Clearly some other solution must be found.

The answer to the problem is to add a *neutral density (ND) spot filter* inside the lens. A neutral density filter is one which affects all frequencies of visible light by the same amount, and therefore has the effect of reducing the overall light level. The term 'spot filter' in this case refers to the fact that the filter does not cover the entire lens area but rather appears like a spot in the centre of the lens. The filter is designed to have maximum effect in its centre, reducing consistently between the centre and the outer edge. The principle is illustrated in Figure 4.9.

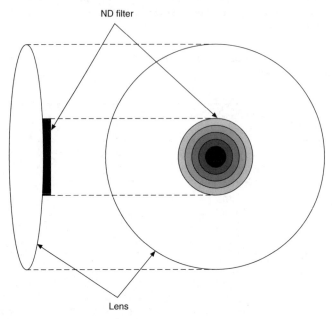

Figure 4.9 *ND spot filter on a lens*

When the aperture is fully open the filter has little effect on the overall amount of light passing through. However as the diameter of the aperture approaches that of the filter, its effect begins to be felt. Consider the effect that such a filter would have on the lens example we have been considering in Table 4.2. Let us suppose that the filter begins to take effect as the aperture diameter reaches 1 mm. As the light input increases from around 2000 lux to 4000 lux there is no need for the iris to close down as far to maintain a 2 lux output, because some of the incoming light is lost through the filter. Further increases in the incoming light level are met with corresponding amounts of filtering as the iris closes, and the centre area of the filter becomes the only part of the lens that is being used.

One option available to lens manufacturers for obtaining lower F-stop figures is to produce *aspherical lenses*. Without going into great detail, these lenses are ground in such a way that they are made to be more of a bell shape, which greatly improves the light-gathering and focussing ability. The increase in light efficiency enables lower F-numbers to be achieved, although this is at some considerable financial cost because these lenses are far more difficult to manufacture.

In practice, lenses using spot filters are often labelled 'F1.4–64'. This means that the mechanical iris offers ten stops (F1.4–F32) unaided, with a further 11 stops (F32–F64) available in the filter ring area. Thus, the lens assembly is capable of 21 stops without the aperture diameter having to close to an impractical amount.

The F-number can have serious implications when selecting a lens for a specific application. From Table 4.2 we see that a 50mm lens with an aperture set at 25mm equates to F.2. However, for a zoom lens with a focal length of 150mm, a 75mm aperture would also give an F-number of $150/75 = 2$. So we see that every increase in focal length requires a larger aperture to maintain a workable lens speed.

In the case of a manual iris lens, the situation can arise where the picture quality is perfectly acceptable during the daytime, but as soon as the light level begins to fall the lens is unable to pass sufficient light to maintain image quality. Clearly it is impractical to manually adjust the iris every time the light level changes, and any camera located either outdoors, or indoors in a situation where there will be large fluctuations in light levels, should be fitted with an automatic iris lens.

An auto lens is one where the aperture mechanism incorporates some form of motorized drive which closes the iris when the light level is high and opens it as and when it falls, maintaining an optimum light throughput for the camera pick-up. The principle of operation is illustrated in Figure 4.10. The video signal emerging from the CCD is sent to an auto iris amplifier circuit which detects and monitors the average level of the video signal. Whilst the video level falls within a range deemed acceptable, nothing happens. However, should the light level increase, the average video level will rise and the circuit will produce a d.c. output to activate the motor drive circuit, and hence the motor. The greater the light input, the higher will be the d.c. control, and the motor turns faster to close down the aperture.

This action is illustrated in the time-related graphs in Figure 4.10. At point (a) the light input becomes too high (large video signal), and the monitor circuit produces a positive d.c. output to operate the iris motor. Between (a) and (b) the iris is closing, the light level is falling, and the d.c. output from the monitor circuit falls accordingly until, at (b), the aperture setting is correct and the motor stops. Between points (b) and (c) the light level, although varying, remains within acceptable levels, and the iris remains stationary. At (c) the light level suddenly falls, and the monitor circuit produces a negative d.c. which will cause the motor to turn in the opposite direction, opening the aperture. At (d) the light falling onto the CCD is once more within acceptable levels, and the monitor circuit removes the negative d.c. control, and the motor stops.

With the arrangement shown in Figure 4.10, the servo motor, gearbox, and auto iris amplifier circuit are all incorporated within the lens, which is commonly known as an AI lens. A connection is made from the camera to the lens to provide a video signal input to the monitor circuit. This link may use terminal connectors, or it may be made using a plug and socket arrangement. Some cameras have just one single socket with a selector switch labelled something like 'Video/DD Iris'. We shall come to DD in a moment, but where an auto iris amplifier circuit is located in the lens assembly, the selector must be set to the 'Video' position.

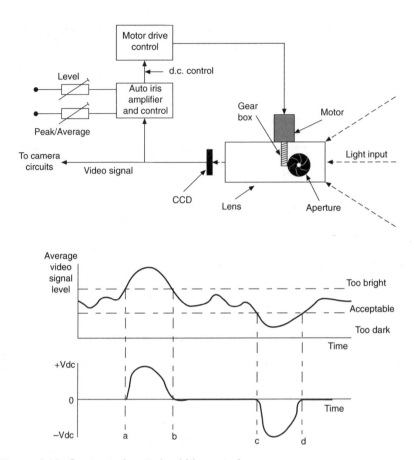

Figure 4.10 *Concept of motorized iris control*

Although AI lenses incorporating a motor and monitor circuit are still used, they are very large and expensive. In recent years an alternative to the motorized drive has been developed called the *galvanometric drive*. The galvanometer is by no means a new invention; it was used as a movement in very sensitive moving-coil measuring meters many years ago, and operates on very similar electromagnetic principles to the analogue meter movement used today. However, instead of moving a pointer needle, it moves the plates of an iris mechanism. The principle is shown in Figure 4.11. The d.c. output is fed to the galvanometer plates, holding the aperture at the correct position. However, the d.c. must be maintained otherwise the plates will simply fall fully closed, and thus the signal monitor produces a varying d.c. as shown. Two advantages of employing galvanometric drives in preference to d.c. motors are a reduction in the physical size of the lens, and a much lower current consumption.

The lens size can be further reduced by incorporating the AI amplifier circuit within the camera. These compact lens types are known as *direct*

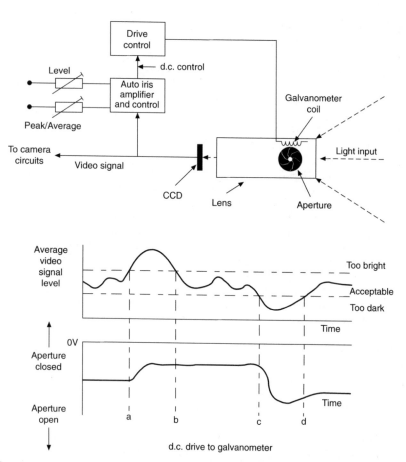

Figure 4.11 *Unlike the motor, a galvanometer requires a constant current to maintain the aperture setting*

drive (DD) lenses and are widely used in the CCTV industry. Where a DD lens is employed, the Video/DD selector switch on the camera must be set to the 'DD' position.

The two controls labelled 'Level' and 'Peak/Average' in the arrangement in Figure 4.11 give the installer some control over the iris action and thus the image on the screen. These controls may be found in either the lens or the camera, depending on where the AI amplifier circuit is located. They are required because there is no camera/lens combination yet devised which can automatically cope with every possible lighting scenario, and sometimes compromises need to be reached.

The level control performs a similar function to the manual iris ring in that it allows the engineer to set the sensitivity of the lens. The control is usually labelled 'H–L' or 'Hi–Lo'. Setting the control towards the high end tends to produce satisfactory results in the day, but the picture may be dark at night. A low setting will allow the iris to open in the dark, producing a clearer picture, but this may lead to excessive brightness in the day. Unless the system incorporates a facility whereby an operator can control the iris via telemetry, the level has to be set taking account of the extremes under which the lens will be expected to operate, and the particular requirements of the customer.

The peak/average control, often labelled 'P–A' or 'Pk–Av', enables the installer to introduce a degree of compromise with regard to large differences in lighting levels within the picture area. Consider the two situations shown in Figure 4.12. The wall light in Figure 4.12a would cause the iris to close down, resulting in a very dark image across the rest of the viewing area. In this situation the peak/average control may be used to open the iris up (by adjusting towards the 'average' position) in order to give a reasonable contrast across the picture. The compromise is that there will be a 'hot spot' in the area surrounding the wall light.

For the situation in Figure 4.12b, if the control were set for 'average' the iris would open fully to bring out the tarmac area, causing the person to bleach out. The problem would be particularly acute in low light conditions. Adjusting the control towards the 'Peak' setting causes the iris to close down to a point where the tarmac is not really visible, but the person becomes more clearly discernible on the screen.

You will frequently see another setting on many cameras labelled 'EI', meaning Electronic Iris. This is a circuit within the camera that maintains the correct video signal level using electronic means, and has nothing to do with the iris in the lens. This principle will be discussed in Chapter 6.

The final parameter we need to examine is the *depth of field*. This is the range (in distance) in front of the lens where objects remain in sharp focus.

As much as we would like a lens to display everything, both far and near, within the field of view in perfect focus, this is not possible. Look at Figure 4.13 where a lens is focused at a particular distance. Items closer and further away than the true focussing distance may also appear to be in focus. This range of field is called the depth of field.

Depth of field is dependent upon two things: the angle of view of the lens and the aperture setting. When considering the depth of field it is important to remember that either *a wider angle of view, or an increase in the F-number (reduced size of aperture) increases the depth of field.*

In general, wide angle, short focal length lenses have a very large depth of field, even when the F-number is low. However, the advantage of the large depth of field is somewhat offset by fact that distant objects appear very small on the monitor screen. As focal length increases, the lens view narrows and distant objects become larger. However, the depth of field reduces.

The problem now is that once the lens has been trained onto a target, and the focus has been set for that target, as soon as the lens is made to zoom onto a target at a different distance the focus has to be readjusted. This is illustrated in Figure 4.14 where a zoom lens has been set to a target (object A) at distance D_1, and the focus has been adjusted accordingly.

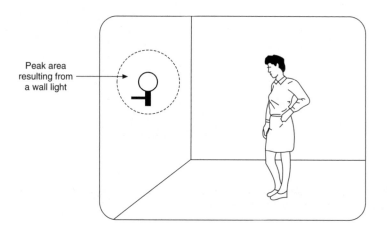

Figure 4.12a *Peak levels allowed to burn out, average levels are viewable*

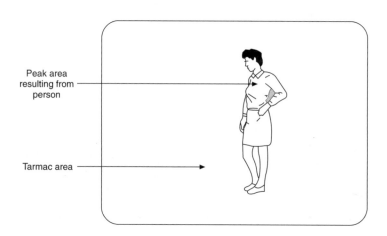

Figure 4.12b *Average area appears dark, peak areas are viewable*

The depth of field around that object would be that shown by the dotted lines. However, when the focal length is readjusted to zoom in on object B at a distance D_2, the focus is incorrect. This is why the more powerful zoom lenses need to be re-focused when moved from one target to another.

Another related problem is when an auto iris, long focal length (telephoto) lens is used where there is insufficient lighting after dark. During the day the aperture will set to a high F-number, and there will be

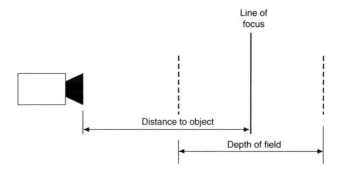

Figure 4.13 *The depth of field is the area on either side of the object in focus where correct focus is still maintained*

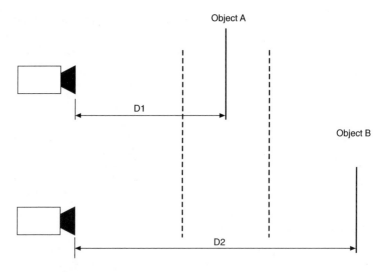

Figure 4.14 *When the zoom is altered, the focus will be incorrect*

an acceptable depth of field. However, after dark the auto iris will reduce the F-number in an attempt to maintain the light throughput. When this happens the depth of field reduces. Of course, if the engineer only visits the site during the day he may wonder what the customer is complaining about!

Zoom lenses

Fixed focal length lenses are all right for locations where the area we wish to view is only a few metres square. However, as soon as we attempt to view a larger expanse such as a car park or shopping mall, then the limitations of a fixed lens become patently obvious. To attain the field of view a wide angle lens must be used, but then everything and everyone appears so small on the screen that the image is useless for evidential purposes. On the other hand, if a zoom lens is fitted the field of view is lost meaning that, unless the lens is motorized and can be operated from a control room, it is of little use. This in turn means having to employ staff to operate the CCTV system. For situations where the level of risk and the size of the business where the system is to be installed does not warrant employing full-time CCTV operators, let alone investing in expensive zoom lenses and telemetry systems, it is possible to obtain a reasonable coverage by installing two cameras at the same location, one fitted with a wide-angle lens and the other with a zoom lens. However, the installer must be certain that such a system will provide the level of cover required before selling the idea to the client.

When manufacturers quote the performance of a zoom lens, it is common practice to state it in terms of a ratio of the change in focal length. For example, a lens having a focal length from 16 mm to 160 mm would be quoted as being a 10:1 zoom lens. However, just describing the ratio gives no clue as to the range of views provided, i.e. 10:1 could mean 10 mm to 100 mm or 15 mm to 150 mm.

The principle of a zoom lens is shown in Figure 4.15. Within the assembly, the zoom lens group is the most complex part of the mechanism because the optical devices within this group have to move in such a way that the image remains undistorted and in correct focus. It would be very difficult to maintain correct focussing over a large change in focal length, and therefore a manual focus control is provided by making the front lens group adjustable.

Specifying the optical speed of a zoom lens is not as straightforward as for a fixed lens because, as shown earlier, the F-number is dependent on the focal length and aperture, and in this case the focal length is variable. To keep the specifications simple, the majority of manufacturers simply state the F-number for a lens at the two extremes of its focal length. So, for example, a $\frac{2}{3}''$ 6:1 zoom lens having a focal length range between 12.5 mm and 75 mm may be quoted as having an F-number between F:1.2–F:560.

When a zoom lens is set to its maximum focal length (telephoto), it must be fixed firmly in position because the slightest movement results in a very large picture shake on the monitor. The longer the focal length, the more acute the problem. Where the camera is fixed to a solid structure there is not usually a problem, however when it is mounted on top of a tower the slightest wind can throw the picture all over the monitor screen when the lens is at a high telephoto setting. Gyroscopically corrected lenses are available (at considerable cost). The optics are mounted in a mechanism that moves in the opposite direction to the motion of the main lens casing. Needless to say, because of their high cost these devices are not commonplace.

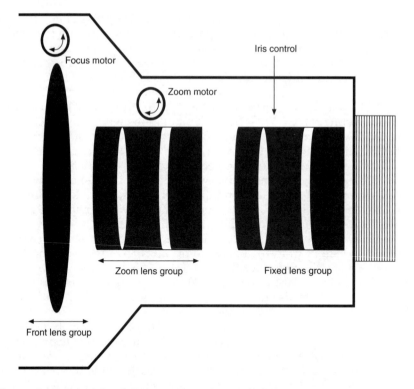

Figure 4.15 *Principle of the zoom lens. In a manually operated lens, the two motors are omitted and two small levers are available to turn the focus and zoom controls*

Electrical connections

Correct electrical connection between the various lens drive circuits and the lens is very important. Connection methods, terminology and drive potentials can differ between lens types and manufacturers, and an engineer must be able to decipher the wiring diagrams provided in the manufacturers' technical information.

The most popular lenses for use in smaller installations are either fixed focal length or varifocal types, employing a DD or AI iris control. In this case the only electrical connections between camera and lens are for the iris. Terminal connectors may be used on some cameras, however many lenses come with a pre-fitted connector plug. When using one of these with a camera from the same manufacturer it is usually very difficult to get the connections wrong. However, where a mix of equipment is being installed it is important to check for compatibility because, although some standardization has taken place with the acceptance of the 'P Plug' (illustrated in Figure 4.16), there are still a number of wiring configurations.

It is also essential that, if fitted, the selector switch on the camera for iris control output is set to 'd.c.' and not 'video' drive.

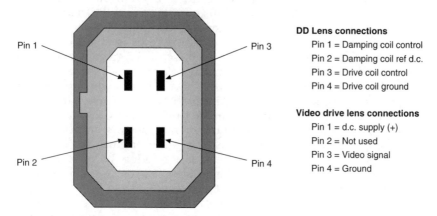

DD Lens connections

Pin 1 = Damping coil control
Pin 2 = Damping coil ref d.c.
Pin 3 = Drive coil control
Pin 4 = Drive coil ground

Video drive lens connections

Pin 1 = d.c. supply (+)
Pin 2 = Not used
Pin 3 = Video signal
Pin 4 = Ground

Figure 4.16 *Standard connection configurations for the P-Plug. (So called because it was developed by Panasonic)*

A galvanometric iris usually has a four-pin connector. Two terminals connect the d.c. drive voltage from the camera to the actuator coil, which controls the aperture. The other two carry a control voltage to a second coil in the iris assembly which is used for damping. The damping coil is necessary because the galvanometer is a very sensitive device and is prone to overreaction to the drive voltage. Because the iris control is effectively a closed loop servo (the light input forming the feedback), this would result in a condition known as hunting. Hunting is where a servo continually overcompensates and the unit that it is controlling, in this case the iris, oscillates. Thus the iris control circuit in the camera outputs not only the drive voltage but also a damping voltage which is fed to the damping coil. The arrangement is shown in Figure 4.17.

In cases where the iris control circuit is located within the lens, then three connections are required: one for the video signal, one to provide a

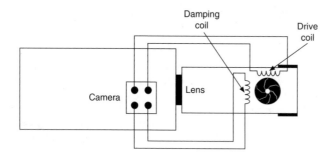

Figure 4.17 *Connections between camera and a DD auto iris lens*

12 V d.c. supply from the camera to power the control circuit, and one for a common negative (ground) return. Although not a guaranteed standard, the wiring colours for these functions are normally white for video, red for +12 V and black for 0 V. A green wire is often found in the lens connector cable. This is only used when the system incorporates fully functional telemetry controlled cameras where the operator is able to manually adjust the iris from the control room. In this case the green wire connects a varying d.c. control from the telemetry receiver to the lens.

The lens connector cable may have a braided screen which is intended to reduce the possibility of RFI entering at this point. In theory this would be connected to the earthed body of the camera, or an alternative earth point in cases where the camera body is non-metallic. In practice this screen is often left disconnected because it can produce an earth loop, and as the connecting lead is so short it is rare for RFI to be induced. Where interference is proving to be a problem then one test which should be performed would be to connect the screen to earth.

When we come to look at motorized zoom lenses, the electrical connections become a little more involved. A zoom lens usually employs low voltage d.c. motors to move the zoom lens group (focal length) and the front lens group (focus). Typical operating voltages for these motors can be between 5–12 V d.c., the control voltage being provided by the telemetry controller, which may vary depending on the type of system employed. It is important to check that the lenses selected for use with a control system are compatible. For example, if the lens employs 5 V motors, and the control unit is applying 12 V when zoom and focus are operating, you will find that the lenses might react very quickly(!), but also fail soon after installation because the motors have burnt out. On the other hand, operating 12 V motors at 5 V will mean that the lens reaction is very slow, if there is any reaction at all.

The motors drive the lenses via gearboxes, and they must not be allowed to over-drive the mechanism, otherwise permanent damage may occur. Take, for example, the zoom mechanism. When the motor has moved the zoom lens group to the maximum focal length position, the power to the motor must be cut immediately. This can be achieved using *limit switches*. However, there is no point in simply placing a switch in series with the motor, otherwise once it has opened there is no way of applying a reverse voltage to move the lens in the other direction. The solution is to place diodes across the switches. A typical circuit arrangement in shown in Figure 4.18.

In this circuit, switch S_1 opens when the lens reaches maximum zoom (telephoto). When the operator wishes to zoom out again it is necessary to reverse the motor direction, which means reversing the polarity of the drive voltage at terminals A and B. The current path will now be from terminal A, through diode D_1, through the motor, returning through switch S_2 which will still be closed. Moving from the 'wide' position is simply the reverse, because S_2 will now be open, and diode D_2 provides the current path.

It is not uncommon to find potentiometers in a zoom lens for *pre-set*

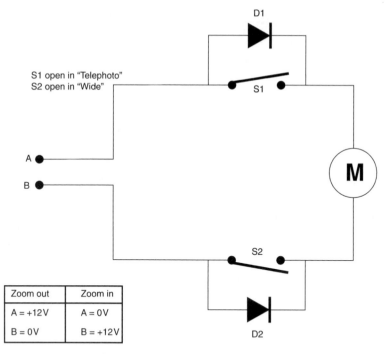

Figure 4.18 *Limit switch circuit for a zoom motor. The same arrangement can be used for focus and iris motors*

zoom and *pre-set focus*. These potentiometers rotate as the zoom and focus motors are operated, thus deriving a range of voltages corresponding to the zoom/focus ranges. The output voltage from each of the potentiometer sliders is connected back to the control unit, making possible a facility whereby the control unit can have programmable pre-set zoom positions. A typical potentiometer wiring arrangement is shown in Figure 4.19.

When setting up the pre-set positions, the engineer or operator moves the zoom to a desired position (it may be that the pan/tilt is also moved at this point) and adjusts the focus. This position can then be stored into the memory of the control unit, which does this by converting the d.c. value from each potentiometer into a digital value. During normal operation, when the operator instructs the control unit to move the camera to the pre-set position, the zoom and focus motors (plus pan/tilt motors) are operated until the d.c. from the potentiometers reaches the pre-determined value.

Modern control units can memorize more than one pre-set position; indeed, some can store up to one hundred pre-sets. Yet in reality five is about the most that is required because, when you think of it, when would you need one camera to have a hundred zoom positions, and how can an operator remember where they are anyway?

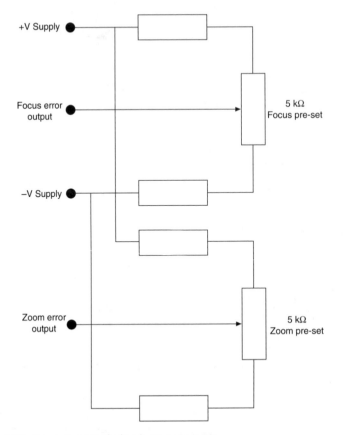

Figure 4.19 *Pre-set control circuit arrangement*

Lens mounts

A type of lens mount referred to as C mount has been used for many years in the ciné industry, and because these lenses were already in manufacture they were adopted by the early CCTV industry. The term 'C mount' refers to the type of screw thread on the lens.

C mount lenses are comparatively large, and as the size of CCTV cameras continued to reduce, it was necessary to have a more compact lens. Furthermore, the lenses can be the most expensive part of a CCTV system, and as the size of systems increased in terms of the number of cameras possible, a more cost-effective lens was called for. It was with these factors in mind that the CS mount lens was developed.

The CS mount lens is much smaller, however this is not without some sacrifice in performance. Compared to C mount lenses, CS mount types suffer greater optical distortion because nearly all of the glass area is employed, whereas a C mount only makes use of the inner area where there is minimal distortion.

From an engineer's point of view, the main difference between these lenses is the distance from the back of the lens to the image device in the camera. For a C mount this distance is 17.5mm, whereas for a CS mount it is only 12.5mm. In practice this means that these lens types cannot simply be interchanged because the focussed image will not fall onto the pick-up device.

CCTV cameras are specified as being either C or CS mount, although some have a mechanical adjustment which moves the pick-up device between 12.5mm and 17.5mm. Where the mount cannot be adjusted, the following rules apply.

A C mount lens can work on a CS mount camera as long as a special 5mm adapter ring is fitted to extend the distance to 17.5mm. This is illustrated in Figure 4.20. However, a *CS mount lens will never work on a C mount camera* because there is no way of reducing the 17.5mm distance.

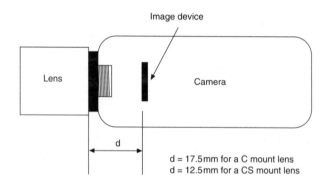

d = 17.5mm for a C mount lens
d = 12.5mm for a CS mount lens

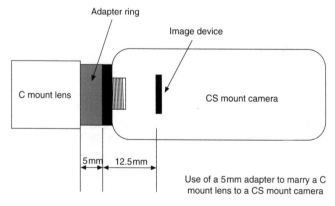

Use of a 5mm adapter to marry a C mount lens to a CS mount camera

Figure 4.20

Filters

There are occasions where it is useful to fit a light filter to the lens. For example, where a camera is required to look through a glass window pane, a *polarizing filter* can be fitted to remove the effects of glare or reflections. This type of filter is fitted to the lens and then rotated until the desired result is achieved.

Another type of external filter is the ND type, which we discussed earlier in this chapter when considering the action of the spot type filter, which is used to increase the possible number of F-stops. Full-sized versions affecting the entire lens area are available, and in a range of attenuation factors. However, it is not often in CCTV applications that these would be a permanent fixture to a camera. A practical application of the ND filter is in the adjustment of back-focus, which will be discussed later in this chapter.

Infra-red cut filters are used where it is desirable to remove IR light from the camera. All colour cameras have an in-built IR cut filter, however some monochrome models are designed to respond to IR light. Sometimes where there is a lot of infra-red light in the viewing area it is necessary to negate this feature because parts of the picture become slightly burnt out. Fitting an external IR cut filter often results in a picture with an improved grey scale contrast range. Another application for IR cut filters is when adjusting the focus. Removal of infra-red light from the lens enables the focus to be adjusted using only visible light. This produces a slightly different focussing point, but one which is perhaps more accurate for a camera which is expected to rely largely on visible light.

Opposite to the IR cut filter is the IR pass filter which removes the majority of visible light so that the camera can only 'see' infra-red. In the case of cameras that are intended primarily for night-time operation using infra-red lighting, adjustment can be performed in the daytime if an IR pass filter is used to remove the visible light. The reliability of the adjustment can be further improved by adding an ND filter, in addition to the IR pass filter, to further block visible light.

Lens adjustment

One of the biggest problems in CCTV installations is incorrect adjustment of the *back-focus*. This refers to the 17.5mm/12.5mm distance between the back of the lens and the camera pick-up device. Where fixed lenses are involved this is not as critical as long as the engineer is able to obtain a correctly focussed image. However, when a zoom lens is employed, if the back-focus is not correctly adjusted, the operator will find that the focus moves out every time the zoom function is used. Another problem can be that the zoom lens functions satisfactorily during the day when the auto iris is closed down, however when the light begins to fade and the iris opens, the focus becomes poor due to the reduced depth of field.

We have already touched on this problem earlier when we discussed depth of field, and the ideal solution is to perform back-focus adjustment at dusk when the adjustment is far more sensitive. However, in reality this is not always practical, and therefore another method is to fit an external ND filter to the lens whilst performing the adjustment; the filter simulating twilight conditions by reducing the amount of light input.

There is more than one acceptable method for obtaining correct back-focus adjustment, and engineers will adopt their own preferred routines as they become proficient at this. However, when starting out, the generally accepted method for adjusting the back focus on a camera which is fitted with a zoom lens is.

1. Manually open the iris, or fit an ND filter, or work in low light conditions.
2. Select a target at the maximum operational range for the particular camera/lens (a target with a lot of detail such as a wall is ideal).
3. Adjust the lens focus to 'far'.
4. Set the zoom to maximum wide angle.
5. Move the back-focus adjustment on the camera forwards and back until optimum focus is obtained.
6. Set the zoom to full telephoto.
7. Adjust the lens focus for optimum focus.
8. Set the zoom to maximum wide angle.
9. Readjust the back-focus for optimum focus.
10. Repeat steps 4 to 10 until optimum focus is obtained at all points between wide and telephoto.

In some cases the back-focus is fixed with a locking screw or nut. Be sure to slacken this off before commencing adjustment, and be sure to secure it again afterwards, otherwise vibrations from the pan, tilt and zoom (PTZ) action may move the back-focus adjustment.

From a practical point of view, it has been assumed all along that the engineer is looking at the picture on a monitor whilst performing focus adjustments, however this is not always as straightforward as it might seem, especially when working on a camera assembly mounted atop a 7m tower. There are a number of ways of overcoming this issue. One of them is to adjust the back focus before mounting the camera, perhaps even in the workshop. When performing the adjustment in this manner, remember to reduce the lighting somehow, otherwise you might find yourself performing the adjustment again, but this time from the top of a ladder!

Another approach is to use a portable, battery-powered monitor. There are test monitors made specifically for this purpose, and they can prove very useful in the field for performing all manner of tests and adjustments. The one drawback at times can be when using these in direct sunlight, as this can make viewing somewhat difficult.

Another device that is useful for performing focus adjustment is the focus meter (Figure 4.21). This is designed to connect to the video output from the camera, where it analyses the high frequency video components in the signal. The sharper the focus the greater the amount of hf, and thus if the engineer moves the focus adjustment to one end of its travel and then progressively moves it back once again: the meter will indicate an increasing hf content up until the point where the optimum focus point has been passed, whereupon the indication will begin to fall off. The engineer is therefore able to set the focus adjustment for the peak indication.

Figure 4.21 *A focus meter (Courtesy of NG Systems Ltd)*

Lens finding

Earlier in this chapter we saw how we can calculate the required lens size for a given application, however there are alternatives to using mathematics and an electronic calculator. Perhaps the simplest of these is to use one of the lens calculators which are often available free of charge from lens manufacturers or suppliers. These differ slightly in the both the way that they function and the data they produce, but they are simple to use, are quite accurate and are adequate for the majority of applications. A typical lens calculator is illustrated in Figure 4.22. This particular type requires

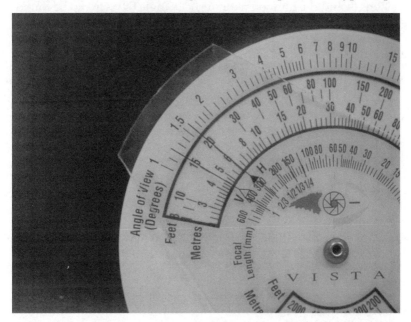

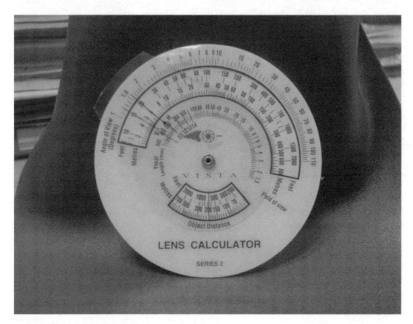

Figure 4.22 *Typical lens calculator*

you to know the primary target height or width, and the distance from the camera to the target. By adjusting the cursors on the calculator, the focal length and the horizontal or vertical angle of view can be found for any given camera format size.

Another method is to use one of the look-up tables produced by various lens manufacturers, however these often quote the horizontal angle of view produced by a range of lenses when fitted to different camera formats. In this case the engineer still has no idea of the object width or height for any given distance from the lens, but this can be calculated using trigonometry.

$$W = d \, \tan\theta$$

where W = width of area across the image
   d = distance of object from lens
   θ = horizontal angle of the lens

Example

A look-up table states that a 30mm, $\frac{1}{2}''$ format lens has a horizontal angle of approximately 11°. Find the image width at a distance of 40m.

Solution

$$W = 40 \times \tan \, 11°$$

$$= 40 \times 0.19$$

$$= 7.6\text{m}$$

Of all the tools available for lens finding, perhaps the most effective are the optical viewfinder types. The engineer positions himself where the camera is to be located and looks through the device, adjusting it until the desired image is obtained. Calibrated markings on the side of the device enable the focal length to be read off. The scales include the various format sizes. One bonus of using these is that the customer can be shown what he is getting before agreeing to the installation. Indeed, the customer can set the viewfinder to show the engineer/surveyor what he requires, and if the engineer is seen to log the agreed lens size at the time he need have no worries about come-back at a later stage in the installation.

5 Fundamentals of television

Before we can look at the operation of cameras and monitors, it is important to have an understanding of the make-up of the television picture and the signals required to produce the picture.

Development of television really began during the 1930s with different ideas being tested, with differing degrees of success. However, all of the ideas had one thing in common; they were all designed to produce a picture using a *cathode ray tube* (CRT). The broadcast analogue television system that emerged in the post-war years is still the one in use today, albeit with many improvements, and CCTV is simply a spin-off of this system.

Because television was designed around the cathode ray tube, this is perhaps a useful place to begin our examination because, without an appreciation of the drive requirements of the CRT, it is not easy to understand the reasoning behind other parts of the system.

The cathode ray tube

People often refer to the thermionic valve as a thing of the past, something that went out during the 1970s with the rapid introduction of the transistor and silicon chip. Yet the cathode ray tube *is* a thermionic valve, and despite many attempts to replace it with a smaller and thinner alternative display device, there is still nothing that can produce an equivalent picture quality for the same price.

A diagram of a monochrome CRT is shown in Figure 5.1. The operating principle is quite straightforward. The cathode, which is connected to a positive d.c. supply, is heated up. This causes the electrons present within its molecular structure to accelerate to an escape velocity, creating a negative space charge in the area just in front of the cathode.

A very high voltage, referred to as the extra high tension (EHT), is connected via the final anode to the screen. The size of this voltage depends upon the screen size, but for a 30 cm (12″) monochrome tube, the EHT is typically 10 kV. If there were nothing between the cathode and the screen, the negative electrons in the space charge would make their way towards the EHT at the screen, and return to their power source via the final anode connection. Because electrons are moving from the cathode to the screen, we can say that there is a current flowing through the CRT. It is important to note that current flow only takes place because the tube has been completely evacuated of all air. Otherwise the electrons would impact with the molecules of air and rapidly lose their momentum, causing them to fall back to the cathode once again.

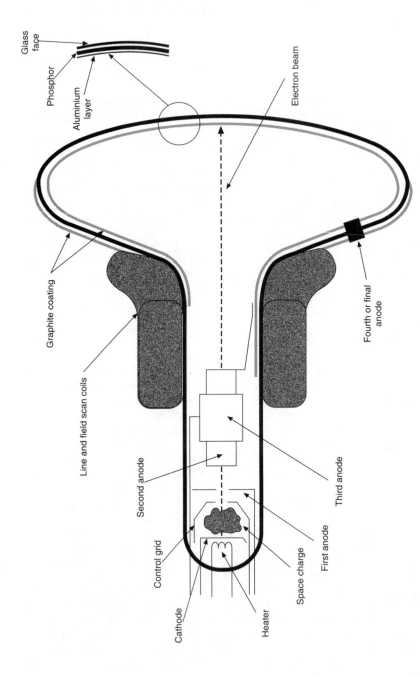

Figure 5.1 *A monochrome CRT*

The problem is that the electrons would not be travelling fast enough for our purposes and, furthermore, they would be spreading out as they travelled towards the screen due to the effect of their like charges. To overcome these problems, anodes 1, 2, and 3 are added. The first anode (A1) is connected to a d.c. potential of around +100V. This has the effect of attracting the electrons away from the cathode, giving them velocity in the direction of the screen. The electrons are travelling so fast by the time they reach this anode that they pass straight through a hole in its centre, and move at high velocity towards the EHT potential. Another name for the first anode is the accelerator anode. Unfortunately it can also be referred to as the screen grid. This is a name that goes back to the days of the valve, but today it can cause confusion for the unsuspecting engineer who might think that it makes reference to the screen on the front of the CRT.

Anodes 2 and 3 form an electrostatic focussing lens. Focussing is necessary to counter the divergence of the electron beam caused by the electrons moving apart. Anode A2 is connected to the EHT, whilst A3 is connected via a variable resistor (*focus control*) to a potential of around +200V. These two largely differing potentials produce an electrostatic field between anodes A2 and A3. Altering the potential on A3 changes the shape and strength of the electrostatic field, and hence the effect on the electron beam passing through the centre. The principle is illustrated in Figure 5.2. The focus control is adjusted until the angle of the converging beam is such that the electrons all hit the same point on the screen. In other words, the picture will appear at best focus.

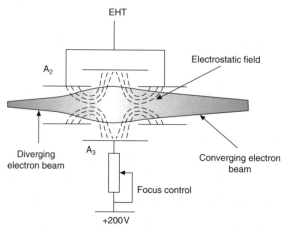

Figure 5.2 *Principle of electrostatic focussing. Cross-sectional view; the anodes are three metal cylinders*

The CRT screen is coated with phosphor, which glows when hit by the high-velocity electrons. Behind the phosphor is a thin aluminium layer which serves both to protect the phosphor from burn, and act as a reflective screen to ensure that all of the light produced by the phosphor is projected forwards.

The assembly comprising the heater, cathode, control grid and anodes is known as the *electron gun* assembly although, as we have seen, it does not actually fire electrons but rather it emits them as a result of the high EHT potential on the CRT viewing screen.

So we see how a CRT produces an electron beam current which flows from the cathode to the final anode, producing a small white spot in the centre of the screen. We shall now look at how the brightness of the spot can be controlled.

The brightness is dependent on the number of electrons hitting the phosphor, so by controlling the beam current we can control the brightness. This function is performed by the control grid, the action of which is illustrated in Figure 5.3.

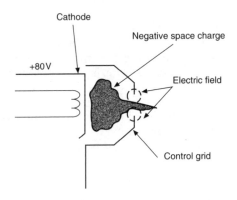

Cathode potential	Grid potential	Grid with respect to cathode	Effect
80 V	80 V	0 V	None. Maximum current through the grid aperture.
80 V	50 V	−30 V	Size of aperture reduced by the effective negative charge (w.r.t. cathode). Beam current reduced.
80 V	20 V	−60 V	Grid is so negative that the aperture is closed. Zero beam current; no display.

Figure 5.3 *Electric field produced by the grid/cathode potential effectively closes the aperture in the grid*

If the cathode is maintained at a constant potential and the control grid is set at the same potential, there is no effect on the electron beam and maximum brightness still exists. Making the grid less positive causes it to appear negative to electrons leaving the cathode, resulting in those electrons close to the sides of the aperture being repelled. However, some electrons still pass through the centre of the aperture, and thus the beam current and brightness is reduced. When the grid potential becomes approximately 60 V lower than the cathode, the repelling action is so strong that the aperture in the grid is effectively closed. All beam current ceases, and there is no spot on the screen. Connecting a variable resistor to the control grid provides a means of brightness control.

The beam current can also be controlled by varying the cathode potential. Increasing the cathode voltage makes the grid appear more negative, causing a reduction in brightness. Reducing the cathode voltage makes the grid appear less negative, and the brightness increases. Thus, if the video signal waveform is connected to the cathode, the electron beam will be modulated by the rapidly changing video signal.

For the CRT to produce a picture, the electron beam is made to deflect both vertically and horizontally at high speed causing it to scan the screen, producing a blank white display known as a *raster*. Applying a video signal waveform to the cathode causes the beam current to be modulated, producing a picture as the screen is scanned.

Deflection of the electron beam is performed by the line and field scanning coils which are placed around the CRT neck. Alternating currents are passed through the scan coils which in turn set up alternating electromagnetic fields. These fields interact with a magnetic field that exists around the electron beam, and thus deflection takes place. The line scan coils perform horizontal deflection. The field scan coils perform vertical deflection.

The graphite coating inside the CRT is used to form connections between the final anode, the CRT screen and the second anode.

The colour CRT

In Chapter 3 we saw that white light is made up from the three primary colours, red, green and blue. Thus, for a colour CRT to work effectively it must reproduce these three colours, which it does by having three separate cathodes, each driven by separate red, green and blue signals derived in the colour camera.

The CRT screen is coated with three different types of phosphor which emit different frequencies (colours) of light when struck by electrons; these colours being red, green and blue. The phosphors are laid on the screen face in a tight pattern, illustrated in Figure 5.4. Each electron gun is targeted at just one set of phosphors, and so in effect we can say that one gun is creating the red light output, another the green, and another the blue.

When all three guns are emitting electrons, all the phosphors are illuminated and the eye receives red, green and blue light. However, because the phosphor spots are so small, at normal viewing distance the eye is unable to discern them and the brain is tricked into thinking that it is seeing a white screen. The individual spots are visible if you move

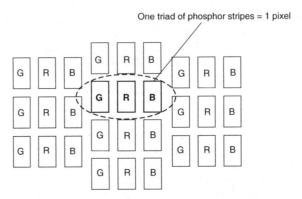

Figure 5.4 *Typical phosphor stripe formation on a colour CRT screen*

very close to a colour monitor screen and focus your eye on an area of white picture content.

Colour can be introduced by turning the guns on and off. For example, if the blue gun is turned off, the eye receives only red and green light and, as we saw in Chapter 3 (Figure 3.3), the brain will interpret this as yellow.

The principle of the colour CRT is shown in Figure 5.5. The actual operation is a little more complex than this diagram reveals because special magnets are required around the tube neck, either external or internal, to ensure that each electron beam only ever strikes its own colour phosphor. This is called *convergence* of the CRT, but it is not necessary to look at this in any more depth as it not something that the CCTV engineer will become concerned with.

The other main difference between colour and monochrome tubes are the operating voltages. For a colour CRT they are generally higher than

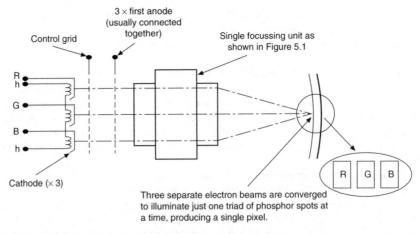

Figure 5.5 *Principle of a colour CRT*

for their equivalent size monochrome counterparts. The cathodes typically require a signal drive voltage of around 80 V pp (swinging between 70–150 V), the first anode potential is around 300–500 V, the focus is approximately 1 kV, and the EHT can be approximated as being equal to 1 kV per inch of screen size, and so for a 24″ colour CRT the EHT will be around 24 kV.

Producing a raster

We saw earlier how by making the spot (or three spots in the case of a colour CRT) deflect vertically and horizontally at high speed across the CRT screen, a white display called a raster is produced. The principle of sequentially scanning the screen to produce a raster is illustrated in Figure 5.6. For simplicity a raster with only nine lines has been drawn, although, as we shall see later, both broadcast TV and CCTV in the UK use a 625 line raster (525 lines for NTSC systems, see later in this chapter).

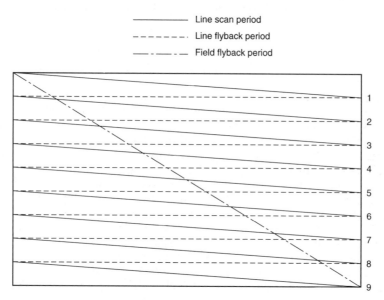

Figure 5.6 *Nine line sequentially scanned raster*

The horizontal (line scan) speed is made to be many times faster than the vertical (field scan) speed, and so the spot zigzags its way down the CRT screen. However, the *line scan* period from left to right is much longer than the *line flyback* period when the spot moves rapidly from right to left. Similarly, the *field scan* period is many times longer than the *field flyback* period.

During both the line and field flyback periods the electron beam is cut off, and so only the solid lines numbered 1 to 9 in Figure 5.6 are actually displayed. This is why the flyback periods have been shown dotted. The line scan period is often referred to as the *active line period*.

Remembering that the electron beam is deflected by passing currents through the scan coils, during the flyback periods the currents are being reversed to produce an equal but opposite magnetic field. This cannot be done instantly because of the inductive effects of the scan coils, hence the reason for having to turn off the beam and wait for flyback to complete.

So we see how a nine line raster is produced using sequential scanning. But what scanning speeds would we require to produce a practical 625 line or, for NTSC, a 525 line raster? The answer to this question is not as straightforward as it may appear. During the development of the television system there were a number of factors the designers had to take into consideration when determining the scanning speeds. Primarily these were the picture rate, the picture resolution, the system bandwidth, and the problem of picture flicker.

It must be remembered that the television system had to be designed around the existing cinema system, because at the time it was accepted that much of the transmitted material would be taken from movie sources. Even television newsreel was sourced on celluloid film (there were no camcorders in the 1940s!). So, before we can begin to look at the rationale for constructing television pictures using a CRT, we need to look briefly at the structure of the source material that was to come from the cinema industry.

The 'moving pictures' we see at the cinema are actually a series of still photographs being flashed onto a screen at high speed. Early systems used a frame rate of 16 pictures per second, however this produced poor quality, jerky pictures, and a 16 Hz brightness flicker was very discernible. It was generally accepted that a picture rate of between 20 Hz and 25 Hz would cure the problem of jerky pictures, but the eye could still resolve some flicker at these rates. This problem could only be overcome by increasing the picture rate to something in the order of 45 Hz to 50 Hz, but this meant a doubling of film consumption. The solution was (and still is to this day) to block the light output from the projector lamp not only whilst the frame is being pulled into the gate, but also once again whilst it is being held stationary in the gate. Thus each frame is flashed onto the screen twice in succession. A picture rate of 24 per second was decided on as the industry standard, and so the cine flicker rate is 48 Hz, which is indiscernible to the eye.

The flicker is a product of how the eye functions. The eye has a characteristic referred to as the persistence of vision. There is a time delay between a part of the retina being excited by a light input and the retina output fading once the light input has been removed. In the case of the 24 Hz cine picture rate, the eye was able to distinguish the projector light output being strobed as the frames were advanced. By strobing the lamp at twice the rate, the retina is unable to resolve the flicker.

Because the UK mains frequency is 50 Hz, there were reasons relating to receiver design why a picture rate of 25 per second rather than 24 was chosen for the television system. (In the United States, where the mains frequency is 60 Hz, the picture rate is 30 per second.) However, displaying the pictures at a rate of 25/30 Hz using sequential scanning would produce the same flicker problems as a cine film flashed at 24 Hz. To overcome the problem of picture flicker, a technique known as *interlaced scanning* was developed. The principle of interlaced scanning is illustrated in Figure 5.7 where, again for simplicity, a nine line raster has been shown.

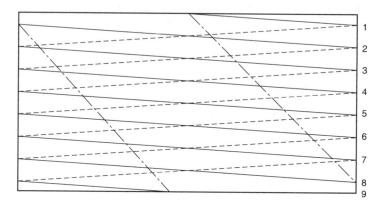

Figure 5.7 *Nine line interlaced raster*

In this case the spot begins at the top centre of the screen and makes its way down, finishing at the bottom right-hand corner. The field flyback now returns the spot to the top left-hand corner, where it once again scans downwards to end in the bottom centre. During the first vertical scan period, known as the *odd field*, the odd TV lines are scanned, and 50% of a cine picture frame is displayed. During the *even field* period, when the even line numbers are scanned, the other 50% of the frame is reproduced. So we see that *two TV fields equal one TV frame*. The principle is illustrated in Figure 5.8, where for simplicity an eleven line raster has been used.

The flicker is eliminated because all areas of the screen are being illuminated at a rate of 50 Hz (60 Hz NTSC). At a normal viewing distance

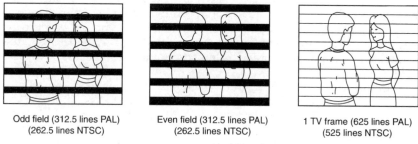

Odd field (312.5 lines PAL)
(262.5 lines NTSC)

Even field (312.5 lines PAL)
(262.5 lines NTSC)

1 TV frame (625 lines PAL)
(525 lines NTSC)

Figure 5.8 *Two interlaced fields build up a complete TV picture frame*

the eye cannot discern the individual TV lines and so, just as one line would be appearing to fade, two more are scanned, one on either side.

In the PAL UK TV system (see later in this chapter), the vertical scanning rate is made to be 50Hz, twice the 25Hz picture rate. Thus during the first field scan the spot reproduces the odd 312.5 lines, and during the second field scan the even 312.5 lines are reproduced. So in $\frac{1}{25}$th of a second (i.e. 40ms, or 25Hz) a complete picture is built up on the screen.

For the NTSC system, the vertical scanning rate is made to be 60Hz, twice the 30Hz picture rate. Thus during the first field scan the spot reproduces the odd 262.5 lines, and during the second field scan the even 262.5 lines are reproduced. So in $\frac{1}{30}$th of a second (i.e. 33ms, or 30Hz) a complete picture is built up on the screen.

Returning to the question, 'what scanning speeds would we require to produce a practical 625 line raster?', having dealt with the issues of picture rate and picture flicker, let's now see where picture resolution and system bandwidth come in.

Picture resolution

This relates to the definition of a TV picture, and can be expressed in terms of either vertical or horizontal resolution. The vertical resolution is determined largely by the number of lines that make up the picture. The horizontal resolution is determined by the number of black and white elements that the system is capable of displaying along any TV line, or in other words, the speed at which the system can switch the electron beam in the CRT on and off. Ideally, the maximum horizontal resolution for a television system should be at least equal to the vertical resolution; that is, where the width of each black or white square is equal to the thickness of one TV line. This display situation is illustrated in Figure 5.9.

Although the vertical resolution is determined by the number of TV lines in the picture, it is also dependent on the position of the camera in relation to the image in view. The more horizontal lines a system has, the more squares we can reproduce. However, it does not necessarily hold that a 600 line raster would always give a 600 line resolution. Looking at Figure 5.9, consider what happens when the camera is positioned such that each line is scanning equally between two sets of squares. The line cannot be black and white at the same time, and so the entire checkerboard would appear mid grey. This is an extreme situation, but it does make the point that in any picture there will almost certainly be some loss in vertical resolution.

Ignoring widescreen television, which has yet to make an inroad into CCTV, all CRT screens have an *aspect ratio* of 4:3. That is, although the screen size of any TV/monitor (e.g. 30cm, 51cm) is measured diagonally, the ratio of the sides is always 4:3. Because the horizontal resolution must be at least equal to the vertical resolution, for any given number of TV lines (vertical resolution) the horizontal resolution will be the number

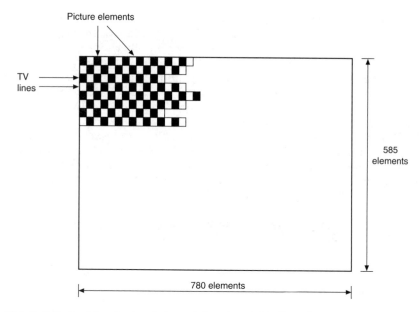

Figure 5.9 *Deriving horizontal resolution for a 625 line picture. (Pixels are not drawn to scale as they would appear too small)*

of TV lines multiplied by 4/3. Let's see how this works for the 625 line system employed in UK broadcast and CCTV.

As we have seen, a 625 line raster is constructed from two fields, each having 312.5 lines. One field scan period is 20ms, however this includes the flyback period which is (approximately) 1ms, during which time the electron beam is cut off to prevent it being seen moving up the screen. In 1ms approximately 15 horizontal lines will have been scanned, but the beam is switched off for 20 lines to ensure a clean flyback. In other words, out of the 312.5 lines per field, only 292.5 are active.

This means that over two field periods 40 lines are unused, and so, out of 625 lines, only 585 actually contain picture information. Looking again at Figure 5.9 we see that if the vertical resolution is 585 squares (pixels), then the horizontal resolution should be at least $585 \times 4/3 = 780$ pixels.

We can now turn things around and look at them from a different point of view and ask the question, why was 625 chosen for the number of lines? It was derived from the decision to begin the calculations with a horizontal resolution of 780 pixels. So how was the figure of 780 arrived at? This is the maximum frequency of the signal drive voltage required at the CRT cathode to reproduce the checkerboard display, a portion of which is shown in Figure 5.10.

In the UK TV system, the horizontal scanning speed is set at 64µs; 52µs for the scan period (also referred to as the *active line period*), and 12µs for the flyback period. This equates to a horizontal line frequency of 15625Hz. For the electron beam to switch on and off quickly enough to reproduce 780 pixels during the 52μs active line period, the periodic time for one cycle of the signal would be 133ns. In terms of frequency, from the formula $f = 1/t$, this equates to 7.5MHz. In other words, in order to reproduce a horizontal resolution of 780 pixels, the system, including everything from the camera to the video amplifier driving the CRT cathode in the monitor, would require a bandwidth of 0Hz to 7.5MHz. This exceeds the 5.5MHz bandwidth originally allocated to broadcast TV, but it was found that the bandwidth could be reduced by applying something called the Kell factor. This is a figure of 0.7 which was derived as a result of extensive work in 1933 by a man named Kell who, after performing many viewing tests, concluded that a reduction in horizontal resolution of 0.7 would not produce an appreciable deterioration in picture quality.

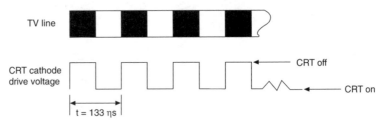

Figure 5.10

Applying the Kell factor reduces the bandwidth to a more practical figure of 5.5MHz, and so it is that the UK TV system has a video bandwidth of 0–5.5MHz, which equates to a resolution in the order of 546 pixels.

For NTSC the horizontal line frequency is 15734Hz which produces a line period of 63.6μs. The horizontal flyback period is approximately 10.3μs which gives an active line period of around 53.3μs. The vertical flyback period is typically 15 lines per field (30 lines per frame) resulting in 495 active lines per TV frame. Therefore, applying the rule that the horizontal resolution should be at least equal to the vertical resolution, an ideal system should be capable of reproducing 495 × 4/3 × 0.7 (Kell factor) = 462 pixels along one line. This would equate to a video signal bandwidth of 0–4.3MHz. In practice the video bandwidth for NTSC is specified as being 0–4.2MHz, which would produce a horizontal resolution of around 450 pixels.

It is more common to express horizontal resolution in terms of 'Television Lines', or TVL. This measurement is related to the number of horizontal pixels that we have just been looking at, and will be discussed in Chapter 6.

It must be remembered that the figures quoted above are for broadcast television and, whilst in times gone by CCTV has in general fallen short of these specifications, with modern technology cameras and monitors, coupled with fibre-optic or other broadband transmission techniques, CCTV is actually capable of producing a superior image resolution to broadcast television, which is dogged with bandwidth restrictions.

However, it must be stressed that to achieve a high resolution everything from the lens to the monitor must be of a high specification and the installation must be sound; one weak link in the system, for example poor cabling with multiple connectors or a poor quality lens, will degrade the resolution.

Synchronization

The image which has been focussed onto the pick-up device by the lens is scanned at a rate of 50Hz, or 15625Hz (PAL). It is essential that the monitor scans at the same rate as the camera, not just in terms of frequency, but also in terms of the precise position of the spot on the screen.

Consider the two conditions in Figure 5.11. In condition A, the electron beam in the monitor begins to scan a field at precisely the same time that the camera begins a field scan, so the displayed picture appears on the screen in exactly the same position as it would if you were looking directly through the camera lens.

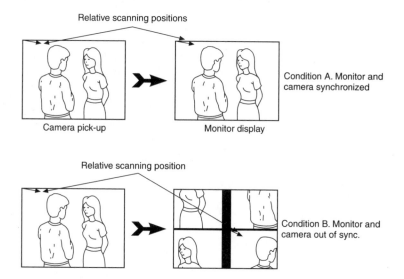

Figure 5.11 *Effect on the display when camera and monitor are unsynchronized*

In condition B, the beam in the monitor CRT is in the centre of the screen when the camera begins a field scan. In this case the top left corner of the image is displayed in the centre of the screen, with a corresponding displacement of the rest of the image. The vertical and horizontal dark stripes appear as a result of the camera flyback periods being displayed;

remember that during the flyback period the beam is meant to be cut off, and so the camera outputs a black level signal.

The monitor must be synchronized to the camera, and to achieve this the camera generates a series of pulses which are added to the video signal at the output. At the end of each horizontal scan, at the instant that the camera is initiating line flyback, a *line synchronization (sync) pulse* is generated by the camera and added to the video signal. Likewise, at the end of each field scan a *field sync pulse* is added to the video signal. Thus, during one 20ms field period the camera will output 312 line sync pulses and one field sync pulse. During one complete TV frame (40ms) a total of 625 line and two field sync pulses will be output from the camera.

The shape and timing of the line and field sync pulses is complex, and it is out of the scope of this book to look into the reasons behind this complex make-up. However, it is important that a CCTV engineer can recognize these signals when viewed on an oscilloscope.

The line sync pulse is shown in Figure 5.12. The monitor will initiate line flyback at the instant the first falling edge, immediately following the front porch, of the pulse appears. Note that the total duration of the pulse is 12µs, which is equal to the line flyback period. The porches are set to be at a level in the video signal waveform equal to black to ensure that the beam is cut off during the flyback period. This is called the *blanking period.*

When viewed on an oscilloscope at the output from a camera, the field sync pulse actually appears nothing like a pulse at all. This is because it is made up from a series of pulses beginning with five equalizing pulses,

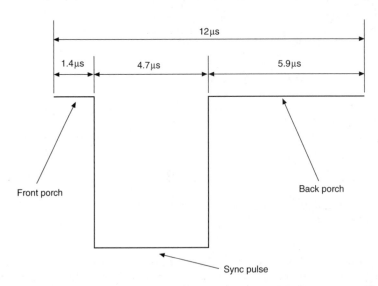

Figure 5.12 *A line sync pulse. The timings relate to a 625 line system. For a 525 line system, the blanking period is 10µs, with similar proportions for the porch and sync periods*

followed by five pulses which we refer to as the field sync period, and finally five or four (depending whether it is the odd or even field) more equalizing pulses. At the monitor, after separation from the video signal, this series of pulses is passed through a low pass filter which integrates them into a single pulse which is the field sync pulse. The complete field sync period is shown in Figure 5.13.

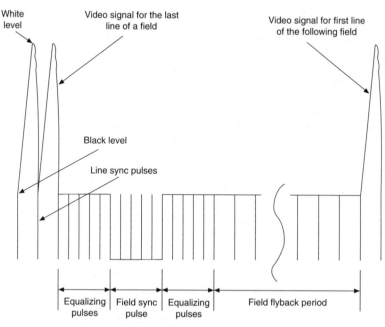

Figure 5.13 *Field synchronizing and flyback period*

Following the field sync period, a series of black lines are sent out. These are essential to ensure that the beam is cut off during the field flyback period. As discussed previously, there are *20 lines in the field blanking period (15 for NTSC)*. It is during this period that teletext information is transmitted, and although this might not appear significant for CCTV engineers, the idea of transmitting data during the field flyback period has been taken up by some manufacturers of CCTV telemetry control equipment, and camera control data is sent out during this period in a very similar way to broadcast teletext data. This will be considered further in Chapter 10.

Synchronization is very important and any loss, distortion or attenuation of the sync pulses will result in vertical jittering or rolling, and/or horizontal pulling or rolling. Such problems are all too common in CCTV installations, and can be the result of many things. To mention but a few, there can be different earth potentials between various points in the system, faulty or incorrectly installed cables and/or connectors, incorrect cables or connectors, poor quality camera switching units which interrupt the sync signals, and incorrect positioning of terminator switches on monitors or other equipment. All of these are covered in the relevant chapters in this book.

The luminance signal

The *luminance* signal, usually abbreviated to *luma* and represented by the symbol Y, is the black and white information required to satisfy the rods in the eye. It contains information relating to brightness and contrast changes. A monochrome camera outputs a luma signal, plus sync pulses. A colour camera produces the luma component by adding red, green and blue in the correct proportions.

It can be shown that one unit of white light is made up from proportions of red, green and blue light following the expression.

$$1Y = 0.3R + 0.59G + 0.11B$$

The signal processing stage in the colour camera employs a matrix which adds the R, G and B signals in these proportions to produce a luma component.

A common test pattern used in television is the eight bar colour display. The order of the colours is such that when the colour is removed, the bars appear with white on the left and black on the right, and descending order of grey in between. This is termed the *grey scale*. The luminance signal required at the CRT cathode to produce this display is termed the *staircase waveshape*, and a quick look at Figure 5.14 reveals how the name was derived.

Remember that an increase in the voltage at the cathode makes the control grid appear more negative with respect to the cathode, and the brightness is reduced. Thus, when the 70V level is applied to the cathode the brightness will be high, and bright white is produced on the screen. At the other extreme, when the 130V level is applied the beam is virtually cut off, and black is produced. Note that the sync pulse is arranged so that it biases the CRT beyond beam cut-off, ensuring that no unwanted display is produced during the line flyback period. Bear in mind that a single staircase produces only one TV line, and to produce a complete frame a total of 585 of these, plus 40 black lines for field flyback blanking, are required.

The luminance signal shown in Figure 5.14 is 60V pp, which is the voltage required at the cathode to drive a CRT. However, when the signal leaves the camera it is at a much lower level. The CCIR standard for transmission of luminance signals along a cable requires that the voltage level should be 1V pp (measured from the peak white to sync tip levels) when the input/output impedances of the equipment are 75Ω. In this 1V signal, the picture content will be no more than 0.7V (70% of the total signal level), and the sync pulse will be a constant 0.3V (30% of the total signal level).

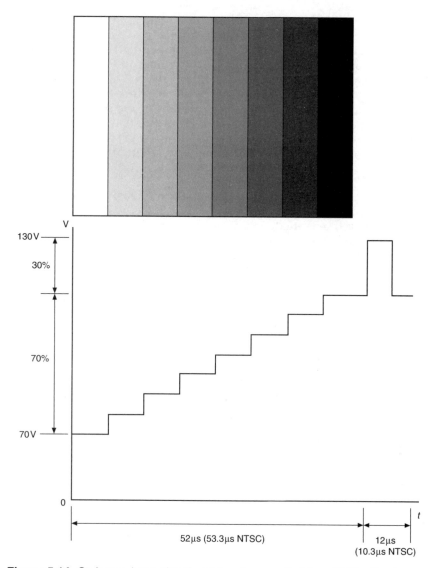

Figure 5.14 *Staircase luma signal which, when applied to a CRT cathode, produces eight grey scale bars*

The chrominance signal

The chrominance, or *chroma* (C), signal containing the colour information is far more complex than the luma component, and although it is not necessary for the CCTV engineer to be fully conversant with the theory, there are some essential features which he must be aware of.

The colour system employed in the UK is known as the *PAL system;*

PAL being the abbreviation for Phase Alternating Line. PAL evolved out of the earlier American NTSC (National Television System Committee) colour television system which is used throughout the USA, Canada, Japan and parts of South America. A forerunner to PAL is the French SECAM (Sequential Couleur Avec Memoire) system, however this is not widely used throughout the world. None of these three television systems are directly compatible and engineers must be aware of this when they are confronted with equipment that has switches (either mechanical or menu driven) which allow different systems to be selected. For example, a VCR switched to operate in NTSC mode will record in black and white if it is connected to a system comprising PAL cameras and control equipment.

In order to produce a colour picture at the monitor, it is not necessary to transmit all three primary colours. This is because the Y signal is already being transmitted, and remembering that $1Y = 0.3R + 0.59G + 0.11B$, then we can see that if we transmit any two of the primary colours, the third can be recovered by matrixing the other two and the Y signal. For example, if we do not transmit the green, a matrix circuit in the monitor can be made to perform the function $G = 1Y - 0.3R - 0.11B$. Any of the three colour signals can be omitted, however green was chosen because, after it has been processed in the PAL colour encoder, it is the smallest of the three colour signals and is thus more prone to being swamped by noise during the transmission process.

To aid transmission of the red and blue colour signals it is necessary to reduce their amplitude. Because the luma is sent independently of the colour, it is possible to achieve this reduction by removing the luma content from the red and blue signals, producing *colour difference signals*, R–Y and B–Y. However, further attenuation of the colour difference signals is necessary and thus the camera applies a weighting factor to each of the colour difference signals. The weighted signals are referred to as *u* and *v*. The *u* contains the B–Y information, and the *v* contains the R–Y information.

In order to transmit the *u* and *v* signals they must be modulated onto a carrier. Modulation is a process where two signals are added together in a certain way to enable them to be transmitted either through space or along a cable. One signal is the desired information and the other is a high-frequency carrier which is used to 'transport' the information to the receiving equipment, after which it is dispensed with. The principle is illustrated in Figure 5.15.

For the PAL colour system the carrier, known as the *colour subcarrier*, has a very precise frequency of 4.43361875 MHz, although it is usually referred to as the 4.43 MHz subcarrier. Similarly, for NTSC the 3.579545 MHz colour subcarrier may be referred to as the 3.58 MHz subcarrier. These exacting figures were chosen to ensure that the colour signal would offer minimum interference with the high frequency luma components because, as we can see in Figure 5.16, the colour is positioned within the luma passband.

The name PAL was given to the system because of the fact that the *v* signal changes its phase by 180° at the end of every TV line. This is

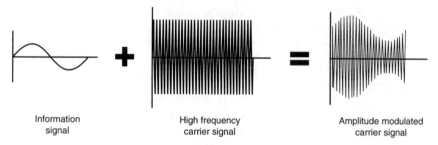

Information signal   High frequency carrier signal   Amplitude modulated carrier signal

Figure 5.15 *Principle of amplitude modulation*

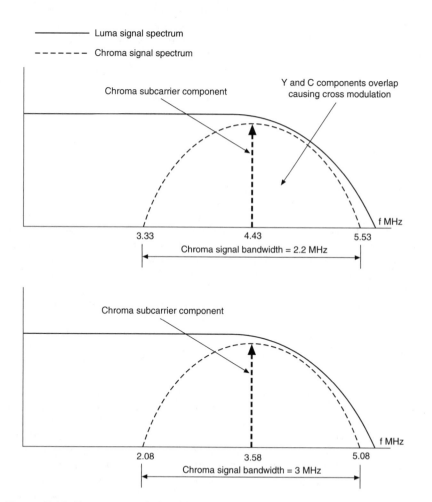

Figure 5.16 *Frequency relationship between the luma and chroma signals for PAL and NTSC transmissions*

unique to the PAL system and is employed to provide a built-in correction for phase errors which occur in the chroma signal as it passes through the transmission medium. Such phase errors would result in noticeable colour errors.

A colour monitor or VCR, for reasons which are beyond the scope of this textbook, uses a crystal oscillator to generate a precise 4.43 MHz (3.58 MHz NTSC) subcarrier. However, this oscillator must not only produce an accurate frequency, its output must be in exactly the same phase as the subcarrier coming from the camera. To achieve this a *chroma burst* signal is generated in the camera. This burst comprises ten cycles of the subcarrier and is placed onto the back porch of each line sync pulse. The chroma burst can be considered to be a sync pulse for the colour processing circuits in the monitor or VCR, and if for any reason it is lost, the decoders in all monitors and VCRs will default to black and white operation.

If a camera were producing a picture of the standard eight bar colour display, then the chroma signal, when viewed on an oscilloscope, would appear something like that shown in Figure 5.17. During the periods of the white and black bars there is no colour signal. Between the yellow and blue bars the amplitude modulated subcarrier is present. Note also the chroma burst signal on the back porch of the line sync period.

Television signals

When it comes to sending the luma and chroma signals from the camera to the monitor there are a number of options available. In the CCTV industry the most common method is to use *composite video* where the luma and chroma are sent simultaneously along the same co-axial cable. The prime advantage of this is the low cost compared with the other options available, because only one co-axial cable is required from each camera and between each item of equipment in the control room.

When the two signals are mixed, the chroma signal tends to sit on the luma voltage waveshape. If we add the chroma signal shown in Figure 5.17 to the luma staircase shown in Figure 5.14, then we have a composite video signal. This addition is illustrated in Figure 5.18, where the chroma signals for the six coloured bars sit on the corresponding luma steps. Note the chroma burst signal positioned on the back porch of the line sync signal.

The disadvantage of composite video is the cross modulation effect. This is where luma signal components at frequencies around 4.43 MHz mix with the 4.43 MHz chroma signal components (3.58 MHz NTSC). Once they are mixed (composite), VCRs and monitors are unable to separate them, and the displayed picture contains interference. This interference manifests itself as a coloured patterning in areas of the picture where there is high-resolution luma. A classic example is frequently seen on broadcast TV when a person appears wearing a suit or jacket with a fine pattern. At certain distances from the camera a rainbow effect appears on the person's clothing.

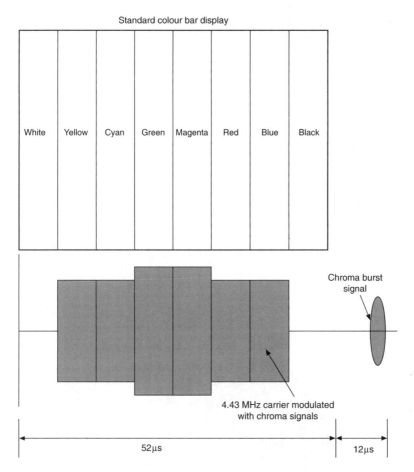

Figure 5.17 *Chrominance signal in relation to the standard colour bar display (PAL system)*

Cross modulation can be avoided by keeping the luma and chroma signals separate at every point between the camera and the monitor or VCR. This method of signal transmission is known as Y/C.

Many CCTV cameras, VCRs, monitors, and other control equipment have optional Y/C provision through the four pin S-VHS socket (Figure 5.19) which carries the luma on one pair of conductors (pins 1 and 3), and the chroma on another (pins 2 and 4). Each pair of conductors is an individual co-axial cable, ensuring that the luma/chroma signals do not mix. This is the good news. The bad news is that to make the system effective every camera requires two co-axial cables and, to further complicate things, adapters are required to marry the large BNC connectors to the very small Y/C connectors, which in reality were never intended for use in CCTV system building. In practice it is generally considered to

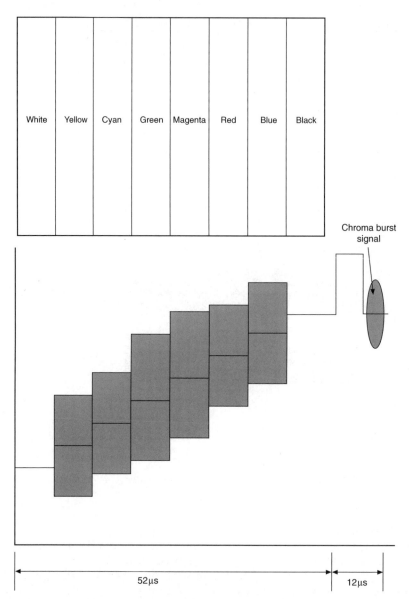

Figure 5.18 *Composite video signal where the modulated chroma carrier sits on the luma signal*

be too expensive and impractical to use S-VHS in a complete CCTV system installation, and use of these connectors is confined to such things as VCR input/output, etc.

In CCTV where picture resolution is of paramount importance, the losses incurred by cross modulation are unwelcome, however there is no

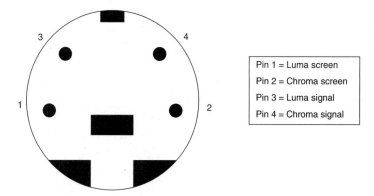

Figure 5.19 *S-VHS connector pin configuration*

cost effective way of avoiding them in analogue transmission systems. Where analogue signals are later digitized, there are methods of detecting and largely cancelling cross modulation effects at the control room, but this equipment is still expensive and is only feasible for larger installations. On the other hand, where the video signal remains in the digital domain from camera to control room, and S-VHS connectors are employed for monitor connection, then the story is somewhat different.

Digital video signals

The concept of converting analogue signals into digital form is not new. In fact, like many of the principles employed in modern computing, the complex mathematics relating to the problem were resolved many years before the technology was available to build even the simplest electronic computer.

We are all now familiar with digital audio, which has been around for a few decades in the form of various tape formats, and for many years in the form of Compact Disc. Yet digital video has seemed to take much longer to make an appearance. There is a good reason for this. A digitized video signal amounts to many times more data than an audio signal of any equivalent time period, and even with the high capacity hard drives of today's computers, without the application of the compression techniques used with digital video, a 10 Gbyte hard drive would store no more than a few minutes of video information. It was the development of video compression techniques that made digital video possible, but it has taken a number of years for this compression to be perfected, and for chip sets to be developed and manufactured in sufficient quantities to make them commercially viable.

The process of analogue to digital conversion is very complex, but a simple overview is shown in Figure 5.20.

Imagine that the video signal is fed into the circuit, and that the switch

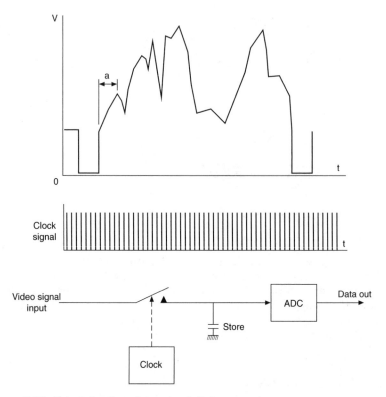

Figure 5.20 *Principle of analogue to digital conversion*

closes for a brief moment every time a clock pulse is present. Let us also assume that the capacitor is capable of instantly charging to the voltage level of the video signal. When the first clock pulse arrives, the switch closes and the capacitor acquires a charge. In the brief period between the first and second clock pulses, the *analogue to digital (A/D) converter* measures the potential on the capacitor and assigns an eight-bit binary word which corresponds to this level. When the second clock pulse arrives, a new voltage level, corresponding to the video signal level at that instant, is stored in the capacitor. The A/D converter now assigns an eight-bit word for this level, and the cycle repeats.

An eight-bit binary word has 256 combinations between 00000000 and 11111111. This means that it is possible for the 1 V pp video signal to have 256 voltage levels. The A/D converter functions by measuring the voltage in the store capacitor, and assigning the binary word that corresponds to the closest of these 256 voltage values.

Of course, for a television receiver or VCR to process the signal, it must first be converted from its digital format back into an analogue waveform. This is known as *digital to analogue (D/A) conversion*. It is at this point where the problems associated with digitizing video signals become apparent. Consider the portion of video signal shown in Figure 5.21. If connected into a monitor, the analogue signal would produce a steadily lightening grey image along part of a TV line. However, after A/D and D/A processing, because the signal was sampled at the clock rate, the linear video waveform is now a series of steps which we know as *pixels*. When viewed on a monitor, this would appear as a series of tiny rectangular blocks of increasing brightness.

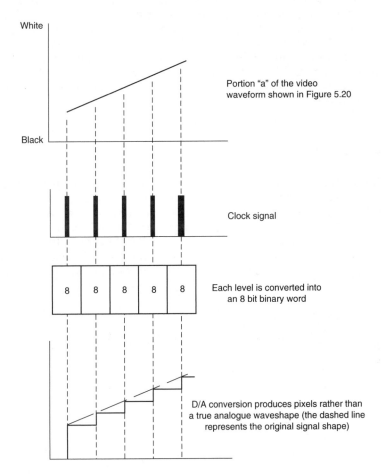

Figure 5.21

The pixels can be made smaller by increasing the clock rate, but this means that we produce more eight-bit words per TV line. For argument's sake, let's suppose that we decide to produce the 780 pixels we looked at in Figure 5.9. This means that for each active TV line we will have 780 eight-bit words which amounts to 6240 data bits. There will be another

1440 bits needed to produce the line sync pulse and blanking levels, giving a total of 7680 bits per 64μs line. Thus, in one TV frame we will produce 7680 × 625 = 4.8Mbits. In one second we will produce 4.8M × 25 = 120Mbits. Dividing by 8 to convert this figure to bytes, we have 15Mbytes per second! So we can now see that if we have a 10Gbyte hard drive, we would be able to store 10G ÷ 15M = 11.1minutes of black and white video information – a colour signal could reduce this time by up to 50%.

The figures above are just an example, but they clearly illustrate how quickly video signals produce data once we take the decision to digitize them. The 'recording time' of our 10Gbyte hard disc can be increased in a number of ways. For example, we do not actually require the signal to be broken down into 256 levels. We could use a six-bit binary word to represent each video signal level. This would still give us 64 levels of grey scale, which would be acceptable, with an increase in the storage time to 14.8minutes.

Video compression

Although this process involves some of the most complex mathematics, it is possible for it to be understood in simple terms. Compression is all about removing any data from a digitized video signal that we know can somehow be restored following 'replay' from the storage device.

There are a number of ways of recovering data (and therefore not having to store it in the first place). One of these is *redundancy*. Consider the television picture in Figure 5.22. This has one thing in common with

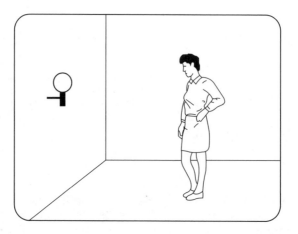

Figure 5.22

almost all other TV pictures and that is that between one TV frame and the next ($\frac{1}{25}$ th of a second) most of the picture information does not alter. Thus, having digitized all of the picture once and stored it, what is the point in storing the same data again and again? Obviously we are referring to the walls and floor areas which for most of the time are stationary; that is, until either the camera pans, or the picture cuts to another shot.

So, one way of compressing a digital video signal is to remove duplicated data, thus making it redundant. To re-build the picture all that needs to be done is to use the same data over and over again to produce the walls and floor in our example.

Another form of compression is *prediction*. Looking again at the example in Figure 5.22, when the camera pans, all of the repeated data will move in the same direction. Upon seeing this, the compression processing chip, instead of passing all of the wall and floor area for storage, produces a relatively small amount of mathematical data which, during the recovery process, will be used to predict where the wall and floor will have moved to on a frame-by-frame basis. In other words, the same data is used over and over just like before, only now it is being moved across the screen.

Of course, we cannot expect to compress a signal and not lose something in terms of quality, and a heavily compressed video signal will show clear signs of deterioration. The compression chip sets are so designed that equipment manufacturers using them can set the amount of compression, and the rule is very simple. A lot of compression results in a lot of redundant data, which means long recording times, but at the expense of picture quality. Minimal compression means that a lot of data needs to be stored, reducing the recording time, but producing high quality (resolution) pictures.

Compression is measured as a ratio of the amount of data entering a compression system to the amount that comes out. Thus, a compression ratio of 1:1 indicates no compression, 5:1 would indicate that there is five times less data at the output, 10:1 indicates a reduction of ten times, and so on.

The process of uncompressing the data involves taking the data that has been stored and applying it to complex mathematical algorithms. The success with which the original signal is restored depends upon the amount of original data that was retained (that is, the amount of compression applied) and the effectiveness of the algorithms (that is, how well they have been derived). The term 'lossless compression' is becoming used more and more, but only where little compression has been applied in the first place. At the time of writing, once even moderate amounts of compression have been applied to an image, some information loss and/or artefacts will be evident, even if only on certain types of picture information. This is because a point is reached where the processor has to make a 'best guess' at what information should be put back into a certain picture location, and where it gets this wrong an unwanted pixel is produced on the picture (i.e. an artefact).

It is difficult to relate a specific compression ratio to any given number of artefacts because there are too many variables. For any given compression ratio, the point at which compression artefacts become noticeable depends on the picture information, the type of compression used, the algorithms employed by the manufacturer and the processing circuitry. Nevertheless, as an aid to installers and end users, manufacturers often compare a given compression ratio with known analogue formats such as VHS, S-VHS, etc. In practice it is difficult to make direct comparisons because the artefacts produced by digital compression errors often manifest themselves quite differently to those produced by analogue processes, but making such comparisons does serve the purpose of giving some idea as to how the reproduced image will appear.

MPEG-2 compression

Digital CCTV equipment employs one of two forms of compression, MPEG or Wavelet.

MPEG (Motion Pictures Experts Group – a body set up by the ISO in 1988 to devise standards for audio and video compression) video signal compression is employed in the broadcast industry for such purposes as digital terrestrial transmission, and is a very robust and reliable compression format. MPEG-2 is a natural evolution from MPEG (or MPEG-1) and is the compression format used in a lot of CCTV equipment.

A TV signal can be said to be four dimensional, having attributes of sample, horizontal axis, vertical axis and time axis. All of these can be explored for redundant information by a compression encoder, and MPEG-2 employs three types of compression to explore these four attributes.

The first type of compression is *temporal redundancy*; also known as *Inter-frame (P frame) compression* because it is applied across the frames. This type of compression takes account of the fact that much of the video information is the same from one frame to the next and therefore it is only necessary to transmit the differences between the frames. Consider the image in Figure 5.23. In this case, assuming that the camera angle is fixed, the only significant changes between frames will be the movements of the vehicle in the centre of the picture. Thus we see that throughout the entire scene when the vehicle is moving round the corner, which for the purpose of this example we shall assume lasts for three seconds, large amounts of data in the 75 frames will be identical. If only data relating to changes in picture information are transmitted, it may be possible to reduce the data content by 90%.

The second type of compression is *spatial redundancy*; also known as *Intra-frame (I frame) compression* because it is only applied within a single frame. Looking at the image shown in Figure 5.24, during each active line period many of the 720 luma samples, or pixels, will be identical and therefore it can be reasoned that it is only necessary to transmit the first pixel in a sequence, plus information to inform the decoder how many times the pixel must be repeated. For example, if we consider line 10 of the image in Figure 5.24, we can see that instead of sending 720 pixels of

Figure 5.23 *The only significant movement in this clip is that of the vehicle, and therefore the majority of the video information only needs to be transmitted for the first frame*

Line 10

Figure 5.24

data at 8-bits per pixel, we need only send the 8-bit value of pixel number 1, along with a small amount of data relating to the position (line 10) and the number of repetitions (719).

Intra-frame compression also makes use of the fact that, in general, the amplitude of video components reduces as their frequency increases. Therefore, if we assign fewer bits to the high frequency end of the spectrum, a further saving can be made. However this *will* lead to increased noise in areas of high picture resolution, but if the process is not pressed too far, the eye will not easily discern this.

The third type of compression is *statistical redundancy,* also known as *prediction* or *motion compensation.* Looking again at the image in Figure 5.23, once the vehicle is fully in shot, it is a relatively simple operation for the encoder to produce a plot of the pixel movements across the 75 frames of the video clip. Therefore it is not necessary to transmit all of the data relating to the changes between frames, but simply the prediction data required by the decoder to move the pixels between the frames.

Further data reduction may be introduced by replacing the line and field sync signals with short codes that will indicate to the decoder the start of these periods. Similarly, short codes may be used to indicate black levels, which occur frequently in most video signals. And finally, replacing long repetitions of '0' or '1' with shorter words that simply indicate the number of repetitions can reduce the amount of data considerably.

Figure 5.25 shows how MPEG arranges the TV frames for storage and subsequent transmission to the decoder. This illustration shows how one I frame is transmitted on every 12th frame to serve as a 'detailed' reference block, with P frames interleaved between I and B frames. The B frames are made up purely from interpolated information from adjacent P and I frames. One weakness with this system is that an error in an I frame will propagate through the following frame sequence until the next I frame. Such an error would persist for about 0.5 seconds. Errors occurring later in the sequence will endure for a lesser time period.

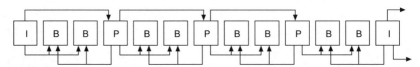

Figure 5.25 *The MPEG frame structure comprising of I, P and B frames*

At this point we may be forgiven for believing that we have reduced the data by as much as possible, however it is here that the mathematicians take over. The remaining 8-bit samples are arrayed into 8×8 matrixes where a process called *Discrete Cosine Transformation* (DCT) is performed. This is followed by a *quantization process,* resulting in a large reduction in data per frame compared with the original 8-bit samples. DCT is a key part of MPEG because this part of the compression process is truly lossless as every bit can be recovered at the decoder by reversing the mathematical process.

Within the encoding and decoding process there are a number of errors that may occur. Data errors can occur even though error correction is employed in MPEG because, if an error is too great, entire 'slices' of picture will be rejected because of the way in which data is arrayed within a frame. De-compression errors, although not an error as such, may occur because of excessive redundancy removal (i.e. a high compression ratio). Where large amounts of information have been identified as redundant there is no way that the original data (and thus image) can be restored. This results in a 'blocky' effect (pixellation) over areas of the picture. Finally, data may be insufficient because of 'Overloading' at the encoder. Overloading describes a situation where the video clip contains a large amount of high definition, fast-moving information. Such footage contains little redundancy and the encoder is unable to output the large amount of data necessary to communicate the images, resulting in large areas of pixellation and/or numerous freeze frames.

Wavelet compression

Signal analysis using wavelets is based on Fourier analysis, which was formulated by Joseph Fourier in the 1800s, although it was not until the 1980s that his findings were developed to create a method of signal analysis. This type of analysis has many applications including astronomy, music, earthquake prediction, radar, neurophysiology and, of course, TV signal compression.

Wavelet analysis does not break the TV frames down into blocks as in MPEG, rather it analyses each entire frame as a whole. In other words, there are no 'P' or 'B' frames. The signal components which make up each frame are separated into a range of frequency bands (typically 42). The higher frequencies which are not deemed to produce image information visible to the human eye are discarded. Spacial compression is then applied to the remaining bands, and algorithms apply further compression to the remaining data. This compression is non-linear, the greater compression being applied to the higher frequencies (Figure 5.26).

Each frame is processed individually in real time, and is scanned three times to determine the optimum compression ratio for that field. This leads to a considerably large data file size, however encoding is very much simpler and therefore less expensive than for MPEG; one factor that can make Wavelet more attractive for CCTV applications. In broadcast television there is only one (MPEG) encoder – at the transmitter – whereas in CCTV we have to build an encoder into every multiplexer, digital recorder, etc. This makes the simpler Wavelet encoder more attractive from a manufacturing point of view, although large scale integration in silicon chips is tending to close this gap.

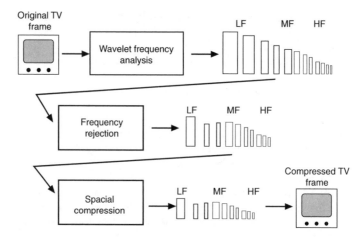

Figure 5.26 *Simplified illustration of the wavelet compression process*

Because each frame is individually processed, wavelet is much simpler to edit. In CCTV, fast-switching multiplexers can result in MPEG having to create a lot of I frames, thus increasing the data capacity. This is not the case with wavelet compression.

Wavelet technology allows much higher compression ratios than MPEG for the same image quality (or resolution). A wavelet compression ratio of 20:1 tends to be comparable to that of an MPEG compression ratio of 10:1, although the losses in both systems are quite different thus making a direct comparison difficult. This being the case, the larger data file size of wavelet compression is countered by the fact that greater compression ratios can be applied.

Because it does not break the picture down into the 8 × 8 blocks, wavelet compression does not produce the 'blocky' effect associated with MPEG when larger amounts of compression are applied. Rather, a heavily compressed wavelet image takes on a blurred appearance, perhaps comparable to looking at a picture produced by a camera with a slightly de-focussed lens.

In conclusion, wavelet compression sees the TV frame as a number of layers of different resolution. Higher compression is applied to the higher resolution layers – however this amount is variable. As one author has put it, wavelet 'sees the trees and the forest'. This is somewhat different to MPEG, which only 'sees the forest'.

6 The CCTV camera

The camera can be considered to have two parts; the pick-up device(s), and the signal processing circuits.

For many years cameras relied on thermionic (valve technology) tubes to derive a signal voltage from the incoming light information. However, the majority of cameras employed in CCTV systems today use a solid state pick-up device known as a *charge coupled device* (CCD).

Similarly, advances in technology have meant that the traditional analogue signal processing techniques which have served us well for many years are giving way to digital signal processing, meaning that cameras are able to produce remarkably clear pictures under very hostile lighting conditions.

Tube/CCD comparison

Generally speaking, compared with their vacuum tube counterparts, CCDs have the advantages of a longer life, no decay in picture quality during their working life, greatly improved low light performance, are less prone to burn when struck by a high intensity light source, are much smaller and compact, and have a much lower operating voltage.

On the other hand, CCDs can have a tendency to overload under bright light conditions, causing light areas of the picture to diffuse into a white mass. This effect is termed 'burn out', however this is not inferring that the CCD itself is damaged, only that the picture quality is degraded. By comparison, tube cameras perform well under bright light conditions, although with suitable filters and a good quality iris, the CCD can be brought up to the same performance levels.

Charge coupled device

The CCD is a silicon device that can store an electrical charge. A chip containing a number of these in an array can be used to store samples of analogue video or audio signals where they can be manipulated. And so, although the CCD chip is not in itself a digital device, when controlled by a microprocessor it can be used to move analogue samples around in the fashion of a shift register.

The CCD design can be modified such that electrons are released when photons (light) fall onto the device. Thus the CCD behaves somewhat like a photodiode. If the light output from a lens is focussed onto an array of these photodiodes, each diode will derive an output voltage proportional to the amount of light falling upon it. Thus the chip is converting light energy into proportional electrical charges.

A typical imaging chip used in a CCTV camera contains many thousands of CCDs arrayed in a rectangular pattern. As we shall see in a moment, the voltages from the cells are integrated to create individual *pixels* ('pixels' is derived from the term *PIcture ELements*). For a CCD image device, the picture resolution is determined by the number of cells in the chip and the density of the cells. In theory a $\frac{1}{2}''$ CCD chip will have better resolution than a $\frac{1}{3}''$, and this is true if we compare like for like. However, a modern $\frac{1}{3}''$ chip (Figure 6.1) can have a greater cell density than an older $\frac{1}{2}''$ device, which means that a new $\frac{1}{3}''$ camera could possibly offer a higher resolution than the old $\frac{1}{2}''$ camera it is replacing. As a general rule, the greater the cell density, the higher the cost of the chip.

Figure 6.1 *A $^1/_3''$ CCD imaging chip employed in CCTV cameras*

Deriving an interlaced raster

The output from the CCD is manipulated to produce an interlaced raster of 585 (495 NTSC) active lines. It would be ideal if a CCD could be employed which contained enough cells to have one row per TV line. However, although such devices are available, their use in CCTV equipment would raise the cost of even the simplest monochrome camera considerably. Consequently the charges from the CCD cells are added to produce the TV lines, different combinations of cells being used for each field. The principle is illustrated in Figure 6.2.

The numbered rectangles represent a group of twenty CCD cells. The video information for line 1 of the odd (first) TV field is produced by

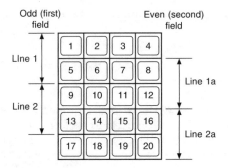

Figure 6.2 *Method of adding CCD charge outputs to derive different TV lines for each (interlaced) field*

adding the charges in the first two rows of cells. Line 2 is derived from the third and fourth rows, and so on.

When it comes to the even (second) field, the first TV line is derived from cell rows two and three, the second from rows four and five, and so on. In this way the picture information on each consecutive line in the frame is different.

Figure 6.3 shows the TV lines derived from Figure 6.2 as they would appear on a monitor screen. The cell numbers used to derive each pixel are indicated on the drawing. The dotted lines in the illustration have been included to identify the individual pixels, although in practice they do not exist because the horizontal line scan is continuous, and one pixel simply dissolves into the next.

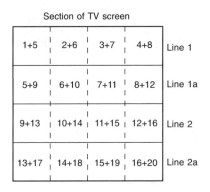

Figure 6.3 *Interlaced raster constructed from the CCD array in Figure 6.2*

The simple mathematical algorithm illustrated in Figure 6.2 demonstrates the principle of CCD charge integration, however there are other more complex algorithms. The actual algorithm employed to produce a TV picture frame for a particular camera will depend on the number of CCD cells in the image device. The greater the number of cells the greater the number of combinations available, meaning less integration and thus better resolution.

CCD chip operation

The charge manipulation we have just examined cannot take place in the photodiode area because of the need to accumulate charges for the next frame whilst outputting the charges for the frame currently being viewed on the monitor. Thus it is necessary to shift the charges into a temporary storage area.

In the early years of CCD development a method known as *Frame Transfer* was used. The principle is illustrated in Figure 6.4.

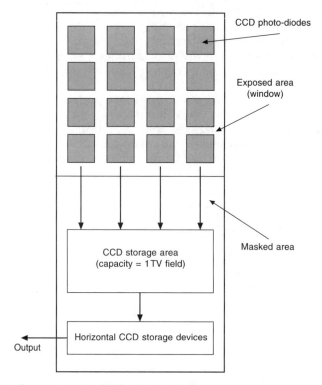

Figure 6.4 *Frame transfer CCD chip principle*

Despite its name 'Frame Transfer', this early chip operated at field rate. Its operation is as follows. During one field period of 20µs the imaging CCDs gather a charge from the incident light. Then, during the field flyback period, the charges are shifted downwards through the image CCD cells into the CCD storage area. During the following field the image devices recharge, whilst the information in the storage area is moved one TV line at a time into the horizontal storage area, from where it is clocked out over a 52μs (one active TV line) period. At the end of the field period, the cycle repeats.

The problem with this method of charge transfer is that the charges have to move down through the image area to get to the store area, meaning that the image CCDs must remain active not only throughout the field period, but also during the charge transfer period. The charges are therefore 'topped up' as they travel down through the image area by the incident light which is still falling onto the chip, resulting in a vertical smear in bright areas of picture content.

The solution to the vertical smearing problem was to re-design the CCD image chip and employ a charge transfer technique known as *Interline Transfer*. The chip architecture for this is illustrated in Figure 6.5.

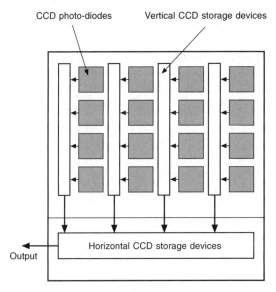

Figure 6.5 *Vertical and horizontal CCDs in an interline transfer image chip. The time that it takes to clock the information out of the H-CCD is 52μs; one active line period*

With this architecture, each CCD charge can be moved directly into its allocated temporary store area without having to travel through the other image cells, thus eliminating the problem of vertical smearing.

The interline operation is as follows. The image cells are exposed for a brief moment during an active field period. A previously acquired TV field will have been moved from the image CCDs into the vertical CCD storage devices (V-CCD) during the field blanking period. Thus, as the image cells are recharging, this information is clocked at line rate, and processed to produce the video information for the field currently being viewed. By the end of the field period, all of the information in the V-CCD will have been clocked out and thus, during the field flyback period when no video signal is required (other than a black level which can be generated by the camera), the image CCD charges for the next field are simultaneously downloaded into the V-CCD area. At the start of the following field period the image CCDs are once again exposed, whilst the stored field is once again clocked out.

The horizontal CCD (H-CCD) has the capacity to store one TV line of information. During each horizontal flyback period one charge from each V-CCD is moved into the H-CCD. At the same time all of the other charges in the V-CCDs are moved downwards. During the following active line period, the charges in the H-CCD are clocked out in serial form. From here they pass into the camera signal-processing circuits to be output as a video signal. The action can be likened to that of a cigarette vending machine. It is during the period when the charges are being moved down through the V-CCDs that the charge addition for field interlacing takes place, implying that the vertical shift operation is somewhat more complex than described here.

The main drawback with the interline transfer chip construction lay in the fact that the image surface is no longer occupied solely by image CCDs. Because the vertical CCDs are adjacent to the image devices, much of the light falling onto the chip is unused. This reduces the sensitivity of the CCD chip, making it less able to cope with low light conditions. However, advances in technology have largely overcome this drawback.

One such advance is the development of a CCD image device known as a *Frame Interline Transfer* (FIT) chip. The FIT chip operates on the interline transfer principle, however instead of holding the charges in the vertical CCDs for the complete field period, they are moved into a lower store area just as in the frame transfer chip. The principle is illustrated in Figure 6.6.

The advantages of moving the charges out of the image area are not immediately obvious, and are only appreciated when we begin to look at the problems associated with charge migration within the molecular structure, and the problem of electron release resulting from thermal action. These considerations are out of the scope of this book, but suffice to say that the FIT chip offers a very high S/N ratio, low smear, and excellent low light performance.

Another development that has done much to improve CCD chip sensitivity is the *micro lens* where a microscopic lens is fabricated over each individual image CCD. Without the micro lens, light falling between cells is lost. The micro lenses gather this light and focus it onto the cells, effectively increasing the chip sensitivity. The principle is illustrated in Figure 6.7. The majority of CCTV cameras used today employ *Exwave technology* CCD chips developed by Sony.

Interline transfer made possible the introduction of *Electronic Iris* (EI). This can be compared to the mechanical shutter in a photographic stills camera, however it is performed electronically by the application of a

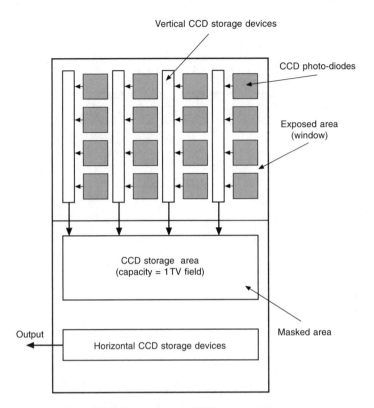

Figure 6.6 *The frame interline transfer (FIT) chip combines the advantages of the frame transfer chip (having a masked storage area safe from corruption from incident light) and the interline transfer chip (adjacent storage areas removing the effect of vertical smear)*

voltage to the cells. The electronic iris circuits in the camera adjust the exposure time of the CCDs to suit the average incoming light level.

The advantage of EI is that, where a fixed iris lens is used, the camera is able to compensate for changes in lighting levels. However, where the lens has an automatic iris (AI), the electronic iris should be switched off to prevent an effect known as 'hunting'. This is where, following a rapid and large change in light level, both iris circuits react. However, the EI normally reacts first, and thus when the mechanical iris closes a moment later the light input becomes too low. This causes the EI to 'open' once again, followed quickly by the mechanical iris, so the light level is once again too high, and the cycle repeats a number of times until the iris circuits stabilize.

CCD image chips are generally sensitive to infra-red (IR) radiation, which is what makes them so sensitive under low light conditions. At first glance this might appear to be good news, and in some instances it may be. However, unrestricted penetration of IR radiation into a CCD image chip can cause problems.

Incident light

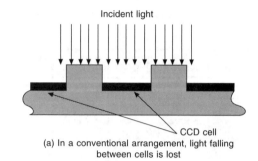

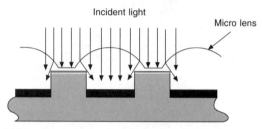

(a) In a conventional arrangement, light falling between cells is lost

Incident light

Micro lens

(b) Micro lens increases the light input to each cell, thus improving the sensitivity of the chip

Incident light

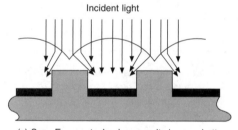

(c) Sony Exwave technology results in even better light gathering ability

Figure 6.7

Because of the longer wavelength, IR radiation penetrates deeper into the silicon substrate of the CCD chip than visible light, and this penetration can lead to the undesirable release of electrons in the charge storage areas, changing the values of the wanted charges, causing smearing and loss of definition. To prevent this phenomenon an *IR cut filter* is placed over the light input window of the CCD chip. This reduces the sensitivity of the chip to some degree, but the improvement in definition and signal-to-noise ratio makes it a worthwhile trade-off.

Monochrome cameras employing chips without an IR filter are available, and find applications where the area is to be illuminated by IR spotlights, or where low light level operation is required. All colour CCD chips must have an IR filter in order to produce accurate colours.

Colour imaging

Up to this point we have only considered the operation of the monochrome CCD image chip, which simply produces a luminance signal. Producing a colour signal is somewhat more involved because the chip must be able to generate three signals, red, green and blue. There are two ways in which this can be achieved; by using three chips, or by using a single chip with a colour filter.

The three chip method, illustrated in Figure 6.8, is by far the best. The incoming light is split into its three component parts using an array of mirrors, including special *dichroic mirrors* which reflect some frequencies of light whilst allowing other frequencies to pass through. Each CCD operates in very much the same fashion as it would in a monochrome camera, producing picture information relating to the colour of light falling onto it. An optical filter is placed in front of each pick-up to correct for deficiencies in the dichroic mirrors.

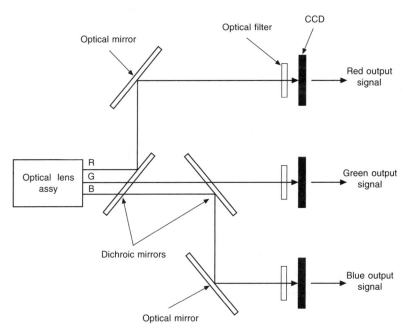

Figure 6.8 *In a three chip colour camera, the light is broken down into its component parts and focussed onto three CCD chips*

Because each CCD is operating in the same manner as a monochrome image device, the resolution and light level performance of a three chip colour camera is comparable to its monochrome counterpart. However, the combined cost of the optics and the three CCD chips make this type of camera very expensive, therefore assigning it largely to broadcast and semi-professional video production use.

Colour cameras for the CCTV industry are generally single CCD chip units. The chip is identical to that used in a monochrome camera, however a filter is placed in front of the CCD window to break the light up into red, green and blue. There are two types of filter in use, the *striped filter* and the *mosaic filter*. Each of these have their strengths and weaknesses and, comparing the two, the striped filter offers better colour reproduction whereas the mosaic filter offers superior resolution.

The striped filter, illustrated in Figure 6.9, forms a mask of alternate red, green and blue strips of filter material in front of the CCDs. Each CCD produces an output for just one colour. These output signals are processed in the same manner as we saw for the monochrome chip in Figure 6.5, however the output from the horizontal shift register has to be further processed to derive the luminance and colour signals.

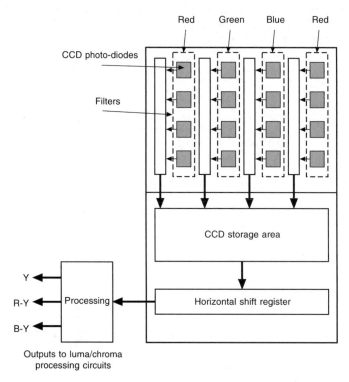

Figure 6.9 *Frame interline transfer (FIT) chip with a striped colour filter*

The reason for the poor resolution with this type of pick-up is apparent when we look at Figure 6.9. In the horizontal direction, three CCD cells are required to produce one pixel, whereas in a monochrome pick-up the same cells would produce three pixels. It might therefore appear as though the horizontal resolution is reduced by two thirds, however when other factors are taken into consideration it can be shown that the resolution of this type of chip is about 50% of that of a monochrome chip.

Another problem which occurs with the striped filter is patterning on areas of fine picture detail. This is caused by the generation of unwanted frequency components when the picture detail falling onto the chip is about the same size as the filter stripes. This interaction between the filter and the picture information, known as *beating*, is overcome by placing a crystal filter between the main optical lens and the CCD chip.

The mosaic filter is considerably more complex, both in terms of the filter construction and the signal processing required. A filter is placed above each CCD cell in a mosaic pattern as shown in Figure 6.10. This sixteen-part block pattern is repeated across the entire chip.

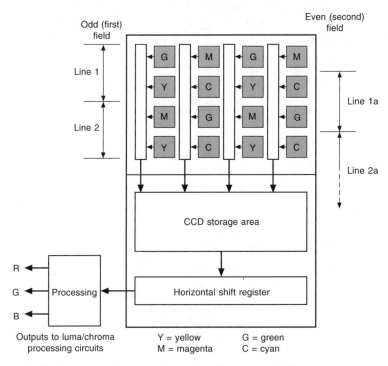

Figure 6.10 *Frame interline transfer chip with a mosaic filter*

Using the three secondary colours yellow, magenta and cyan, plus the primary colour green, the processing block following the horizontal shift register is able to derive red, green and blue signals which can then be further processed to produce the Y and C components. The algorithms used to derive the colour signals can vary, depending on the number of CCD cells there are in the chip; however, the greater the number of cells, the better the CCD performance.

Both the striped and mosaic filters reduce the light input to the CCD cells. This is one of the prime reasons why colour cameras are much less sensitive than monochrome cameras. Whilst it is common to find monochrome cameras with a specified minimum light input level of 0.1 lux, in general the minimum level for colour cameras is in the order of 1 lux.

Camera operation

The principle of the colour camera is illustrated in Figure 6.11. The shift registers which process the CCD charges are contained within the CCD chip, and thus the input to the signal processing block is the output from the CCD horizontal register. The charge transfer process is controlled by the CCD driver which in turn is clocked by an accurate crystal oscillator. Because of the relationship between the charge transfer and the line and field sync signals, the CCD driver takes a reference from the sync pulse generator.

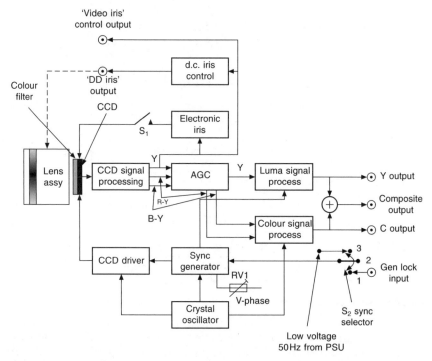

Figure 6.11 *Block diagram of a single chip colour camera (PAL)*

The signal processing is highly complex, however as far as we are concerned it is sufficient to note that there are three signals present at the output; the luma and the two colour difference signals R–Y and B–Y. The average amplitude of the Y signal is determined by the average light input level, and thus the Y is monitored by the electronic iris (EI) circuit. If the light input level is consistently high or low, the EI control changes the exposure time of the CCD accordingly. This function enables a camera to be fitted with a manual iris lens and yet maintain a degree of control under changing lighting conditions. However, it should be remembered that, unlike the manual iris, EI does not affect the depth of field and so, should the engineer set the manual iris to a low F-number, the EI will 'close' to maintain a correct light level, but the depth of field will be poor. The situation will become even worse at night when the depth of field further reduces despite the fact that the EI has 'opened'. Another undesirable effect of electronic iris is the increase in smear when the exposure time of the CCD is reduced.

The EI circuit can be switched on or off by S_1 which may be accessible either on the side of the camera or through the set-up menu. The EI should be switched off when the camera is used with an auto iris lens otherwise the two may tend to fight each other when sudden changes in light level occur, resulting in an iris oscillation effect.

The luma signal is also fed to both the d.c. iris control circuit and the output socket on the camera provided for 'video' iris control. The action of these was discussed in Chapter 4.

The signal voltage level derived by the CCDs varies considerably with changes in light level, and in low light conditions the signal voltage is so small that a large amount of amplification is necessary to produce an acceptable output. However, in order to produce a high quality picture under all lighting conditions, the gain of the amplifier must be made variable so that it can reduce as the light input level increases. The *Automatic Gain Control* (AGC) circuit is an amplifier which includes a signal level monitoring circuit. As the average level of the signal alters, the gain of the amplifier alters accordingly so that, for example, when the signal level is high the gain is reduced, and vice versa.

It should be noted that the CCDs generate noise as well as a signal voltage. Under reasonable lighting levels this noise is hidden by the high signal to noise (S/N) ratio. However, under low light conditions where there is less signal voltage generated, the S/N ratio reduces. At the same time the gain of the AGC amplifier rises to a very high level, and both the video signal and the noise is amplified. This noise appears as a background grain on the picture which detracts from the resolution.

As we have seen, the luma signal is derived in the CCD signal processing circuits, however further processing is required before the luma is ready to be sent to the monitor. Much of this processing is of little interest to the CCTV engineer, however one process which is worth mentioning is *gamma correction* as it has a direct bearing on the output waveshape.

Tubes and CCD pick-up devices are generally linear, and so equal increments of brightness give rise to equal changes in output voltage. Unfortunately the CRT characteristic is not linear but follows a curve like that shown in Figure 6.12. If we were to apply an equal increment staircase waveform (like that illustrated in Figure 5.14) to the cathode of a television CRT, the light output would not rise in equal increments. Instead, the steps in the dark and light regions would give rise to large increments in the CRT beam current, whereas the intermediate (mid-grey) steps would produce compressed levels with little contrast difference between bars. Because of this the luma is passed through an amplifier whose

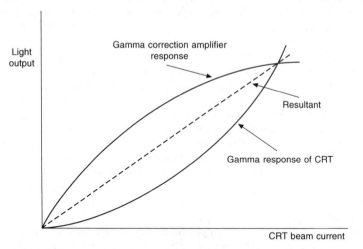

Figure 6.12 *CRT response and associated gamma correction curve*

characteristic is equal but opposite to the characteristic of the CRT. This process is called gamma correction. The effect of gamma correction on the luma staircase waveshape is shown in Figure 6.13.

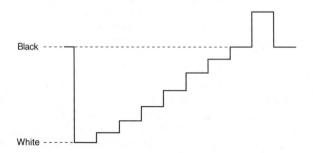

Figure 6.13 *Staircase signal with gamma correction (exaggerated)*

The gamma correction circuit could have been built into the monitors, however when we consider this from the point of view of broadcast TV, where there may be just one or two cameras whose output is being viewed on literally millions of receivers, then it does not make economical sense to put a circuit into every TV.

Switching the gamma on and off on a CCTV camera appears to simply alter the contrast level, but remember that with the gamma turned off the CRT will produce greater contrast changes at the lower and higher brightness levels, leaving the mid-grey levels somewhat bland. As a general rule the gamma correction should be turned on, offering a linear contrast range. However, you may experience cases where the CRT phosphor characteristic does not match that of the gamma correction in the camera and the contrast range appears too stark at the high and low levels. In such cases a more linear appearance may be obtained with the gamma correction turned off. The point to remember is, don't simply use the gamma correction setting as an alternative gain control.

Referring once again to the block diagram in Figure 6.11, the minimum bandwidth of the luma process circuits must be 0–5.5 MHz for a resolution of around 550 TVL, although with modern technology many CCTV cameras are able to exceed this resolution figure.

Once the luma signal has been derived, line and field sync signals are added. These pulses are generated in the sync generator stage which derives an accurate signal by dividing down the crystal oscillator output.

The need for synchronization between the camera and monitor was discussed in Chapter 5, but at that point we only looked at a single camera and monitor. Problems arise as soon as we try to send two or more camera outputs to a single monitor through a switcher or multiplexer because, unless steps are taken to lock the cameras together in terms of synchronization, at any instant in time the scan position of the two cameras would be totally different. Each time the switcher toggles, the monitor would have to lock to the new scan position, the picture rolling and pulling as it does so.

Switch S_2 is a three position switch with a common output terminal connected to the sync generator. Position 2 is not connected to any circuit, and when the switch is in this position the sync generator circuit simply 'freewheels' and generates an independent sync signal. This position is used where the switcher or multiplexer contains circuits that can lock the camera signals together, or where there is just one camera, or where the customer doesn't mind a lot of picture roll!

Position 1 is connected to an external socket (generally BNC) which is usually labelled 'Gen Lock'. This is used where one camera, or perhaps the switcher or multiplexer, generates the line and field sync, which is then sent to each camera via a separate co-axial cable. The poor economics of using this in CCTV are obvious when we consider that each camera requires two co-axial feeds. Gen locking is normally only employed in broadcast television where multicore cables are used, and cable runs are relatively short.

Position 3 is only available on cameras that are either 230 V a.c. fed, or 24 V a.c. fed. A sample of the 50 Hz mains frequency is fed to the sync generator which locks to the zero transit point in each a.c. cycle. If each camera is connected to the same phase of the mains supply, then they will be synchronized. This method of synchronization is called *line lock* (LL). Problems can occur on larger installations where cameras in different locations are fed from different phases of the mains supply, however this can be overcome by adjusting the V-phase control RV1 which is able to shift the sync output from the generator circuit through 120°, which is the difference between any two mains supply phases. Line locking is the most economical method of multiple camera synchronization.

Multiple camera synchronization will be looked at in more detail in Chapter 9.

The colour signal process block takes the R–Y and B–Y signals and applies weighting to produce the *u* and *v* components. It also produces the 4.43 MHz sinusoidal subcarrier which, in the case of the diagram in Figure 6.11, is done by dividing down the master crystal oscillator, thus ensuring that the phase relationship between the chroma, sync and CCD output is always correct.

The *u* and *v* signals are amplitude modulated onto the subcarrier. Normally with AM only one signal can be put onto a carrier, however in a PAL colour TV signal a method called quadrature amplitude modulation (QAM) is employed which enables two separate signals to be placed onto one carrier in such a way that they can be separated in the colour decoder.

To complete the PAL chroma signal package, a sample containing ten cycles of 4.43 MHz subcarrier is positioned to coincide with the back porch period of the line sync pulse. This signal, known as the *chroma* or *colour burst*, is used to synchronze the colour decoders in the monitors and VCRs.

The majority of colour cameras offer a choice of either separate Y/C outputs (S-VHS) or composite video. The relative merits of these were discussed in Chapter 5. All output connectors are terminated at 75Ω to provide correct impedance matching to the 75Ω co-axial cable.

White balance

Up to this point we have assumed that the CCD chip or chips in a colour camera are able to produce exacting proportions of R, G and B for any given light input. Unfortunately this is not the case. Tolerances between chips, and within each individual chip, affect the R, G, B levels to such an extent that the colour quality of the reproduced picture would be at best poor, and in most cases totally incorrect.

Following power-up, the camera needs to be shown what white light looks like. It then uses this information to derive correction values for the processing circuits which ensure that the correct proportions of R, G and B are produced for a white light input. In theory, if the camera is producing the correct proportions of R, G and B for white, then all other colours will be correct.

The majority of modern cameras have an *automatic white balance* (AWB) function. Following power-up, a white card is held in front of the lens to provide a white light input. When the AWB is selected the camera quickly adjusts its circuits and memorizes the correction factors. As an alternative to using white card, if there is a large white object within the field of view, the camera can be trained onto this.

Some cameras have a simpler form of white balancing which uses pre-set correction factors. There is usually a choice of two settings, 'Indoor' and 'Outdoor'. The manufacturer takes the average lighting conditions for these two situations and designs suitable correction factors into the camera. Apart from operating the selector switch, there is no setting up required with this type of white balance, but there are obvious limitations with this system.

The main drawback with automatic white balance is the effect that the different light colour temperatures has on picture quality. Take, for example, an external camera which is to rely on halogen lighting during the evening. If it is balanced using daylight as the light source, the colour may well be incorrect during the evening. Even during the daytime difficulties may be experienced if areas within the field of view have different colour temperature lighting. This situation can arise when fully functional cameras are employed and their panning action takes them across different lighting conditions. These problems associated with AWB are one reason why for many years colour cameras were often considered unsuitable for external applications.

Advances in technology have largely overcome the problems associated with AWB. An automatic tracking circuit is included in many colour cameras which ensures that once AWB set-up has been performed, correct white balance is maintained for all colour temperatures of light.

Camera sensitivity

There are a number of ways in which the sensitivity of a camera can be measured and quoted, which is not helpful to the engineer when trying to decide between cameras of different manufacture, because the figures may not be comparable.

A true sensitivity figure is the maximum F-stop which produces a 1V pp video output when the camera is trained onto a specific test card under specified lighting conditions. The *AGC must be switched off*, and the manual iris is progressively closed down to the point where the video signal begins to fall from 1V pp. At this point the F-number is read, and quoted as the sensitivity.

However this is not the figure that is often quoted, rather, the *minimum illumination figure* is used. This is a measure of the lowest level of light falling onto an object from which a 'recognizable' video signal can be produced. Typically these specifications appear in a catalogue something like, '1 lux – 80% – F1.2'. This implies a light level at the object of 1 lux, where the object has a reflectivity of 80%, and an F-stop of 1.2 was used.

It is the definition of 'recognizable' that causes some difficulty, because it is left to each manufacturer's judgement. This is by no means implying that all manufacturers are attempting to pull the wool over the eyes of installers and specifiers, however it does offer a window of opportunity to some who wish to market what in truth are low spec cameras, whilst quoting high sensitivity figures.

An important consideration when looking at minimum illumination figures is to see if the measurement was taken with the AGC turned on or off. With the AGC turned off the figure is going to be more realistic because the camera will not have been working 'flat out' to produce the recognizable video signal. Be careful when comparing one camera which has been specified with the AGC off with another with the AGC on. This is not a true comparison because it is almost certain that the model with the AGC 'on' will show a much better figure than that with the AGC 'off', yet it may well be that the camera with the AGC 'off' is the better of the two. Unfortunately not all specifications state whether the AGC was on or off when the sensitivity was measured.

Camera resolution

The theory behind the resolution of a video image has been dealt with in Chapter 5, where we saw that ideally a 625 line system should be able to reproduce 780 horizontal pixels (Figure 5.9), but that in practice because of limitations in technology we opted for something less during the design of the original broadcast system. For a 625 line television system with 585 active lines, the maximum number of horizontal pixels along one line is 780×0.7 (Kell Factor) = 546.

The resolution of CCTV cameras is quoted in TVL (Television Lines). This figure refers to *the number of horizontal pixels a camera can produce along a distance equal to the height of the screen*. This point is illustrated in Figure 6.14.

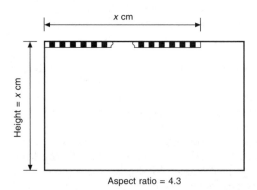

Figure 6.14 *TVL is measured as the number of horizontal pixels along a distance which is equal to the screen height*

In Chapter 5 it was stated that, ideally, the horizontal resolution should at least equal the vertical resolution. Therefore if the maximum number of pixels along a line is 546 (PAL), then the number of pixels along a distance equal to the height will be 546 divided by the aspect ratio, which is $546 \div (4/3) = 409.5$. Thus for a PAL CCTV camera to produce a picture which matches that seen on a broadcast transmission it must have a resolution of at least 410 TVL. Similarly, for NTSC the horizontal resolution in terms of TVL will be $462 \div (4/3) = 346$; although the practical figure quoted is 330 TVL.

In practice other losses in the system often require the CCTV camera to have a much higher resolution than the figures quoted above if the system is to match broadcast performance.

It should also be noted that whatever resolution is quoted, it will not apply to the entire picture area. Neither the lens nor the monitor CRT produce full resolution around the edges of the picture, and when looking at TVL figures it is prudent to assume that this performance will only apply to the centre portion of the displayed picture. This is of particular importance when selecting equipment for a specific operational requirement where the TVL for each image at the control room end has been specified.

The subject of camera resolution is considered in further detail in Chapter 12 when we look at methods of measuring system resolution.

Camera operating voltages

The three common supply voltages for CCTV cameras are 230V a.c. 24V a.c. and 12V d.c. Although at first glance the operating voltage may not appear too significant, the choice of camera supply has a direct bearing on the installation material costs and labour because some supply methods require more wiring than others.

For 12V d.c. cameras the supply is separately fed, meaning that every co-axial cable must be buddied with a d.c. supply cable. In some cases this is not a problem, however where there is a need for all cables to be hidden, losing the extra one can sometimes prove difficult.

Another problem associated with 12V d.c. systems is that of voltage drop on cable runs exceeding (typically) 100m. This phenomenon, along with methods of overcoming the problem, was discussed in Chapter 2.

The 12V supply is derived from a power supply, the rating of which must be suited to the number of cameras being installed. The current drawn by a camera is typically between 350–500mA, and to avoid over-running a power supply a useful rule of thumb is to look at two cameras per 1A supply. From this it becomes obvious that for even a modest system a large power supply is required. There are two schools of thought on this subject. On the one hand a single 12V power supply rated high enough to power all cameras can be employed. On the other hand a number of smaller units can be used, having the advantage that if one unit fails, the whole system is not put out of action. In practice it is not much more expensive to take the second option, and the problem of voltage drop can be reduced by dispersing the power supplies around the site.

230V a.c. systems do not suffer the problems of voltage drop and the need for large power supplies. This supply is particularly suited to external camera applications, and is essential if a pan/tilt unit is employed as 230V is required to operate the motor.

Another advantage of using the 50Hz mains as a power source is that the line lock feature on the cameras can be employed to provide synchronization (see Figure 6.11).

The main drawback of the 230V a.c. supply is the requirement of a fused spur at each camera location which can often make the installation more involved, especially where cameras are mounted on towers and must be supplied using an underground steel wire armoured cable. Under current regulations this work must be carried out by a competent person and final inspection and testing of the circuit must be performed, with a certificate of compliance issued to the customer by the inspector, in accordance with BS 7671. In other words, if the installer is not a qualified electrician, the electrical installation work will need to be subcontracted out, or the installer will run the risk of prosecution in the event of any mishap.

Another problem encountered with mains-powered systems is that of ground loops, although this phenomenon is usually rectified using ground loop correctors. This was discussed in Chapter 2.

For internal use, 24V a.c. cameras are becoming increasingly popular. Being defined as extra-low-voltage (ELV), 24V a.c. does not come under the same regulations as 230V a.c., yet overcomes the problems of voltage drop. As with 12V d.c., a separate a.c. power supply unit is required, however some switchers incorporate a limited a.c. supply which is sufficient to operate a small system.

Some cameras are compatible for both 12V d.c. and 24V a.c. operation. These cameras generally operate at around 9V d.c. internally and use an internal d.c. to d.c. converter power supply to reduce the 12V d.c. input, and an internal bridge rectifier and smoothing circuit to rectify the 24V a.c. input.

A variation of the low voltage d.c./a.c. camera is the *line fed* system where the power to each camera is fed down the co-axial signal cable. The cameras are supplied from a 24V a.c. supply contained within a dedicated switcher/controller. The video signal is superimposed onto the a.c. and the two are separated using filter networks within the controller. This system makes installation very simple, and even lends itself to the DIY market. However, the need for dedicated controllers and cameras means that there is little flexibility in system design, and the system cannot be extended beyond its maximum camera capacity.

Specialized cameras

In addition to the vast choice of monochrome and colour cameras available, advances in both CCD and digital technology have spawned a range of high performance specialized cameras, particularly in low-light and covert designs.

As we have seen, comparing like for like, monochrome cameras always outperform their colour counterparts in terms of low-light ability and resolution, and high performance designs are available with minimum illumination levels well below 0.1 lux. Thus the installer looking for a camera which will perform well in an environment with minimum illumination has never had such an easy task. Even with colour cameras the situation is changing rapidly. For many years it has been generally accepted that colour cameras were unsuited to external use because of their poor low-light performance, and the fact that they would only produce correct colours if the area was illuminated in such a way that it resembled a TV production set! Yet new designs in CCD image chips, along with the production of dedicated digital processing ICs has caused surveyors to rethink.

However, there are still special circumstances where a quality image is required in situations where any form of artificial lighting, visible or otherwise, is unacceptable. In these circumstances a device known as an *image intensifier* may be employed.

Image intensifiers are not new and have been used for many years to enhance the performance of cameras, including tube types which always struggled to operate under low light levels. They function by effectively amplifying the amount of incoming light using electronic means. The basic construction is shown in Figure 6.15.

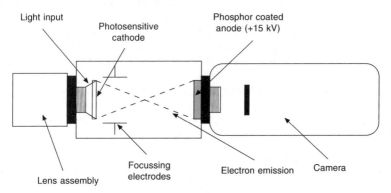

Figure 6.15 *Principle of the image intensifier*

The incoming light is focussed onto a photosensitive cathode, the coating of which has the property of emitting electrons when impacted by photons. The electron emission from any point on the cathode is directly proportional to the amount of light falling onto that point, and thus there is a constant emission of electrons from all points on the cathode, representative to the image produced by the lens.

The electron cloud is attracted towards the anode by a +15kV potential. As the cloud passes through the device it is focussed electronically onto the anode plate which is phosphor-coated in much the same way as a cathode ray tube in a monochrome monitor. Thus a picture of the original image is produced in front of the camera imaging device, however it is many times brighter than that produced by the lens.

Use of an image intensifier makes it possible to obtain a clear picture with nothing more than starlight illumination. However, the cathode and anode materials have a limited operational life (typically 2000 hours), making image intensifiers a somewhat expensive option in any CCTV system. To obtain maximum lifespan, a high F-stop lens should be fitted.

Although image intensifiers are still in use, because of their limited lifespan a more reliable alternative would be most welcome, and it is expected that developments in CCD technology will make them largely redundant.

Turning our attention to covert cameras, these may be employed for any number of reasons, and not solely by the security forces. They are available for use by retailers, employers, entertainment centres and domestic homeowners alike. Some examples of use are: covert cameras can record the activities of an intruder once they have defeated the overt CCTV system, they can be used to produce video evidence of activities which may be later used by either prosecution or defence counsels, or they may be employed in preference to overt equipment in order to maintain the aesthetics of the premises.

Until the advent of the CCD image chip, covert cameras were relatively bulky and difficult to hide. Nevertheless, covert tube cameras were successfully employed for many years. Of course, it is not just the camera which needs to be compact, the lens must also be unobtrusive, and it is this which is perhaps the more difficult to achieve because the words 'miniaturizing' and 'optics' simply don't go well together. As we saw in Chapter 4, ideally a lens must be able to collect and process as much light as possible, and this means using large optical components. Having said this, small lenses offering remarkable performance have been developed for covert use.

The most common type is the *pinhole* lens, although this name is somewhat misleading because these tend to have a diameter in the order of 3.5–8mm. They are generally available in $\frac{1}{3}''$ and $\frac{1}{2}''$ formats and have a CS mounting, making them compatible with any matching format CS mount camera. Additionally, pinhole lenses are available in a right-angled construction to enable the camera to be hidden in locations where there is restricted space. This is illustrated in Figure 6.16.

Another type of lens developed for covert use is the mini lens which, as the name implies, is both short and narrow. However, the small size is achieved at the expense of certain components, and mini lenses generally have no iris, meaning that they are only suited to applications where the lighting conditions are reasonably stable. Also, mini lenses do not invert the image at the output.

When selecting a pinhole or mini lens, the installer should try to choose one with the lowest possible F-number in order to attain the highest

Figure 6.16 *Typical pinhole lenses for covert applications. A right angled lens may be used where a covert camera is to be installed in a restricted space. (Photos courtesy of CBC (Europe) Ltd, manufacturers of Computar Lenses)*

optical speed, bearing in mind that the optical speed will be restricted by the miniaturized optics.

Fibre-optic lenses are available for use in situations where it is necessary to 'see' through thick walls or perhaps beyond a wide void. Both rigid and flexible types are available. The rigid type simply fixes to the front of a camera in the same manner as a conventional lens assembly, the light being carried from the small front optical device to the main lens assembly via a cluster of fibre-optic strands contained within a narrow tube. The flexible type allows the front optical plate to pass through more intricate spaces, and the camera does not have to be fixed adjacent to the field of view. Due to a number of types of losses within the fibre-optic strands, these lenses are not as sensitive as glass pinhole types.

Of course, all of the covert lenses so far discussed are expensive, and when the additional cost of a camera is added to the installation price the majority of would-be users are put off. However, with recent developments in low-cost miniature covert combination camera/lens assemblies, the number of covert installations has risen considerably. Popular off-the-shelf covert CCTV products are the passive infra-red (PIR) camera (some of which include a working PIR), clocks, mirrors and domestic smoke detectors. However, 'bare bones' PCB cameras are available which can be mounted into almost anything. Many of these are designed to be connected using standard four core intruder alarm system cable which is far more flexible than co-axial cable and, despite the lack of screening and the mismatch in impedance, the transmission results are usually quite acceptable; although most manufacturers do not recommend cable runs beyond 100m. The camera modules are generally designed to operate at 12V, which is delivered along two of the four cores.

Another type of specialized camera is a colour camera which switches to monochrome operation when the light level falls below a pre-determined value. This is to take advantage of the much more desirable colour picture when the light level is sufficient, but to revert to the more effective monochrome operation when low-light conditions prevail. Early versions of these cameras tended to be somewhat unstable under some conditions – for example, where car headlights intermittently illuminate the viewing area – but improvements in performance during recent years have made these cameras a popular choice for external operation.

7 Monitors

Having seen how the camera converts light energy into electronic signals relating to the luma and chroma content, we will now see how the colour monitor converts these signals back into light energy, creating the illusion of moving coloured pictures.

Block diagram

The primary stages in a colour monitor are shown in Figure 7.1.

Generally speaking, two inputs are available: composite (CVBS) or Y/C, the latter being included to accommodate an S-VHS input. BNC connectors are normally used for the CVBS input/output, both because of their robustness and because they are designed to maintain the 75Ω impedance of the transmission system, provided of course that the correct BNC type is used. BNC may be employed for the Y/C inputs, however SCART or four pin S-VHS connectors are commonly used.

Some monitors use RCA (phono) connectors for CVBS input/output, however this can present a problem when the monitor input cable is co-axial because RCA connectors, which were originally intended for audio use, do not fit onto co-axial cables such as RG-59. Thus a BNC-to-phono adapter must be used, which creates an added connection in the transmission medium.

The input selector switch S_1 may be mechanical, although electronic selection via the CPU is becoming more common, the advantage of this being improved reliability due to the omission of mechanical switch contacts which are prone to oxidization which can lead to intermittent or permanent poor picture contrast.

The input buffer stage is an amplifier with unity gain, meaning that it actually has no gain at all. This stage performs a number of functions. Firstly, it is designed to present a 75Ω impedance to the input connector. Secondly, its segregated feeds to the monitor and output connector ensure that changes in the load impedance on one output does not have an adverse effect on the signal at the other.

The signal emerging from the buffer is passed to three separate processing sections: the timebase, the luma and the chroma stages, although when the input is Y/C there is no chroma signal present at this point in the monitor.

Dealing firstly with the luma signal process, the input to the luma amplifier contains a filter which blocks the 4.43MHz colour subcarrier. The 1V pp luma signal is amplified by two or three times to overcome

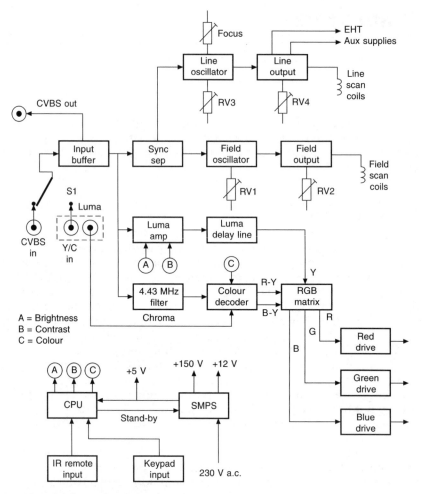

Figure 7.1 *Block diagram of a colour monitor (PAL)*

losses in the following delay line. The luma amplifier also contains variable d.c. control inputs which control the gain of the amplifier (picture contrast), and the d.c. level of the luma signal (picture brightness). The variable d.c. control voltage may be derived via variable resistors accessible at the front of the monitor, or via a D/A converter in the CPU section. In the case of the latter, the control is adjusted either by touch buttons on the front of the monitor, or via an infra-red remote link. The effects on the luma signal of the brightness and contrast controls are shown in Figure 7.2. The brightness control shifts the d.c. level (A), moving the complete waveshape up or down without altering the signal amplitude. The contrast control alters the peak-to-peak value of the signal (B), maintaining the sync pulse at the d.c. level.

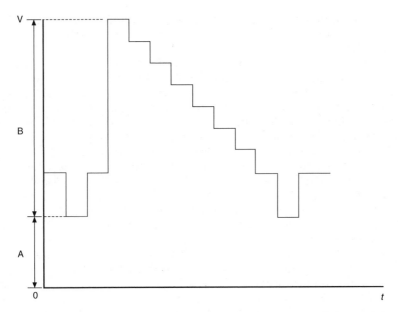

Figure 7.2 *Effect of brightness and contrast control. Brightness alters the d.c. level (A), moving the complete waveshape up or down without altering the amplitude. Contrast alters the peak–peak value (B)*

The luma delay line introduces a 600–900 ns time delay in the luma signal path. The justification for this is somewhat complex; however, in simple terms, it is necessary to compensate for the lack of bandwidth of the chroma signal in comparison to that of the luma signal (2.2 MHz compared with 5.5 MHz for PAL). Without a delay line, the chroma information would be displayed to the right of the corresponding luma detail on the monitor screen.

The luma signal emerging from the delay line is passed to the RGB matrix stage. Before following its progress any further we must look at the colour signal path.

The 4.43 MHz bandpass filter at the input to the chroma stage blocks the path of the luma signal components. The 4.43 MHz chroma subcarrier with its 2.2 MHz bandwidth sidebands is passed to the colour decoder which demodulates the u and v signals. After demodulation the u and v are restored to their original amplitudes, thus recovering the R–Y and B–Y colour difference signals. The PAL colour burst signal serves as synchronization for the colour decoder. If, for any reason, the burst is corrupted or missing, the decoder will cease to function and the monitor will display a monochrome picture. Perhaps the most common cause of burst corruption is defective or poorly maintained VCRs where it is not uncommon to have a situation where normal play operation is acceptable, but a monochrome picture is displayed in still or search modes. VCRs will be discussed in Chapter 8.

The colour decoder has a direct input to accommodate the Y/C facility and, like the luma amplifier, it also has a variable d.c. control input (C) to provide colour control.

In the RGB matrix, the luma is recombined with the two colour difference signals to produce red and blue signals. A further matrix adds proportions of red and blue to derive a green signal. The RGB signals emerging from the matrix are approximately 3V pp, however the CRT requires signal levels in the order of 80V pp to produce adequate variations in beam current. Thus three separate voltage amplifiers are required.

The primary function of the timebase section is to produce the horizontal and vertical scanning currents which are required to deflect the three electron beams in the CRT. As discussed in Chapter 5, it is essential that the timebases in the monitor are in step with those in the camera(s), and to achieve this horizontal and vertical synchronization pulses are sent with the video information. These synchronization pulses are illustrated in Figures 5.12 and 5.13.

The sync separator stage performs two functions. First of all it must remove the sync pulses from the luma information. Referring to Figure 7.3, a circuit contained within the sync separator is designed to conduct when the input is between voltage levels A and B, and to switch off between levels B and C. The output from this circuit is a train of line and field sync pulses known as *composite sync*.

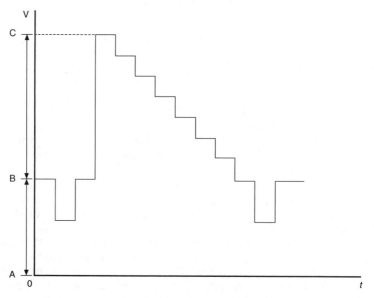

Figure 7.3 *Sync separator action*

The second function of the sync separator stage is to separate the composite sync into its line and field components. Passing composite sync through a low pass filter derives the 50 Hz field sync pulses. Passing it through a high pass filter derives the 15625 Hz line sync pulses.

The scan waveshapes are produced by the line and field oscillators. These are free-running, but their timing is controlled by the sync pulses. Thus each oscillator operates in step with the timebase oscillators in the camera.

Owing to manufacturing tolerances it may be necessary adjust the frequency of the timebase oscillators. In Figure 7.1 this function is performed by variable resistors RV1 and RV3, although in many modern designs timebase adjustment is performed electronically in the same manner as brightness, etc. Where potentiometers are employed it is not uncommon for them to be contained within the monitor, adjustment being performed using a terminal screwdriver. Access to the controls is usually provided via holes in the rear or side of the monitor cabinet. These are labelled 'Hor Hold' and 'Vert Hold', or similar.

Incorrect adjustment of the field oscillator will result in field roll or picture bounce. If the line oscillator is maladjusted the picture may tend to pull to the right, or break up into a series of horizontal black lines. These effects are illustrated in Figure 7.4.

The field output stage is a power amplifier not too dissimilar to that employed in an audio hi-fi system. The small 50 Hz ramp waveshape generated by the field oscillator is raised to a level sufficient to produce the required magnetic deflection field. This will depend upon the screen size, but for a 51 cm (20″) monitor this is typically 40 V pp, with a peak current value of around 2 A. Control RV2 performs *vertical shift*. This is used to centre the picture vertically on the monitor screen.

The line output stage is more complex than the field circuit. This is because it is required to produce a scan waveshape in the order of 100 V pp at around 2 A at a frequency of 15625 Hz. The circuit operates on a switching principle whereby a high d.c. voltage in the order of +150 V is switched at 15625 Hz across a transformer. Each time the electronic switch opens, a large back EMF is developed within the transformer. This is used to derive not only the scanning current, but also the *extra high tension* (EHT) required at the final anode of the CRT, the 1 kV required by the focus electrode, the +500 V for the first anode, and other auxiliary d.c. supplies which are used to power circuits within the monitor.

In Figure 7.1, RV4 performs horizontal shift control, although not all monitors include this adjustment. In addition, the line timebase includes the CRT focus and first anode (A1) voltage adjustments. These adjustments are often made available through the rear of the monitor, although it is not recommended that the first anode (often labelled 'Screen' on the monitor) control is adjusted by the CCTV engineer as the correct procedure for setting this is somewhat involved. It requires removal of the cabinet, and a voltage measurement taken at the A1 terminal on the CRT whilst adjusting the control. The A1 appears to behave as a brightness control, however it is not to be used for this function, and maladjustment of this can result in impaired picture quality, and a possible reduction in CRT life.

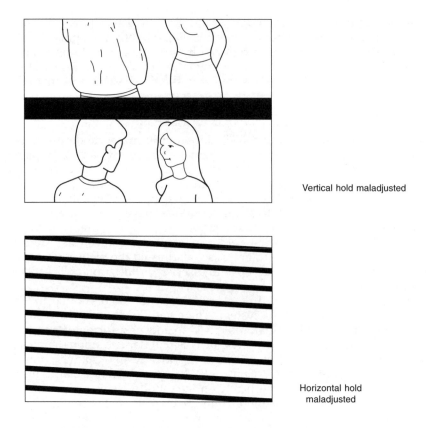

Vertical hold maladjusted

Horizontal hold
maladjusted

Figure 7.4 *Effects of maladjusted timebase controls*

Adjustment of the focus control is not as involved, and can be performed in the field as long as the monitor covers do not need to be removed. The monitor should be made to display a picture containing a high degree of detail, especially in the centre, and the signal source should be known to be sound; in other words, the camera focus should be correct! The focus control is then adjusted for the sharpest picture at the centre of the screen.

Two other controls which may be available are *raster correction* adjustments. All monitors and TV receivers suffer from an effect known as *pincushion distortion*. This picture distortion, illustrated in Figure 7.5, appears at the edges of the display and is caused by differences in the distance between the point of origin of the electron beam (i.e. the CRT cathode) and points along the sides of the screen. Circuits within the line and field output stages are included to correct the effect and, on larger monitors especially, external adjustments are made available.

The monitor requires very stable d.c. supply rails, and for all colour monitors these are provided by a type of power supply known as a *switched mode power supply* (SMPS), which is employed because of its high

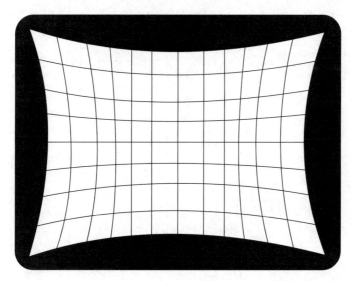

Figure 7.5 *Effect of pincushion distortion. Without raster correction, the edges of the picture become bowed*

efficiency. The 230 V a.c. mains supply is full-wave rectified and smoothed to produce 320 V d.c. This d.c. is then switched at a high frequency (40–80 kHz) through a transformer primary winding. Voltages induced in the secondary windings are rectified and smoothed to produce a variety of high and low voltage d.c. supplies.

The principle of the SMPS is shown in Figure 7.6, which illustrates a very important feature of this type of power supply; *mains isolation*. It is essential that the 0 V side of the d.c. power supply in a CCTV system is isolated from the a.c. mains supply. In items of equipment such as cameras, controllers, multiplexers, etc., this isolation is performed by the action of the mains transformer. However, in the monitor it is possible for the 0 V line to find a return path to the a.c. mains supply through the bridge rectifier. If this were to occur, the chances are that the earth connections to the CCTV system would cause fuses in the monitor to rupture, as well as the RCDs to trip. However, if an earth fault were to exist in the system, all metal parts of the CCTV system would become live, with possible fatal consequences.

By using the arrangement shown in Figure 7.6, the 0 V d.c. line is completely isolated from the 'live' area by the transformer action. Even the feedback from the output to the control circuit, which is necessary to maintain a stable d.c. output, is isolated by means of an opto-coupler. It is essential that no attempt is made to modify the power supply section in a monitor as this isolation may be compromised, and all servicing work in this section must be carried out by a qualified television service engineer, whose role and training is somewhat different to that of a CCTV engineer.

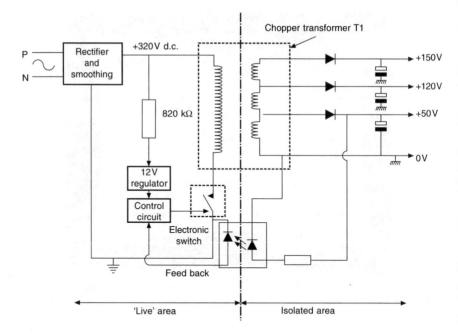

Figure 7.6 *Principle of the SMPs, illustrating the isolating effect of the chopper transformer*

The CPU is a dedicated chip containing input and output ports, ROM, RAM and, of course, the CPU itself. The RAM is used to store the brightness, contrast and colour settings plus other data. The infra-red remote link and the front control buttons are input directly to the CPU, and a switched output from this chip is used to put the SMPS into stand-by mode. A word of warning here. When a monitor is in stand-by the SMPS is not switched off, it simply reduces the 150 V supply to such a level that the monitor is no longer able to function. This is done so that the +5 V supply to the CPU chip is maintained in order that it is able to receive and process a command to come out of stand-by. If an engineer were to remove the monitor covers whist it is in the stand-by mode, there is the very real hazard of receiving a fatal shock from the 320 V rectified d.c., or the a.c. mains input.

A typical colour monitor is shown in Figure 7.7; the primary components are labelled.

Monochrome monitor

In most respects the block diagram of a monochrome monitor differs very little from that shown for the colour monitor in Figure 7.1. Obviously

Figure 7.7 *Primary components inside a colour monitor*

there is no colour decoder or RGB matrix, and there is just one CRT video drive amplifier instead of the three RGB driver stages. Apart from this, the main differences are usually the omission of the SMPS which, because of the much lower power consumption, is replaced with a conventional step-down transformer and regulator arrangement, and the omission of the pincushion correction circuits. This function is achieved by use of permanent magnets placed around the CRT neck. It is also unusual to find a monochrome monitor with a remote control facility.

Monitor safety

Monitor servicing should be referred to a qualified television service engineer, and the CCTV engineer should only perform the picture adjustments outlined in this chapter. However, there are occasions where this involves removal of the monitor cabinet, and in such cases the engineer must be aware that this immediately exposes both him/herself and anyone in the area to the possibility of a lethal electric shock. Supplies such as the 150 V d.c. rail are able to deliver more than sufficient current to kill, and are especially lethal if applied across the chest, which can easily happen if the engineer has one hand on the chassis to hold it steady, and the other hand which is performing an adjustment slips and comes into contact with a component connected to the high voltage supply. This is illustrated in Figure 7.8.

In this illustration the engineer has his left hand on the negative metal case (or chassis) of the equipment on which he is working. If his right hand were to slip and touch a high voltage contact, a current path would

Figure 7.8 *Current flows from the positive supply (right hand), through the body and back to the negative supply (left hand)*

exist between his hands, taking a path straight across his chest and therefore the heart. It has already been stated that this is a very dangerous situation.

Whenever working on a live monitor a 'one-handed' approach should be adhered to. This means that the engineer never has both hands on or in the monitor at the same time whilst it is connected to the mains supply, thus reducing the chance of electric shock across the chest. This point is illustrated in Figure 7.9, which shows the engineer working with one hand away from the chassis (his hand is on the bench, however it could be placed on the plastic or wooden cabinet of the equipment). In this case there is no circuit and hence there can be no current flow.

Of course there is still a chance of shock from the supply to earth, which brings us to the second important point on safety when working on a live monitor. *When working on live equipment connected to the mains supply, the equipment must be connected via a mains isolation transformer.* For a small colour monitor a rating of 500VA is sufficient, however for larger screen models a 750VA transformer must be used.

It is not usually practical to work on a monitor on-site, and since 230V a.c. isolation transformers are not a usual item in a CCTV service engineer's kit, one-handed working can be difficult in what are often confined working conditions. It can also be difficult to ensure the safety of control room/area staff whilst the monitor is exposed. Consequently defective monitors are normally exchanged and serviced in a workshop.

In Europe, following servicing a monitor must be PAT tested to prove its integrity.

Figure 7.9 *There is no circuit so current does not flow, provided that the bench top is insulated*

One point which the CCTV engineer must always test is the integrity of the earthing on monitors which have a metal case. This includes not only the earth in the mains connector plug, but also the earth in the mains supply socket to which the monitor is to be connected. In a worst case scenario, a faulty monitor without an earth can cause not only its own case to become live, but the entire CCTV system including metal camera housings, mounting brackets, etc.

Terminator switches

The diagram in Figure 7.1 has an input buffer stage which maintains a constant 75Ω impedance at both the input and output sockets, irrespective of whether the output socket is in use. However, many monitors do not employ an input buffer, the 'loop out' signal path being through passive components. A typical circuit arrangement is shown in Figure 7.10.

The problem with this arrangement is that the input and output sockets are effectively connected across a parallel resistor arrangement, meaning that a change in impedance at the output will alter that at the input. Therefore the input impedance, which should be 75Ω in order to match the cable and thus maintain a condition of maximum power transfer, is dependent on whether or not another piece of equipment is connected to the video output socket.

To overcome this problem, manufacturers design the input circuit so that correct impedance-matching is achieved when a piece of equipment is connected to the output socket. Where this is not the case, a switched 75Ω resistor is made available. As can be seen from Figure 7.10, with nothing connected at the output, the inclusion of this resistance will maintain correct impedance-matching conditions.

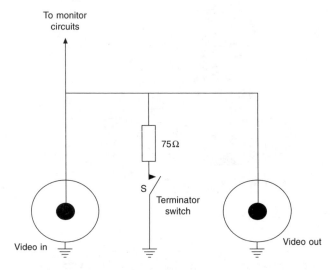

Figure 7.10 *Terminator switch arrangement on a monitor loop circuit*

Correct setting of these switches is important in a CCTV installation. Looking at Figure 7.10, it can be seen that if the resistor is switched into circuit when an item of equipment is connected to the output, the impedance will fall below 75Ω. This will cause an attenuation of the signal, resulting in a poor contrast picture. If the switch is left open when there is nothing connected to the output, the input impedance will increase, causing a high contrast display.

It is easy to think that a low or high contrast picture can be easily corrected by simply adjusting the contrast control on the monitor, however there can be more serious consequences from an incorrectly set terminator switch. In the case where the resistor is switched in when it shouldn't be, the reduced signal is passed onto the next piece of equipment in the chain, and so on. Similarly, when the resistor is omitted when the monitor is the last item in the chain, the excess signal level may result in frame roll due to clipping of the sync pulses.

More serious consequences may become evident in systems where telemetry is passed down the co-axial video cables (see Chapter 10). Remember that co-axial cables behave as LC tuned circuits, and that standing waves exist along their length. As we saw in Chapter 2, when the terminating impedance is incorrect, the standing waves alter, and reflections can pass back down the cable. Such a condition can cause corruption of the telemetry data, resulting in intermittent or permanent loss of control of remote cameras, etc.

The majority of modern CCTV equipment employs automatic termination switching; that is, the switch is operated by the action of inserting a BNC connector on the output socket. Where no connector is present, the switch defaults to the closed position and the resistor is connected into the circuit. In equipment where manual switching is employed, the switch positions are usually labelled 'Open' and '75Ω'. When the video output socket is in use, the switch should be set to the 'open' position. When the monitor is the last item in a chain the switch should be set to the '75Ω' position. Occasionally an engineer may encounter a monitor which has neither an input buffer nor a terminator switch. In such cases a 75Ω terminator should be employed when the monitor is at the end of a chain. These resemble a sealed BNC connector, however they have an internal 75Ω resistor.

Resolution

This is generally quoted in TVL, the definition of which was given in Chapter 6 (see Figure 6.14).

Monitor resolution is governed primarily by the quality of the CRT, although the design of the drive circuits does have some bearing, especially in the case of colour monitors. A quick look through any CCTV supply catalogue reveals a range of monitors with resolutions from 300 TVL to over 1000 TVL, although as with cameras, high resolution monochrome monitors are far less expensive than their medium-resolution colour counterparts.

When selecting a monitor for a particular application, resolution is one factor which must be taken into account. Yet it should be remembered that the TVL quoted for a monitor will not apply to the entire screen area because a CRT suffers problems of beam de-focussing at the sides, and particularly in the corners. In addition, colour tubes often suffer convergence problems in the corners of the screen. If we add to this the problems of image distortion around the edges introduced by the camera lens, then we see that it is highly unlikely that a monitor with a resolution of 400 TVL will be able to produce such resolution across 100% of its screen area. As a rule of thumb, if you imagine a rectangle in the centre of the screen with an area equal to about one third of the screen area, then this is where the quoted resolution will be achieved. Thus, if it is desirable to attain a resolution of 400 TVL at the sides of the picture, then a monitor of around 450 TVL would most probably be required.

Ergonomics

Some monitor designs are derived from domestic TV receiver models where the tuning and RF signal processing stages have been removed, and a range of video (and possibly audio) input/output sockets are added. Being designed around a domestic receiver, these monitors frequently offer high resolution. However, the moulded plastic cabinet does not make them particularly robust, and it is not possible for them to be stacked. The metal-cased rectangular design is often more suitable for CCTV purposes as it is more able to withstand the industrial environment, and it is possible to stack them into banks.

Careful thought should be given to the positioning of monitors during the initial site survey. Such things as viewing height, distance and angle, ventilation, monitor size and monitor resolution should all be considered at this point. At the time of writing, standards are being devised for the ergonomic design of control centres (ISO 11064), and these will have considerable bearing on the design and layout of CCTV control rooms.

Generally speaking, monitors should be positioned so that they may be viewed without causing discomfort to the operator over a period of time. The distance of the monitor from the operator will depend on its size and function, however recommendations are laid down in the new standards which are outlined in Table 7.1, along with the figures quoted in the BSIA Code Of Practice for CCTV (BSIA No. 109: Issue 2: October 1991). In addition to the distance, the viewing angle must not be excessive, and 30° maximum is recommended for monitors located away from the operator, and 15° maximum for a monitor mounted on a desk directly in front of the operator. Also, site the monitor so that the display is not impaired by glare from light sources, otherwise steps must be taken to remove or mask the source of the glare. Alternatively an anti-glare screen can be fixed to the monitor, although this can reduce the light output.

Table 7.1 *Note that some of the BSIA figures relate to slightly different monitor sizes. Where this is the case, the monitor size is shown in paratheses*

Monitor size	Viewing distance (ISO 11064)	Viewing distance (BSIA COP)
23 cm (9″)	0.9–1.2 m	1–2 m
30 cm (12″)	1.2–3.0 m	2–3 m (39 cm/14″)
43 cm (17″)	1.3–3.6 m	–
53 cm (21″)	1.3–4.6 m	3–5 m (51 cm/20″)

One point to consider when stacking or racking monitors is ventilation. The reliability of a monitor may be reduced if it is made to operate continually at a high temperature, and in a large, tightly packed, stack the units in the centre could easily become overheated. Of course it is not always up to the installing or servicing engineer how the monitors are to be mounted, however where a monitor is found to be overheating, the hazards associated with this (e.g. unreliability, fire, etc.) should be pointed out to the customer.

The required monitor size is dependent on such factors as the amount of detail which is to be discerned and the number of images that are to be displayed. For example, it would not be practical to display sixteen images on a 23 cm monitor.

Finally, make sure that it is possible to access the monitor after installation. It will be necessary for operators to routinely clean the screen, as well as make occasional adjustments to compensate for tube ageing, and when the monitor fails it will be necessary for the service engineer to remove the monitor and install a temporary or permanent replacement.

8 Recording equipment

The ability to be able to record CCTV images is of immense importance because it not only enhances the effectiveness of systems which are at times unmanned, but it also provides supporting evidence to control room operators who by nature of their work become eye witnesses to the incidents they are monitoring. On the one hand the video evidence will only be as good as the system performance will allow, on the other, if the specification of the recording equipment does not match that of the system, or the equipment is poorly maintained, then the quality of evidence will be far below the picture quality offered by the system.

There are three recording systems in use in CCTV: analogue video recording in the form of VHS and Super VHS (S-VHS), digital tape recording, and disk-based systems using either PC hard drives built into customized recording units, or CD-R disks. Each of these have their advantages and disadvantages, and an engineer must appreciate the differences between, and limitations of, each of these systems.

Magnetic recording has been around for many years, during which time we have seen it evolve from a crude audio recording format using wire as the recording medium into a sophisticated recording system capable of storing data in either analogue or digital format, and not just on linear tape but also on rotating metal discs (hard drives).

The first video recorders to be used for security applications were reel-to-reel machines which only recorded in black and white. These were not particularly successful owing to their high cost, short recording time, low resolution and high maintenance requirements. It was not until the domestic VHS machine arrived on the scene during the latter part of the 1970s that the security industry had anything like a viable recording system to complement CCTV installations. Further modifications to these machines produced the now familiar time-lapse recorders, and the development of an enhanced VHS format – Super VHS – gave the industry a recording system with an acceptable picture resolution. The main drawbacks being the relatively high maintenance requirements of the machines and the problems of tape management.

Digital recording is rapidly replacing the analogue VCR, however, at the time of writing, there are still a lot of analogue machines in use, and engineers must be aware of all formats if they are to cope with the issues that surround installation, maintenance and upgrading of CCTV installations.

As analogue recording in the form of VHS has provided the backbone of CCTV recording for many years, perhaps it is fitting that we begin by looking at this topic before we move on to examine the more recent developments in digital recording.

Video recording principles

Unlike an audio signal which has a bandwidth in the region of 20 Hz to 20 kHz, video signals contain large numbers of high frequency components extending up to (and beyond) 5.5 MHz. In order to record these high frequencies the tape must pass the recording head at a very high speed – in the order of 1.5 m per second. A 3-hour VHS cassette contains 250 m of tape, so with a tape transport speed of 1.5 m/sec the recording time would be around 167 seconds, or 2.8 minutes! Clearly another answer, other than extremely large cassette tapes, had to be found; and it was.

Helical scanning was developed where the tape transport speed is actually very low (around 2.4 cm/sec), but the tape is wrapped around a head drum which is rotating at a fast rate, producing a velocity at the outer circumference of the drum of around 5 m per second. The head drum is tilted with respect to the tape so that the recording heads scan the tape following a diagonal path up the tape. The head path forms a helix shape, hence the name helical scanning. The principle is shown in Figures 8.1 and 8.2.

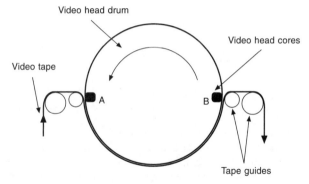

Figure 8.1 *Tape path around a video head drum*

The tape is laced around the drum by 186°, the overlap being included to allow for mechanical tolerances. The drum is made to rotate at 1500 rpm which equates to 25 revolutions per second, and it is no coincidence that this equals the TV frame rate (1800 rpm equating to 30 revolutions per second for NTSC). Two head cores are fixed onto the drum 180° apart so that there is always at least one head in contact with the tape at any time. The drum rotation is controlled such that as the first TV line of the first field is being input at the video input of the machine, the A head core will be in the position shown in Figure 8.1. For a PAL machine with a rotational rate of 25 Hz (40 ms) it will take 20 ms for the drum to move through 180°, this period equalling one field period of 312.5 lines. At the end of this period the B head core will be on the left-hand side, and will proceed to record the second TV field of 312.5 lines (262.5 lines for NTSC).

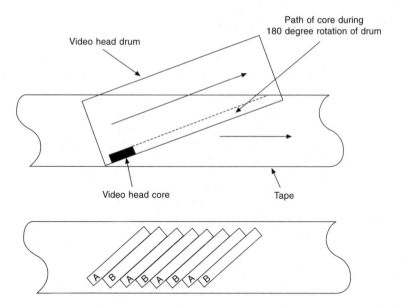

Figure 8.2 *Principle of helical scanning. Magnetic information is laid down on the tape in the form of diagonal stripes*

Thus it can be seen that

- Head A records the first TV field.
- Head B records the second TV field.
- Each single 360° revolution of the head drum records one TV frame.

For a number of reasons, it is not possible to record an analogue video signal directly onto magnetic tape and for this reason *frequency modulation* is used. Like amplitude modulation, which was discussed in Chapter 5, frequency modulation is a process of combining an information signal and a high frequency carrier. In the case of FM, the amplitude changes in the (video) signal waveform alter the frequency of the carrier; the higher the signal voltage, the further the carrier deviates from its fundamental frequency. The principle of FM is illustrated in Figure 8.3.

It is important to note that it is only the luma signal which is modulated onto the FM carrier. The chroma signal is superimposed onto the FM

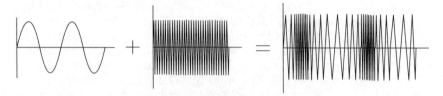

Figure 8.3 *Principle of frequency modulation*

carrier where it is recorded directly, however the frequency of the 4.43 MHz (3.58 MHz NTSC) chroma subcarrier falls within the same range as the luma FM carrier signal components, and unless something is done about this the two signals will become mixed to such an extent that it would be impossible to separate them again during replay. For this reason the frequency of the chroma subcarrier is changed to a much lower frequency in the VCR prior to recording. This system is known as *colour under* because the chroma carrier frequency is now lower than the luma signals, which is opposite to the PAL or NTSC systems. During replay the VCR must re-convert the chroma frequency to 4.43 MHz in order that it will be recognized and decoded by the monitor.

Apart from the video information, a VCR must record audio information (although in CCTV this is a feature which is rarely used). Ignoring a VHS format known as 'High Density' (HD) sound recording (more commonly known as hi-fi sound) which is really intended for domestic models, the audio signal is recorded using Compact Cassette technology where a lateral sound track is laid down along the top edge of the tape.

During replay the machine requires a reference signal to synchronize the drum rotation with the tape transport, which is what is meant when we refer to *tracking*. This reference signal is provided from a *control (CTL) track* which is derived from the 50 Hz field sync, having first been divided down to 25 Hz before being recorded along the bottom edge of the tape (for NTSC, the 60 Hz field sync produces a 30 Hz CTL track). The CTL track is also used to 'clock' the real-time tape counter, and to mark the positions of alarm input activations in time-lapse VCRs.

A video tape, therefore, contains the diagonal video signal tracks positioned in its centre, and lateral audio and CTL tracks along the edges. This track format is shown in Figure 8.4.

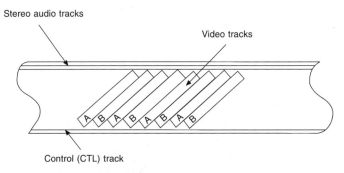

Figure 8.4 *Videotape track format*

Mistracking occurs in a VCR when, during replay, the tape transport and drum rotation motors are both running at the correct speed, but they are not in phase with each other. In this case the heads will be scanning two tracks at the same time. This is illustrated in Figure 8.5. Because of differences between the two heads, when a head scans a track which is not its own there is little or no output, and a white grain or snow appears over the picture. It is quite common for a head to begin scanning along its own track and then drift off onto the adjacent track. This gives the effect of a clear picture at the top of the screen, dissolving into a band of grainy picture at the bottom. These bands are known as *noise bars*. Effects of mistracking are illustrated in Figure 8.6.

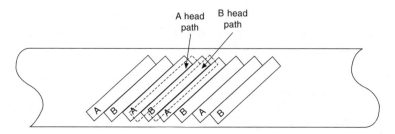

Figure 8.5 *Mistracking. The dotted lines indicate the path followed by the A and B heads during replay*

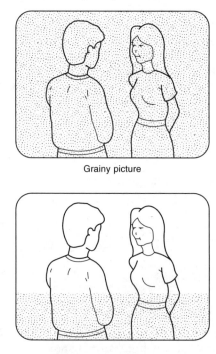

Grainy picture

Noise bar. In this case at the bottom of the picture

Figure 8.6 *Two common effects of mistracking*

Mistracking can occur because of small mechanical tolerances between machines, and in anticipation of this manufacturers include a tracking control circuit which enables the customer to adjust the machine to compensate for these tolerances. Tracking problems can also occur when a tape has become stretched. This alters the angle of the video tracks making it difficult for the heads to follow them. Similarly, the machine may have suffered mechanical wear which makes tracking difficult. Where tracking errors are caused by faulty tapes or machines it is often difficult to correct for this using the tracking control.

Most machines now incorporate automatic or electronic tracking, however the tracking control is more easily explained if we imagine the familiar variable resistor control which was employed for many years. As the tracking control is being adjusted, the speed of either the drum or capstan motor is altered fractionally, returning to its correct speed immediately the operator stops moving the control. Thus, referring to Figure 8.5 once again, if for example the capstan motor were to slow down momentarily as the control is adjusted, then the video heads would be able to catch up so that they are once again following the correct path up the tape. Alternatively, if the drum motor were to speed up momentarily then correct tracking would be restored.

In a correctly aligned machine replaying its own recording on a good quality tape, optimum tracking should be obtained with the control set to the 'fix' position. Therefore if this is not the case, then either the machine or the tape must be faulty. When replaying a recording made on another machine, the tracking control should first be set for the 'fix' position and adjusted as necessary.

VHS (Video Home System)

This format was developed primarily by JVC during the 1970s for the domestic video recorder market, hence the name, 'Video Home System'. Like its rival formats VCR, Beta and V2000, VHS employed many of the technologies developed for professional VCR equipment, but it had to be built for a price that would be affordable to the domestic user, and therefore the quality of picture, sound and mechanism had to be compromised. Interestingly, compared with its rivals, VHS had the poorest performance, and yet it was the format which became adopted in Europe. There are a number of reasons for this, but mainly it came down to a well-thought-out product range coupled with a sound marketing strategy on the part of JVC. Yet VHS was never intended to be an industrial format. This role was, and is in many cases, to be played by formats such as High Band U-Matic, Digital Beta and Hi-8.

However, during the 1980s these formats were all somewhat expensive, and the cheap and cheerful VHS machine offered the CCTV industry a chance to include video recording at an affordable price.

The reasons for the poor resolution offered by VHS become apparent when we examine the frequency spectrum for the FM luma and down-converted chroma signals shown in Figure 8.7.

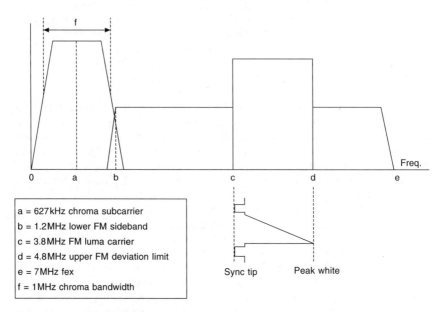

a = 627 kHz chroma subcarrier
b = 1.2 MHz lower FM sideband
c = 3.8 MHz FM luma carrier
d = 4.8 MHz upper FM deviation limit
e = 7 MHz fex
f = 1 MHz chroma bandwidth

Sync tip   Peak white

Figure 8.7 *VHS signal spectrum*

For VHS *the FM carrier frequency is 3.8 MHz*. The luma signal is presented to the modulator circuit so that the sync tip equals 3.8 MHz, and every corresponding step towards white level causes the carrier frequency to increase, up to peak white which produces a deviation of 4.8 MHz. When a carrier is modulated, signals known as sidebands are produced, and in the case of Figure 8.7 these are shown extending down to 1.2 MHz and upwards until the extinction frequency occurs at around 7 MHz.

In order to keep the sideband frequencies between 1.2 MHz and 7 MHz, it is not possible to record a luminance signal bandwidth of 0–5.5 MHz. In fact, for VHS *we are only able to record luma signals up to 2.8 MHz*, which reduces the resolution of the replayed video signal to around 240 TVL.

The chroma signal also suffers in the down-conversion process because it is not possible to fit the 2.2 MHz bandwidth PAL chroma signal into a space which is only 1.2 MHz wide. Thus, prior to recording, *the chroma signal bandwidth is reduced to 1 MHz* (+/− 500 kHz). Also note the region of overlap between the luma and chroma sidebands around 1.2 MHz. This can result in an amount of patterning on the replayed picture which further degrades the resolution.

The implications of these figures for VHS are that even where a system is capable of high resolution and picture quality, once this has been recorded onto VHS format the best that one can expect is a colour picture resolution of 240TVL, with a narrow bandwidth chroma resolution and patterning. In some cases the quality of the replayed picture is not that important, however where the tape or a print taken from the tape is to be used in court as evidence to support witness testimony, the loss of resolution can in a worst case scenario result in the images becoming meaningless.

Some improvements have been made to the picture quality since the launch of VHS, and the inclusion of certain noise cancelling circuits allows a manufacturer to use the VHS-HQ logo. This implies 'high quality' VHS recording, and when a good quality video tape is used in a well-designed HQ machine the picture quality will appear to be very clean. However, it must be remembered that the TVL resolution for a colour recording will only be in the order of 240.

Many machines incorporate a 'colour/mono' switch. When this is moved to the 'mono' position the machine will only record monochrome no matter what signal input is provided. At first this might appear to be something of a waste of time, because the machine will only record monochrome if there are no colour cameras in the system, and if there are colour cameras, why would anyone wish to record in black and white?

However, there is a good reason for including this switch because, when it is moved to the 'mono' position, the filters which are used to limit the recorded luma bandwidth to 2.8MHz are altered to allow a wider bandwidth luma signal to be recorded. The additional sidebands produced by this action are able to occupy the area that would otherwise have been taken up by the chroma signal. Thus, by switching the machine to monochrome recording it is possible to obtain a picture with a TVL of anything up to 300, depending upon the machine design. Even where colour cameras are employed, the engineer or owner has a choice between 240TVL colour recording or 300TVL monochrome recording.

Super VHS

The designers of the original VHS were aware that it would be possible to record a much better picture resolution if the FM carrier frequency could be increased, because this would offer more space for the necessary sideband components. The problem they had was that the recording tapes of the day were not capable of retaining magnetic information relating to signal frequencies above around 7MHz; however, by the earlier part of the 1980s tape manufacturers had developed an oxide coating which could retain frequencies up to around 10MHz. This laid the foundation for a new and better version of the original VHS format; VHS mark II if you like, although the official name is Super VHS.

An S-VHS machine is capable of reproducing video signal frequencies up to 5MHz, which equates to a TVL in the order of 400. The reasons for this are seen when we consider the S-VHS signal spectrum shown in Figure 8.8. First of all, the carrier frequency is much higher at 5.4MHz, and there is greater frequency deviation between the sync tip and peak white levels; 1.6MHz compared with the 1MHz for VHS. In any FM system, increasing the deviation improves the signal-to-noise level (S/N) ratio. Also note that there is no overlapping of the luma and chroma signals. The one thing that remains unchanged between the two formats is the chroma signal, which has the same carrier frequency of 627kHz and reduced bandwidth of 1MHz.

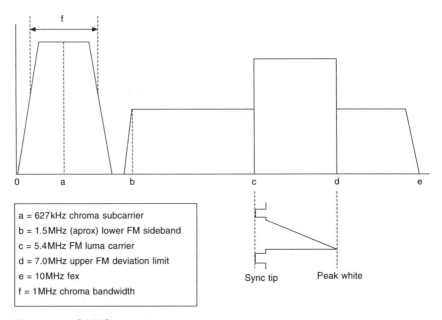

a = 627kHz chroma subcarrier

b = 1.5MHz (aprox) lower FM sideband

c = 5.4MHz FM luma carrier

d = 7.0MHz upper FM deviation limit

e = 10MHz fex

f = 1MHz chroma bandwidth

Sync tip   Peak white

Figure 8.8 *S-VHS signal spectrum*

Another feature of S-VHS machines is the option to input and output the Y/C signals on separate links via the special four pin S connectors. These were discussed in Chapter 5 (Figure 5.19) where it was noted that the advantage of using these in preference to composite video connections is the absence of cross modulation which results in coloured pattering in areas of high picture definition. However, it must be remembered that in CCTV the system will almost certainly be using composite video signal transmission at some point, and therefore cross modulation will already have been introduced, and once it has occurred the use of Y/C connectors at the VCR will do nothing to remove it. Even where fibre-optic cabling has been employed there is a good chance that a composite co-axial link between the fibre-optic equipment and the control room equipment will exist. Nevertheless, if Y/C signal transmission can be maintained throughout the system, then S-VHS recorders will reproduce a clean, 400TVL picture.

Remembering that it is the special tape oxide which makes S-VHS recording possible, then it is important that S-VHS cassettes are used. All S-VHS machines are built to be dual standard; that is, they will record and replay in both Super and standard modes. However, whilst it is possible to record in standard VHS on an S-VHS tape, it is not possible to record in Super format on a standard VHS tape because of the frequency limitations, and to prevent this from happening by accident manufacturers fit a sensor in the machine which looks for a small identification hole in the bottom of the cassette (see Figure 8.9). If a standard format cassette is inserted into the machine, then even if the record selection is set for Super format, the machine will revert to standard format recording. Engineers should make the customer aware of this, pointing out that they are compromising the quality of the system if they use the much less expensive standard cassettes.

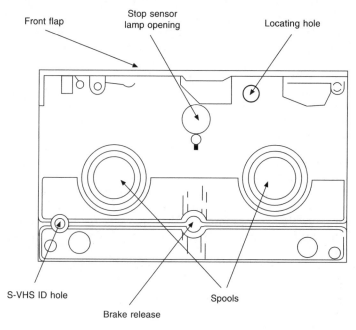

Figure 8.9 *An S-VHS cassette. Standard format cassettes are identical except for the ID hole*

Although it is possible to record in standard format on S-VHS cassettes, this is not advisable because of the differences in pre-emphasis levels between the two formats. Pre-emphasis circuits are included in VCRs to improve the S/N ratio of the luma signal, and to sharpen the rise times of the luma waveform, which amounts to a sharpening of the edges in the picture information. However, when an S-VHS cassette is used in the standard format these levels become incorrect, giving rise to overemphasis of any light-to-dark or dark-to-light transitions in the picture content, making them appear to have black outlines. Where a high quality standard VHS recording is required, it is advisable to use a 'professional' quality standard tape rather than a Super tape.

Time-lapse recording

The need for VCRs in CCTV installations to operate in time-lapse mode is obvious. No matter to what extent current VCR formats are modified, they will never be able to offer more than a few hours of recording time, which is woefully inadequate where many installations require 24 hour recording.

By making use of the still frame function, in the recording mode time-lapse machines record a single frame or field, pause momentarily, and then record another frame/field. Whilst the machine is in the pause mode the head drum continues to rotate, but the heads are switched off. On the other hand the tape must be moving at 2.4cm/sec whilst a frame is being recorded, and then stop the instant the recording is made. This requires some very exacting control on the part of the VCR electronics, and a robust, well-maintained deck in order to record the tracks accurately. Note that because the tape stops regularly, it is not possible to record an audio track whilst the machine is operating in time-lapse mode.

By operating in time-lapse mode a 3-hour cassette can be made to last much longer. Of course the tape only contains a series of still images, but this is often sufficient for CCTV purposes, and if the tape is replayed in a faster mode than that in which it was recorded a form of fast motion film can be viewed. The number of still pictures available on one 3-hour cassette is quite staggering. In the 3-hour mode a machine is recording 25 frames per second, and thus during 3 hours this amounts to a total of 25 × 60 × 60 × 3 = 270000 frames. In time-lapse mode each of these frames is an individual picture, and thus the cassette may be considered to be like a photograph album containing 270000 photos. And bear in mind that any of these photos can be produced as a hard copy if a video printer is available.

The time-lapse track format is illustrated in Figure 8.10, where the number at the top represents the TV frames. In this example it is assumed that the machine is operating in the 12-hour mode, thus the machine

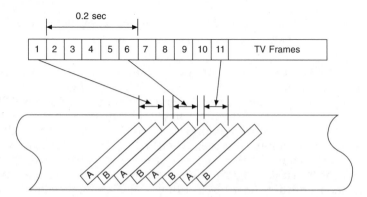

Figure 8.10 *Frame recording format for the 12-hour time-lapse mode*

records frame number 1, pauses during frames 2 to 5, and then records frame number 6. Hence one frame in every five is recorded, the cycle taking 0.2 seconds (5×40ms frames = 0.2s).

Note the anomaly in the figures, because in fact a time-lapse machine operating in the so-called 12-hour mode actually runs for 15 hours. The reason for this becomes clear when we look at the time from the point of view of the number of frames recorded on the tape. We have just seen that the figure for the time delay is 0.2s, and there are 270000 frames stored on the tape, hence $0.2 \times 270000 = 54000$ seconds, which equates to 15 hours. Similar calculations for other time-lapse modes prove that the recording time is always 3 hours more than the mode quoted. Now consider this, if the machine were to have a delay time of 0.2–0.04s (one frame period) = 0.16s, then the recording time would become $0.16 \times 270000 = 43200$ seconds, which equates to 12 hours. However, to record in this manner would mean recording every fourth frame and not every fifth, but in order to maintain a particular track format in relation to the chroma signal this is not possible, and one extra frame delay period must be introduced. This applies to every time-lapse mode.

The method of recording one TV frame per interval is in fact very wasteful, because when a VCR replays a still frame it actually only scans one field of the frame, and the other field is effectively ignored. This point is illustrated in Figure 8.11.

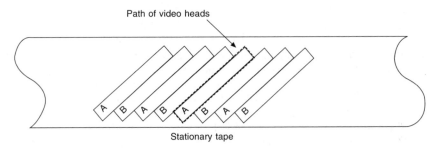

Figure 8.11 *In still mode the tape is stationary, and thus both video heads scan the same track*

When a VCR enters still mode it ensures that when the tape pauses an 'A' track is presented to the video heads every time. Remembering that video heads can only read their own tracks, this means that the 'A' head will derive an output signal, but the 'B' head will not. This is where the extra heads on a four head VCR come in. These are switched in to provide an output signal in still mode (and visual search) when the 'B' head is ineffective. This explains why many budget domestic VCRs do not produce a watchable still frame; they only have two video heads.

Returning to the time-lapse interval, manufacturers decided that if the second field of each frame is ignored in the time-lapse mode, then why bother recording it? Thus modern machines actually only record one TV field out of each frame, which means that for the 12-hour mode the delay period can be halved to 0.1 seconds. The tape will still run for 15 hours, but will have recorded twice as many pictures; i.e. $2 \times 270\,000 = 540\,000$ still fields. This principle is illustrated in Figure 8.12.

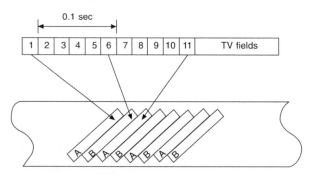

Figure 8.12 *Field recording format for the 12-hour time-lapse mode*

The one drawback with recording TV fields is the very poor replay effect when a time-lapse recording is played back in the 3 hour (real time) mode. Because each video track is no longer related to the same TV frame, the monitor is effectively interlacing fields from different frames all of the time. However, in relation to the improved recording duration, this is a small price to pay.

Another important consideration with time-lapse operation is the loss of vertical picture resolution. In Chapter 5 we saw that a TV picture contains, at the very best, 625 lines less 40 vertical flyback lines, equalling 585 active lines. However, when we consider that these lines are contained within two fields, then clearly when a VCR is in still mode, although it is still producing two fields of 312.5 lines, they are in fact the same lines. In other words, the vertical resolution is reduced by 50%. This loss may be crucial where a recorded picture is to be used as evidence.

Not all machines have the same number of time-lapse modes, although the more elaborate models offer a very wide range. Some typical modes, along with the delay periods for both frame and field operation, are given in Table 8.1.

The delay period between each recorded field is important, because if it is too long vital information may be missed. As an extreme example, look at the situation in Figure 8.13. If a field recording machine were set to the 720-hour mode, the delay period between recorded fields would be 4.82 seconds. This means that, if the machine were to record picture number 1, then the next picture to be captured would be number 6. The most important activity has been completely missed. Setting the machine to the 240-hour mode would produce a delay period of 1.62 seconds, meaning that either picture 3 or 4 would be captured, producing a more valid account of the activity.

When setting up a time-lapse VCR, the engineer must consider carefully the delay period, and hence the mode of operation. There are a number

Table 8.1 *Time-lapse modes*

Mode	Running time	Delay (frame rec.)	Delay (field rec.)
12h	15h	0.2s	0.1s
24h	27h	0.36s	0.18s
48h	51h	0.68s	0.34s
72h	75h	1s	0.5s
120h	123h	1.64s	0.82s
240h	243h	3.24s	1.62s
480h	483h	6.44s	3.22s
720h	723h	9.64s	4.82s
960h	963h	12.84s	6.42s

of factors which must be taken into consideration; for example, is the machine recording a single camera, or a multiplexed or switched camera arrangement? Does the system have alarm detection? And if it does, is the alarm feature on the VCR being used? The relation to multiplexed and switched systems will be considered in more detail in Chapter 9.

Time-lapse VCR features

Apart from the various time-lapse modes, there are a range of features which almost come as standard on any quality VCR, although some of these may be excluded on budget models.

Linear slow speed is a form of 'continuous' time-lapse where 12- or 24-hour recording is achieved not by pausing the tape but by running it continuously at a speed that is four or eight times slower than normal. This was introduced solely to enable audio recording. Because the tape is running continuously, a lateral sound track can be laid down at the top of the tape, albeit of very poor quality owing to the slow tape speed, which results in a poor frequency response and a lot of wow and flutter (an audio term for the warbling produced by rapid tape speed fluctuations).

The delay periods for linear slow speed are the same as for time-lapse modes. When the first field has been recorded, the video heads are switched off for the duration of the delay period, although the drum continues to rotate. When the time comes to record the next field, the tape will be in the correct position in relation to the heads for the next track to be laid down, and one head is switched on to record the field. The problem with linear slow speed is that, during replay, the signal-to-noise level is changing continuously as the heads move from one track to another, scanning each track a number of times as they progress. A high S/N ratio is achieved whilst the heads are following along the centre of a track, however as the tape moves forwards the heads track along the edge of the video track

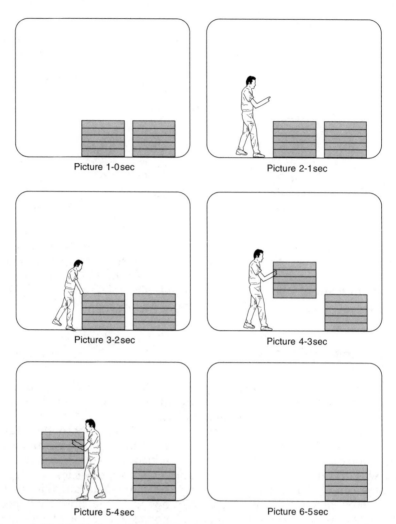

Picture 1-0 sec

Picture 2-1 sec

Picture 3-2 sec

Picture 4-3 sec

Picture 5-4 sec

Picture 6-5 sec

Figure 8.13 *Vital information may be lost if the time-lapse mode is set to be too long*

and the S/N ratio falls. Where the audio recording facility is not required, it is better to use the time-lapse mode of recording.

Shot mode is another feature found on some VCRs, although manufacturers have different names for this same feature. When this mode of operation is selected, the machine remains in pause mode until an external trigger signal is received, whereupon the machine records about a half-a-dozen fields in the 3-hour mode before returning to the pause mode once again. Because the machine cannot remain in the pause mode indefinitely (the tape would be worn out by the continuously rotating heads) it records a few fields every few minutes so that the tape is able to move past the heads.

The shot mode input is generally a normally open (N/O) type which is taken to ground for activation. Any manually or electronically operated N/O switch connected to this input will suffice.

A feature similar to shot mode is the alarm input. However, in this case the machine operates in the selected time-lapse mode, but when the alarm input terminal is connected to ground the machine reverts to the 3-hour mode for a pre-set period of a few minutes, thus ensuring that maximum information is recorded. The alarm input may be triggered manually by an operator using a simple push switch, or it could be connected to some form of electronic alarm system. On a larger system where the machine is expected to record the output from a number of cameras, the alarm activation signal can also be connected to the multiplexer or switcher. The normal recording pattern can then be interrupted so that only the cameras in the activation area are connected to the VCR input during the alarm period.

Where an alarm input activation has taken place, the machine marks the position on the tape so that the operator can use the index search facility to quickly find the position on the tape. One common type of 'marker' is a momentary change in the mark-to-space ratio of the CTL pulse. When an alarm input occurs, the duty cycle changes from 60:40 to 27:73. During replay when the index search feature is selected, the tape is put into a fast wind mode, however the CTL track is still read and the system controller chip looks for the change in duty cycle, at which point it places the machine into the replay mode. A more elaborate marker system is where a digital time code is recorded in addition to the CTL track. With this system, the operator can key in a specific time and date, and the machine will search for that exact position on the tape.

The number of alarm events may be displayed on the monitor screen, along with a reference number. In addition, the machine may have some form of indication on the front panel, and/or it may have an alarm output terminal to drive an audible or visual warning device to alert the operator.

Auto re-record is a feature which is particularly useful for unmanned systems. As the name implies, when the tape comes to the end, the machine rewinds and re-records. Options are usually built into this feature to prevent erasure of important evidence, for example, the machine can be set so that it will not auto re-record should an alarm input activation have taken place.

The clock output signal found on many machines can be used to control a camera switching unit. On a multi-camera system which employs a sequential switching unit, it is important that there is some corroboration between the camera switching sequence and the time-lapse recording periods, otherwise it is feasible that, due to the timing of the two units, some camera outputs may rarely, if ever, be recorded. If the switcher has a clock input facility, the clock signal from the VCR can be connected to this so that each time the VCR has recorded a field, a clock pulse is sent to advance the switcher. In more elaborate systems employing certain multiplexers, communication between the VCR and the multiplexer is far more involved, and is performed via an RS port.

Some machines incorporate a small camera controller. These may be ideal for smaller installations because the control area is more self-contained and the installation cost is reduced. The drawback with relying on an integral camera controller is that it can prove difficult to expand the system, and should the VCR have to be removed for servicing practically the entire system becomes inoperative unless a similar VCR or temporary controller is installed.

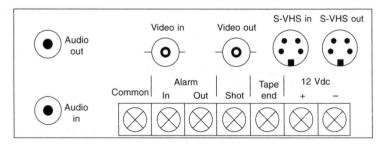

Figure 8.14 *Typical terminals and connections at the rear of a time-lapse VCR*

VCR maintenance

Perhaps the biggest criticism of VHS when employed in the CCTV industry is the need for mechanical maintenance. And this criticism is justified because mechanical parts in a VCR deck do wear out with constant use. Numerous CCTV engineers can recite stories of customers who have invested thousands of pounds in CCTV equipment, only to penny pinch on tape replacement, and it is not uncommon for a customer to complain to an installer that, following an incident, the tape has been replayed only to produce a snow storm. Upon inspection it is often found that the tape in question is the one which was provided during the system handover a number of years previous! In such circumstances, not only will the tape be next to useless (the oxide coating will be thin and the backing material stretched) but the machine will desperately require a major mechanical overhaul before it is capable of reproducing anything like an acceptable picture.

The frequency at which routine servicing should be performed on a time-lapse VCR is the matter of some conjecture, and in reality will depend upon a number of factors such as the quality of the VCR, the number of hours per day/week the machine is actually recording, and the quality of the tapes being used. However it is generally accepted that a VCR in a CCTV system should be overhauled *at least once every twelve months*.

In practice, a machine that has been operating continually for twelve months will be in need of a service. Even if the picture quality still appears to be satisfactory, there is no telling how much longer this will be the case and, furthermore, the performance of a VCR cannot be properly determined by looking subjectively at the replayed picture. Only by using an oscilloscope to monitor the off-tape (FM) signal whilst replaying an alignment tape can an engineer be certain that the signal level and tracking are correct.

When considering VCR servicing, video head drum checking and replacement is often singled out as the primary concern, yet this is not the only item that may be showing signs of wear after a machine has operated continually for one full year (8760 hours). Items such as the pinch roller, rubber belts, back tension band (if used) and head cleaning rollers will all require checking and/or replacement, and the condition of the lower video drum, tape guide posts and audio/control head should all be verified. Furthermore, the tape path must be cleaned of all dirt and tape oxide deposits, and the alignment of tape guides checked and adjusted as necessary following video head drum replacement. In some cases, manufacturers provide service kits containing all of the mechanical components which should be replaced after a period of no more then 10000 hours. Clearly the level of servicing being discussed here can only be performed by competent VCR servicing personnel, and for this reason it is expected that a machine will be removed from site and returned for (annual) servicing.

Where the machine is known to be operating for a lesser period, say 12 hours per day, then it might be agreed with the user that full servicing is performed once every two years; although to comply with the Code Of Practice the performance of the machine should be verified every twelve months as part of the routine system maintenance, and the average machine would benefit greatly from having the heads and tape path cleaned. Of course it can be argued that there is no way of knowing how long a machine has been operating, but this does not have to be the case. Some machines incorporate timers which log the operating times of such things as tape transport, head drum rotation and POWER ON. This log is generally available through the on-screen menu. A simpler but less reliable alternative to software-based timers is to replace one of the fuses in a switched supply rail with a timer fuse. These devices still offer fuse protection, however they also contain an indicator which moves along as current passes through. The scale is usually marked between zero and 10000 hours, and the device must be replaced after this time. The problem with using these is locating an appropriate switched supply in which to fit the timer.

Some basic servicing can be performed on-site. For example, where it is suspected that a machine is malfunctioning because of a foreign object such as a detached cassette label in the mechanism, the machine cover can be removed. Tape path cleaning can also be performed on-site, however this should only be done by those who have been trained in basic VCR servicing, as components such as video heads are extremely fragile and will be damaged if care is not taken. Where the machine cover is to be removed with the mains power connected, the same health and safety issues apply as for monitors (see Chapter 7), and a mains isolation transformer should be employed.

Video head cleaning

The frequency at which video heads require cleaning can be a matter of opinion, and in reality is dependent upon a number of factors including the quality of tapes being used, the number of times a tape is to be used, the tape storage method and conditions, whether the machine has an automatic cleaning facility, and a degree of luck! But before we consider the frequency and methods of head cleaning it is important to understand what a 'dirty head' is, and recognize the symptoms.

The 'dirt' we refer to is not the airborne dust that we see collecting on monitor screens and cabinets. It is particles of tape oxide which have detached from the tape and have either adhered to the side of the video head drum or become lodged in the head gap. This is illustrated in Figure 8.15. Oxide on the side of the drum reduces the tape/head contact which in turn reduces the record/replay signal levels. The overall effect is poor tracking symptoms. Where the oxide is lodged in the head gap, the effect on the picture is the same as if one video head has failed (see Figure 8.6) because the oxide presents a low reluctance path across the gap to the magnetic flux, creating a form of a short circuit in the magnetic circuit. Thus, during record, the flux does not pass from the head into the tape, and during replay it does not pass from the tape into the head core. This effect is shown in Figure 8.16.

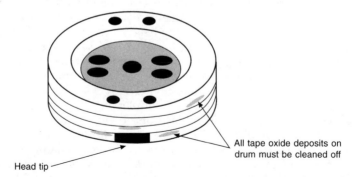

All tape oxide deposits on drum must be cleaned off

Head tip

Figure 8.15 *Typical oxide build-up on a VHS video head drum*

In conclusion, the symptoms of a dirty head/head drum are mistracking or a grainy picture. Where both heads have become clogged there will be no output from either head and the replayed result will be snow on the screen. Note that some machines have a mute circuit which inserts a blank screen in place of the snow effect. This hides the true symptom and is not at all helpful to the engineer, but where this symptom is evident head cleaning should be the first port of call.

Head cleaning is the removal of the oxide from both the head gap and drum surface. However, this is not as simple as it might first appear because the video head tips are extremely fragile, and the slightest pressure

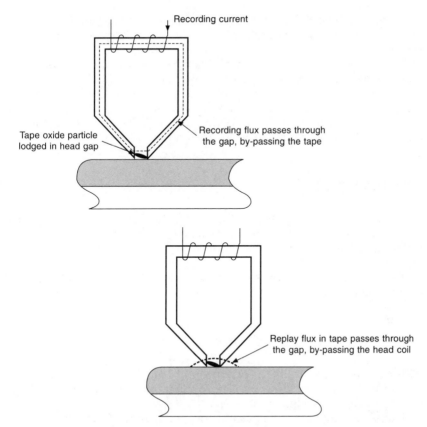

Figure 8.16 *Effects of tape oxide in the head gap*

in the vertical direction will break them off, necessitating replacement of the entire drum assembly. Furthermore, the video head gap is in the order of 0.3μm (0.3 of one thousandth of a millimetre), and so we are trying to remove a piece of oxide of these dimensions. Oxide on the drum surface can become well-adhered, and there is a temptation to try to scrape this off. However, the smallest scratch on the drum surface will alter the aerodynamics to such an extent that the tape will ride off the drum, producing a permanent line across the picture.

Head cleaning cassettes are available, and some manufacturers supply one of these with each time-lapse machine. During handover the customer should be instructed in the use of these, but should be warned that excessive use may lead to early head wear, as some of these can be somewhat abrasive. As a general rule, if the picture is perfectly all right, don't bother cleaning the heads!

Some machines employ an automatic head cleaning facility. This usually operates on the principle of a felt wheel that is pressed against the head drum each time the tape loads and unloads. Where this is the case, the customer can be instructed to load and unload a tape a number of times to force this cleaning operation in the event of apparent dirty head symptoms.

The problem with both cleaning cassettes and automated systems is that, where the oxide is lodged into the gap or fixed firmly onto the drum, there is insufficient pressure to dislodge it. In this case the only option is to clean the head drum manually, and because of the delicate nature of the head drum this operation should be performed only by those who have been trained in the technique.

DAT recorders

The DAT (Digital Audio Tape) machine evolved from the VCR. Indeed, the earliest version was a Sony Betamax recorder with an A/D and D/A interface connected between the video in/out sockets and a sound system. Because of this, the DAT machine has very similar servicing needs to the VCR, and a recorder that has completed a few thousand hours' use will usually require a clean-up and overhaul of the mechanism.

Tape management and care

Although this is primarily the responsibility of the operator, the engineer should make their customers aware of the implications relating to tapes during the initial system handover.

A tape passing through a machine operating in the time-lapse mode is subjected to far more stress and wear than when it is used at normal speed because each part of the tape spends much more time stationary against the rotating heads. Thus it is necessary to use tapes that have a strong backing material which will not stretch, and a well-bonded oxide coating. Not all VHS cassettes are of the same quality in this respect, and this is why only tapes marked as being of 'professional' quality should be used for CCTV applications.

Another reason for using quality tapes is that not all oxide coatings have the same magnetic qualities, the budget versions often suffering from high frequency losses and lower signal output levels (poorer S/N ratio).

The number of times that a tape should be used is a matter of some contention, however experience in the industry indicates that for tapes being used in the 24-hour time-lapse mode, twelve passes through the machine is the maximum. Thus, if a customer is going to operate the machine in the 24-hour mode, purchasing 31 tapes will allow a suitable rotation over a twelve month period. However, this does not allow for any losses incurred when tapes are subsequently removed from the system because they contain vital evidence.

The Data Protection Act 1998 requires that a detailed log of all CCTV tape movement is maintained, and the engineer should encourage the customer to use an auditable tape logging and management system. For smaller installations it is often possible to make use of systems that are provided with some of the video cassettes which are manufactured specifically for CCTV use. However, where a manned control room is in operation, a more sophisticated tape management system will be required. These may be purchased ready-made, and include a secure storage cabinet which is designed to aid tape rotation, and a complete set of logging sheets.

With regard to tape storage, advise the system owner to store tapes flat and not vertical, to have a storage environment that is not too hot or too cold (tapes are designed to live in 'normal' room temperatures, just like ourselves!), and to ensure that that there are no stray magnetic fields in the area which will cause at least some degree of erasure; video monitors leak magnetic fields from all sides, so keep tapes well away.

Digital video tape

In addition to the poor resolution offered by analogue video recorders, another serious problem for the CCTV industry is the fact that the signal degrades every time the tape is replayed or a copy is made. To overcome all of these problems a number of digital video tape recording formats have been developed and, although digital video recording is by no means faultless (it suffers from digital noise and compression losses), it provides a clean, quality picture which does not degrade either with time or through generations of duplication.

One such format is the Digital Time-Lapse VCR (D-TL) developed by Panasonic and Sanyo. This digital recorder employs a normal S-VHS tape cassette and in many respects functions as a traditional analogue machine. However, the digital signal processing means that a horizontal resolution of up to 520 TVL is possible. The D-TL combines the advantages of digital video recording with the relatively low cost of S-VHS tapes. Perhaps one disadvantage is the fact that the recordings can only be replayed on D-TL format machines meaning that, when data is required for evidential purposes, it will more than likely have to be copied down to S-VHS or even VHS. Nevertheless, because the original material is of a high quality in terms of resolution this does mean that the copies will be of a high standard.

Another digital video tape recording format, known as 'DV', has been developed by Sony with both industrial and domestic applications in mind, and its resolution of up to 500 TVL makes it attractive to the CCTV industry.

There are two versions of the DV cassette; DV and Mini DV. Both cassettes use a 6.35 mm wide ($\frac{1}{4}''$) tape, but the Mini DV cassette is much smaller, with a correspondingly shorter recording time. The Mini DV tape is used in the majority of domestic digital camcorders because it keeps the size of the machine to a minimum, however for CCTV applications the 60 minute recording time is somewhat restrictive, and many archive machines take the full-size cassette which provides 4.5 hours of recording time. Some models have the facility to take either size of cassette.

There are some Mini DV machines available that have been developed with covert CCTV in mind, and these are becoming a satisfactory alternative to the Hi-8 analogue format which has previously performed this role.

The DV machine mechanism is still based on the analogue VCR system of tape lacing and helical scanning, however in the case of a DV machine the head drum rotates at a rate of 9000rpm; six times faster than in a VHS machine. This means that during one TV frame period of 40ms, the drum will rotate six times, and the two heads will record or replay twelve tracks. The data is placed onto each track in a particular format, illustrated in Figure 8.17.

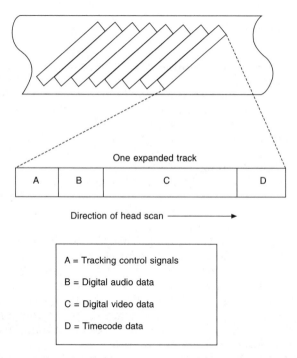

Figure 8.17 *The DV track format. Three such tracks are required for one TV field*

The luma and chroma signals are processed separately, which gives outstanding colour definition and Y/C correlation compared with analogue systems. The compression system used is a modified MPEG-2, with a compression ratio of, typically, 5:1 which gives good still frame performance, an important factor in CCTV recording.

Disk-based video recording

In the CCTV industry the primary form of digital recording medium is the magnetic hard disc, where a computer hard drive is employed. Early versions introduced during the mid 1990s were limited by the relatively small storage capacity of the hard drives of the day and, due to the volume of digital data produced when digitizing video signals (see Chapter 5), were only capable of a few hours recording time. Because of this, some means of archiving was needed and the most common solution was to employ a DAT (Digital Audio Tape) recorder. Although this combination retained the advantage of no signal degradation over both time and generational copying, the advantage of quick data access was lost, and a tape management system was still required. Furthermore, because the DAT recorder is in effect a spin-off of the domestic VCR and employs helical scanning, it has the same servicing requirements as a VCR; perhaps with the exception that, because it is reproducing a digital signal, head wear does not produce the slow degradation in picture quality that is common in analogue VCRs. Rather, the picture quality is consistent until the wear becomes excessive, at which point the picture breaks up continually.

The rapid advances in computer technology, coupled with the reductions in the cost of hardware and improvements in video compression techniques, have enabled disk-based recording to evolve considerably in recent years. By employing a form of time-lapse recording where only a certain number of frames per second are stored, machines are available with storage capacities of many days. If true time-lapse features are employed, then a number of weeks of recording time is possible without the need for any tape archive system. Of course we must remain mindful of the need for some control rooms to archive video material for at least three months, and in these cases it may still be necessary to maintain some form of back-up, be it either tape or optical disk-based.

Recording capacity

In general, hard disk video recorders are set up in such a way that they will continue recording until the disk is full and will then proceed to over-write the earliest recordings, thus providing continuous recording. Of course, problems will arise when the disk capacity is insufficient to provide the required archive period and thus the installer must ensure that the intended equipment is up to the job. This is more difficult for disk-based recorders than it is for VCR installations, because for VCRs all that is required is to look at the recording time (e.g. 12 hours) and ensure that the owner has enough tapes to cover the archive period. For example, for an archive period of 31 days, VCRs operating in the 12-hour time-lapse mode will require 62 tapes per machine plus, say, 5% to cover for tape extractions for evidential purposes.

In the case of hard disk recorders the recording time is dependent upon a number of factors. First of all there is the picture recording rate. This is equivalent to the time-lapse period in a VCR where, on many machines, the installer or user can set the number of pictures per second that they wish to record. Secondly there is the file size for each picture that is recorded. Because the images must be digitized and compressed prior to recording, each picture in effect becomes like an individual file that is then recorded onto the hard disk. The file size will be dependent upon the amount of compression that is applied, and this can be set by the installer or possibly the user. The more compression that is applied, the smaller will be the file size and thus the greater will be the recording time. However, increasing the compression also reduces the image quality. Finally, the recording time is determined by the capacity of the hard disk.

It is important not to confuse the *picture recording rate* with the *picture update rate*. The recording rate is the number of pictures per second (PPS) that the machine is recording, whereas the picture update rate is the rate at which each camera image is updated when reviewing the recording. The update rate (in seconds) can be determined by dividing the number of cameras by the record rate. Or

Pic update = $n \div$ PPS

where n = number of cameras

      PPS = recording rate

For example, for a system having just one camera, if the recording rate is set to 25 PPS, then the update rate will be $1 \div 25 = 40$ ms. In other words, the replayed images for the camera will be updated every 40 ms, which is equal to the TV frame rate – that is, real time 25 pictures per second. If 25 cameras are now connected to the recorder and the record rate is maintained at 25 PPS, then the update rate now becomes $25 \div 25 = 1$ second. So now we see that when the recording is replayed the images from each camera will only be updated once per second.

The PPS setting for any system will be determined by two factors: the number of cameras connected to the recorder, and the rate at which the user requires the replayed images to be updated. Let's consider a more extreme example. A hard disk recorder is required to record the information from 30 cameras. Because of the nature of the security risk, the user requires a picture update of at least twice per second. Thus, from the expression Pic update = $n \div$ PPS

PPS = $n \div$ Pic update

    = $30 \div 2 = 15$ PPS

The required disk capacity for a system can be calculated from

Disk capacity = $86400 \times$ days $\times$ PPS $\times$ file size

where   86 400 = number of seconds in one day
          days = number of archive days required

PPS = number of pictures per second to be recorded
file size = size of each picture file (in kilobytes)

For example, a CCTV system requires an archive time of 14 days. It has been decided that the recorder must operate at a rate of 5PPS and, for the proposed machine, the file size must be 20kB per picture in order to obtain an image quality comparable to that of an S-VHS recorder. Thus, the recording equipment would require a hard disk capacity of at least

$$86400 \times 14 \times 5 \times 20000 = 121\,\text{Gigabyte (GB)}$$

This example, which is typical of current disk-based recording equipment, illustrates just how much disk space is required. And yet the figures used in our example would really only relate to a smaller installation because of the low picture recording rate (PPS). Let's now consider the larger system that we looked at earlier. This used 30 cameras and required a picture update rate of twice per second, which led to a required PPS of 15. Let's now say that the archive period for this system has to be 31 days. How much hard disk capacity would be required if the recording quality were to be similar to that of S-VHS?

$$86400 \times 31 \times 15 \times 20000 = 803\,\text{Gigabyte (GB)}$$

This capacity could be reduced by reducing the file size for each image, however this would result in a reduction in image quality. The only alternative is to employ equipment capable of supporting a large hard disk capacity.

One method of providing a large storage capacity is to employ SCSI technology which enables a number of hard disk drives to be daisy-chained in such a way that they behave as a single drive unit with enormous capacity. There are different approaches to this; some units simply contain a number of internal SCSI drives, whereas others have external connections which enable the installer to add drives as necessary. The principle of a SCSI-based CCTV recording system is illustrated in Figure 8.18.

An alternative to SCSI is the RAID (Redundant Arrays of Independent Disks) technology where hard disk drives are grouped into arrays, each array acting as a single drive unit. Although this might sound very much like SCSI, the system protocols are somewhat different and many would argue are more reliable and robust.

The development of the DVD-ROM (Digital Versatile Disc) format has caught the eye of more than one CCTV equipment manufacturer, and there are a number of disk-based recording systems available which incorporate a DVD unit (see Figure 8.18). The data is initially recorded onto magnetic hard drive(s) which store the data until the user decides to archive it onto the DVD or another external storage medium. Programmable options are usually available to select automatic archive routines. For example, following an external alarm input activation, the unit automatically copies to DVD the data relating to the activation, beginning from a few minutes prior to the alarm. The DVD disc is removable and can be stored in the same manner as a video cassette, however because

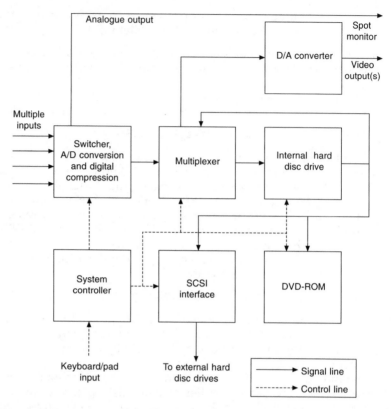

Figure 8.18 *Typical disk-based recording unit comprising a MUX, hard disk and DVD-ROM archive system*

the recording is in the form of a digital disc the advantages of no signal degradation and instant access to any point in the recording are maintained. It should be noted that in many cases the disks cannot be replayed on the standard DVD player incorporated in a PC without special viewing software. This software is provided by the manufacturer and is often free, but it may not be immediately available in every police station or court room, which is where evidential material needs to be viewed.

It is common to find manufacturers equating digital image quality with analogue recording performance, for example, stating that a file size of 20 kB will produce an equivalent picture performance to that of an S-VHS machine. Whilst it is understandable that they are attempting to use a familiar image quality to help the installer and end user appreciate the sort of quality they should expect for a given file size, in truth it is difficult to accurately equate analogue and digital images in this way; especially where the compression method used is MPEG. This is because the losses in digital recording appear somewhat different on the screen to those of analogue recordings.

Where MPEG video compression is employed, as the amount of compression is increased the image begins to break up into pixel blocks, a feature that will never appear on an analogue recorder. Yet these blocks may only be evident in areas of very fine picture detail which would never have been recorded by an analogue machine. Thus, a comparison of the performance of the two formats may reveal that although neither format is capable of reproducing a particular part of an image, the loss is manifest in quite different ways. Furthermore, in most cases a comparison of the areas of picture that can be resolved reveals that the digital images are cleaner and have a greater contrast ratio.

Security of digital information

Perhaps one of the most useful features of a disk-based recording system is where the recorder can be accessed from another site using a LAN or WAN connection. For the installer and end user alike such access can save a lot of time and money as well as increase the flexibility of the CCTV system. Installers can 'return' to a site via a network connection and perform adjustments, check fault symptoms, reprogramme system parameters, etc. The end user can look at his/her site at any time from anywhere in the world, again being able to perform adjustments if necessary.

The main issue surrounding such access is one of security. Is a closed circuit television system really 'closed' once it is accessible via a network connection? To offer security, password protection is included and often special software is required to view images. However, these measures do not guarantee complete security. Nevertheless, remote access will continue to increase in popularity as end users see its advantages.

The issue of accessing CCTV data remotely brings us to another point, watermarking. This is another feature of digital video recording in the security sector. When digital recording was first introduced, the legal profession made much of the fact that (it was felt) digital material could be tampered with more easily than analogue. Whilst there were grounds for concern, it was felt by many that rigid control procedures in the CCTV control room would provide a sufficient safeguard. On the other hand, many digital recorders are not located in control rooms but at unstaffed sites and thus it was felt necessary to develop methods of identifying the original material and proving that it had not been edited in any way. To achieve this, many manufacturers of digital recording equipment have built in some form of 'watermark'. This takes the form of additional data in each image file which can be read using special software that is not normally available to the average installer or end user. If the information is copied or edited, this data will be altered in such a way that anyone checking the data will know.

9 Camera switching and multiplexing

On larger installations it is clearly impractical to have one monitor for each camera, and therefore some means of image selection must be employed. There are basically two options available: we can sequentially switch between cameras, or we can display a number of camera images on a single monitor screen. Both of these methods have their strengths and weaknesses. Switching implies that the operator is only able to watch a single picture at a time (although, as we shall see later, more than one monitor may be used) and therefore each area has a period during which it is not being monitored. Multiple imaging perhaps removes the blind spots, however, where there are too many images on display, it becomes difficult for an operator to maintain the concentration required to look at all of these images, and the reduced size of the images often leads to a loss of definition.

Of course, these are very much generalizations, and developments in technology have done much to overcome the disadvantages, often by bringing the two concepts together.

Sequential switching

The principle behind the simplest form of sequential video switcher is shown in Figure 9.1 where S_1 is an electronic switch. The rate at which the switch scans the inputs, known as the *dwell time*, is set by the operator,

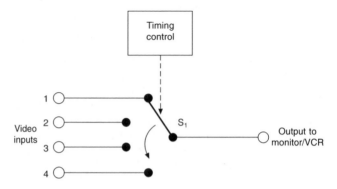

Figure 9.1 *Principle of a sequential analogue switcher*

either by means of a potentiometer or via a simple keypad input. There are usually additional controls which enable the operator to override the automatic switching and manually select an input, as well as inhibit the selection of inputs to which there are no cameras connected.

A more advanced form of sequential switcher is shown in Figure 9.2. This arrangement makes provision for alarm inputs. Under normal circumstances S_3 is closed and the timing control circuit operates S_1 and S_2 in tandem. Hence the VCR is recording whatever the operator is viewing. Upon receipt of an alarm, for example on input 3, switch S_3 opens, S_2 is moved permanently to position 3 and the warning output is activated. In this condition the main monitor continues to display all four cameras sequentially, however the operator can investigate the cause of the alarm on a spot monitor, whilst the VCR records the activity. The operator can be alerted to the alarm by a light and/or buzzer connected to the alarm

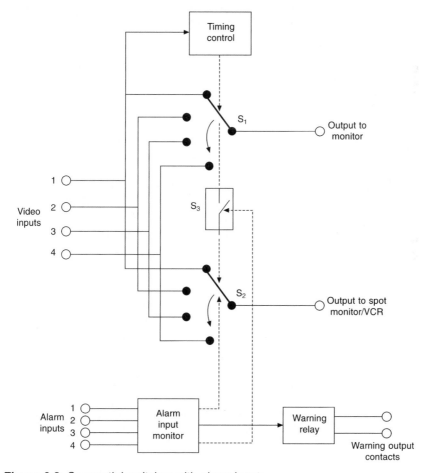

Figure 9.2 *Sequential switcher with alarm inputs*

output, which may also be used to activate the alarm input on a time-lapse VCR (see Chapter 8).

Before proceeding it is worth reminding ourselves of the importance of output termination, which was discussed in Chapter 7 (see Figure 7.10). Any unused outputs should be correctly terminated using either the termination switch on the back of the equipment (if fitted), or a 75Ω termination device. In some cases the switching is automatic, the 75Ω resistor being switched out of circuit as the BNC connector is pushed into place. The rules for termination apply to all of the equipment that we shall be looking at during the course of this chapter.

Although 'cheap and cheerful', sequential switchers have no means of maintaining synchronization between cameras, and therefore the picture is likely to roll each time the switch toggles because of the difference in the scanning positions at each camera. This is illustrated in Figure 9.3 where the phase relationship between the video signals from two unsynchronized cameras is drawn as they would appear if they were displayed on a dual beam oscilloscope. From this illustration it can be seen that camera synchronization is a matter of ensuring that each camera begins scanning the first TV field at precisely the same instant. When this condition exists between every camera in an installation there will be no picture roll when a switcher toggles between cameras, because the monitors and VCRs will not see any change in the timing of the vertical sync pulses.

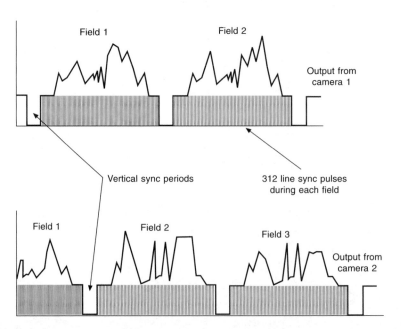

Figure 9.3 *Relationship between two unsynchronized cameras as they would appear on a dual beam oscilloscope adjusted to the field rate*

One common method of camera synchronization is to *line lock* the cameras using the 50/60 Hz mains cycle as a reference. To achieve this a sample of the mains frequency is passed into the sync pulse generator circuit within each camera (refer to Figure 6.11). Of course, all of the cameras in the system will require a mains frequency reference, which means that they will have to be fed from either a 230/110V mains or 24V a.c. supply. The sync generator is designed to trigger to one of the two points in the mains cycle where it is passing through zero, which in the example given in Figure 9.4 is at each negative-going transition. If every camera is triggering to this same point in the mains cycle, then the field sync pulses will be aligned. Problems occur when cameras are fed from different phases of the mains supply, and to compensate for this many cameras with the line lock facility incorporate a *vertical phase control* which, when adjusted, alters the timing of the sync generator circuit. The adjustment normally has a range of at least 120°, which is the difference between any two mains supply phases. This control may be set by trial and error, however where this is done it is possible that some cameras are set 'just on the edge', and when changes occur in the mains supply voltage these cameras may manifest problems of picture roll during switching.

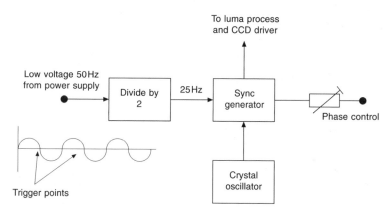

Figure 9.4 *Line lock arrangement in a camera*

A more sure method of adjusting camera phase is to use an oscilloscope to display the vertical sync phase as shown in Figure 9.3. One camera must be selected as a reference, and the output from every other camera is then checked against this, the V-phase control being adjusted as and when necessary until the sync pulses are aligned. Of course, this operation is not as simple as it may sound, because the oscilloscope will be located at the control room where the camera inputs are available, and is therefore not usually visible from the camera location. Using two people with a mobile radio or mobile phone is one solution to the problem. Alternatively, where the distance from the reference camera to the camera under adjustment is not too far, a temporary co-axial link between them can be reeled out.

Another method of maintaining synchronization between cameras is to use *genlocking*. This is where a vertical sync pulse is fed to an input at each camera which is labelled 'Genlock', 'Ext Sync', etc. (see Figure 6.11). Not all cameras have this facility, and it is therefore important that suitable models are chosen for installations which are to employ genlocking. There are two ways of deriving a master sync pulse. One is to take the video output from one camera and distribute this to all of the other cameras in the system. In this case the sync selector switch at the first camera would be set to the 'Internal' position, and the switches on all subsequent cameras set to the 'Ext Sync' position. This method is illustrated in Figure 9.5. The second source of a sync pulse is to use a master sync generator which would be located in the control room, the sync signal being distributed around the system.

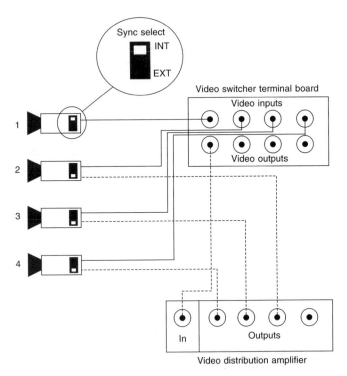

Figure 9.5 *One method of genlocking cameras. In this case all cameras are locked to the vertical sync pulses generated by camera 1*

Genlocking is a very robust method of synchronization, however it requires the installation of two co-axial cables to each camera location which increases the cost. The only way that this can be avoided is to employ camera/switcher combinations which send a sync signal through the video signal cable and into the video output socket on the camera. Such systems tend to be self-contained in that you can only use the cameras and equipment that have been specially designed to operate together, which is not a problem as long as you are not intending to extend an existing conventional system, or are required to extend the system beyond its capacity in the future.

Matrix switching

As the term matrix implies, this equipment is capable of selecting any one of a number of inputs and connecting it to one of a number of outputs. The principle is illustrated in Figure 9.6 which shows an 8 in–2 out matrix.

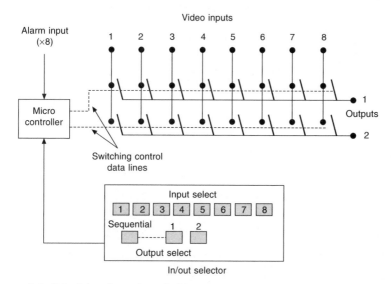

Figure 9.6 *Principle of matrix switching*

The switches are electronic and are controlled by the microcontroller chip. The chip is programmed such that only one switch on each line may be closed at any one time. Thus, if the operator selects output 2, input 4, then the switch corresponding to these co-ordinates is closed, and the signal from input 4 will be present on output 2. In this example the control module is simple and does not offer many features other than an alarm facility similar to that shown in Figure 9.2 (the activated input being made available on output 2) and a sequential switching option on output 1.

One essential feature of a matrix switcher is that it can be designed to be expandable in terms of both inputs and outputs. Taking the example in Figure 9.6, if the manufacturer adopts a modular design, then the number of inputs can be increased to 16 by the insertion of an 8 channel input card identical to the first. Further cards may be added to give 24,

32, 40, 48, etc., inputs. Some larger units are capable of expanding up to many hundreds of inputs. Similarly, output expansion cards enable the number of available outputs to be increased. An expanded version of the unit in Figure 9.6 is shown in Figure 9.7.

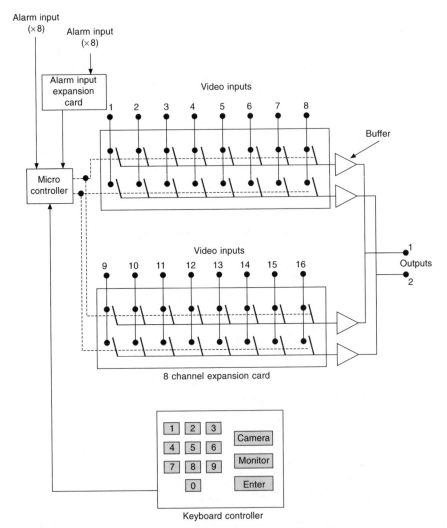

Figure 9.7 *An 8 channel matrix with 8 channel expansion cards installed*

In this arrangement the expansion card mimics the first input card (in this example an output expander has not been installed). The alarm input facility may not be required in all systems, therefore the alarm expander may be separate to the video card so that it can be included as an option. Beyond 16 inputs the switch selector type shown in Figure 9.6 becomes impractical because of the number of buttons required, and a ten digit keypad is found to be more practical. The method of selecting inputs and outputs varies between types of equipment, but typically the operator keys in a sequence such as 'Camera - 09 - Monitor - 02 - Enter' to place input 9 onto output 2.

The type of equipment shown in Figure 9.7 is a vast improvement on the sequential switcher, however as the number of inputs is increased certain limitations become apparent. Most noticeably, it would be difficult enough for a single operator to switch through 16 cameras, but to cope with any more would make the task impossible. This problem is overcome by enabling the system to have more than one control keyboard, and hence more than one operator. However this creates another problem; how to prevent a number of operators from trying to access the same inputs at the same time. This can be taken care of in the system programming whereby each keyboard is given access to only certain cameras (inputs), i.e. each operator 'patrols' a given area within the CCTV system. Furthermore these inputs will only be placed onto the monitors (outputs) associated with that operator, thus preventing one operator from bringing images onto another operator's screen. The programming can be further enhanced to allow two operators access to the same inputs, however one of them will always have priority so that in the event of both attempting to access the same input, the operator with priority will always gain the access.

As can be imagined, the programming for very large systems is often involved, and to make the operation simpler for the installer or commissioning engineer manufacturers have devised methods utilizing pull-down on-screen menus. Effective as these are, as the system capabilities have become ever more complex, manufacturers have taken the logical step and have moved towards the use of a PC running software designed to work in Windows™. Initially this may appear daunting for the engineer, however, as with many PC applications, with a little practice the basic process becomes second nature, and for the more involved programming procedures manufacturers frequently support their product with training courses and technical support.

Another limitation of the simpler matrix systems is the inability to control the cameras. It is to be expected that a CCTV system with many dozens of cameras must require some of them to have pan, tilt and zoom (PTZ) facility. This is why the larger matrix units have the capability to offer telemetry control. Because the number of PTZ outputs required will vary from system to system, the telemetry capacity is usually expandable in a similar way to the alarm input capability. Telemetry control will be discussed in more detail in Chapter 10.

A large matrix system illustrating many of the features we have been considering, such as multiple operators, levels of operator access and telemetry control, is shown in Figure 9.8. Note the inclusion of a VCR at each operator position, enabling incidents to be recorded whilst still being able to continue monitoring. Also note the inclusion of an on-screen text generator. This is essential for two reasons. In a large system it would be impossible for the operator to know what he/she was looking at without some form of camera and/or area identification facility, and in the UK it is a requirement for all videotape evidence presented in court to have a time and date displayed on the screen and, although the VCR is capable of producing this, it makes sense to include the camera/area ID information as well.

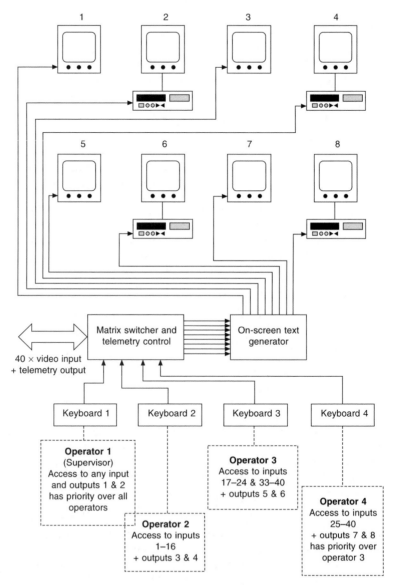

Figure 9.8 *A large matrix controller with multiple operator facility*

The problem with such a system is that, despite the sophistication of the switching control, each operator is still only able to view one scene at a time, and for a large number of cameras it is simply not possible for a person to take in a large number of changing images for any length of time. The problem can be alleviated to some degree by making use of the alarm inputs in such a way that each operator only scrolls through a small number of areas, selecting the others only if and when an alarm signal is received. However, reliance on an alarm detector may not be satisfactory for some situations, and the system could never be made to work in a town centre situation where all of the alarms would be triggering all of the time! It is clear that the operator needs to see a number of images simultaneously, and for this we need some form of screen splitting equipment.

The quad splitter

As the name implies, this equipment allows four camera images to be displayed on a screen simultaneously. In order to be able to achieve this the incoming analogue signals must be digitized and stored in a frame store. Once in the store a central processor unit (CPU) has to reduce the size of each image to $\frac{1}{4}$ of the original and arrange the data so that when it is clocked out and converted back into analogue form, the monitor will display four images in four quadrants on the screen. To do this, each horizontal line will contain video information for one picture during the first 26μs, and for the adjacent picture during the second 26μs (remember that, for UK television, one active line period equals 52μs). Likewise the top and bottom halves of each field contain information from different cameras. The process is illustrated in Figure 9.9.

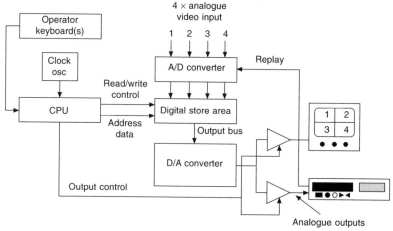

Figure 9.9 *Basic signal process in a quad splitter*

The fact that each horizontal line now contains information that has been derived from two horizontal lines belonging to two different cameras implies that the horizontal sync pulses must have been removed by the quad unit, and a new sync pulse inserted. The same applies to the vertical sync pulse. This means that, because the quad is acting as a form of master sync generator (although it is not actually synchronizing the cameras themselves) there is no requirement for the cameras to be synchronized by any other means.

The problem with compressing a 52μs line into 26μs is that the horizontal resolution must be reduced, in theory by 50%. In *basic* quad switchers this is precisely what happens and so, although the operator can view four cameras simultaneously, it is at the expense of picture quality. Also, because it takes time to process the information, it is not possible to show four live action images, rather the images move in a succession of frame jumps. To enable the operator to view high resolution live images, the quad normally has the ability to display any selected input in normal full size, and alarm inputs may be included to prompt an operator to select this mode.

In the basic quad the problem of resolution loss becomes more acute when the signal is recorded onto video tape, because each helical track (one TV field) contains the compressed information for four pictures. This is illustrated in Figure 9.10. The implication is that, when the tape is replayed, the four images are permanently compressed, and even though the quad unit may have a VCR input facility which enables any one image in the replayed quad format to be separated and displayed at full screen size, the resolution is still only 50% of the original.

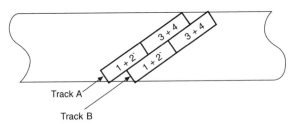

Figure 9.10 *In a basic quad, the VCR records all four compressed pictures in one frame period*

Earlier quad units were limited by the speed at which the CPU could manage the data process. If we examine this process in relation to Figure 9.9, we see that when the unit is operating in the quad mode the CPU has to clock four unsynchronized TV frames into the data store, strip out the line and field sync pulses, compress the data into 26μs horizontal line periods, add new line and field sync pulses, and clock the data out of the frame store and into the D/A converter in the order that it is to appear on the screen. For this to be done in real time takes a considerable amount of processing speed and power, and the relatively low clock speeds of the early microchips meant they were simply not up to it.

Developments in microchip technology have brought about giant leaps in processor clock rates, and this has enabled quad splitters operating in real time to be developed. Some of these are capable of accommodating eight inputs. In normal quad mode the images are arranged into two groups of four, each group display being alternated on the screen, with a variable dwell time.

By increasing both the memory capacity of the digital store area and the CPU clock speed, the rate at which pictures are processed is increased, enabling a much faster rate of update. But perhaps the most significant improvement is in the fact that, although the resolution is initially lost when the images are converted to quad mode, because modern digital compression techniques are used (i.e. MPEG or Wavelet), the resolution can usually be recovered when the images are restored to full screen size.

Video multiplexers

The multiplexer (MUX) can be said to take over from where the quad leaves off. Taking advantage of the faster picture processing made available through high speed CPUs and digital compression techniques, multiplexers offer a whole range of facilities that greatly enhance the effectiveness of a CCTV system. A typical multiplexer will offer a range of screen displays; some typical examples are shown in Figure 9.11. However, as we shall see later in this chapter, the multiplexer is not only capable of producing some clever screen displays, sophisticated models are capable of delivering two completely different picture sequences or structures to the monitor and the VCR, a facility which may be further enhanced when used in conjunction with alarm inputs.

The operating principle of the multiplexer is illustrated in Figure 9.12. Following the process through, the analogue composite video signals coming from the cameras are immediately converted into digital signals and stored in a temporary frame store area. Working at very a high speed, the video compression encoder reduces the amount of data per TV frame before placing this data into another store area. The video compression and expansion process is a complex operation requiring a lot of processor power, and to prevent the system from being slowed down, or even prone to lock-up (crashes), it is common for the compression circuits to have their own control CPU, freeing up the main CPU to deal with the multiplexing and other housekeeping operations. The compression circuits also have their own dynamic RAM (DRAM) memory stores to avoid clashes within the frame store areas. Another point about video compression is that the process is more complex for colour signals than it is for monochrome, where less memory is required for frame storage. For this reason some manufacturers produce monochrome multiplexers for use with monochrome CCTV systems. Because of the reduced cost of the processing and memory chips, the customer is not having to pay for a facility which they are never going to use.

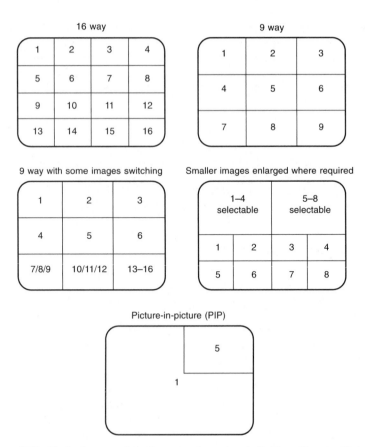

Figure 9.11 *Typical examples of screen layouts available with a multiplexer*

Multiplexing takes place as the pictures are moved out from the digital store area 1 by the main CPU, which clocks the data to the D/A converter in an order that will produce the desired picture layout on the monitor screen. When the operator alters the layout via the keyboard, the CPU simply changes the order in which the data is clocked out. Fast address and control buses are required between the CPU and the memory chips to sustain such complex data control.

Where a camera input signal is lost, the MUX will usually detect the loss of sync pulses and display a warning prompt on the screen. When a sequential switching mode is selected, the MUX skips any missing or unused channels; a feature that is also found in many sequential switchers.

In units which have the provision for different monitor and VCR outputs, a second store area is required (Digital store 2 in Figure 9.12) so that this data can be output to the D/A converter in a different sequence.

The main implication for VCR recording is that, unlike with the quad, the machine is able to record one full field per helical track. This recording method is shown in Figure 9.13. Replaying a tape with this recording

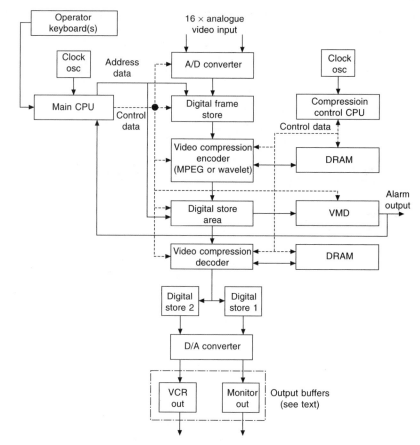

Figure 9.12 *Signal processing in a multiplexer (simplified)*

pattern directly into a monitor would produce an unintelligible image because each picture contains only one field, and therefore the monitor will interlace two different images to produce each TV frame. However, when the recording is replayed through the multiplexer, the images are able to be manipulated into whatever format the operator desires, i.e. full screen, quad, 9-way, etc. Note that in full screen mode the movement may appear jerky because the VCR has not recorded every field, and therefore the multiplexer is effectively having to display a series of still frames. For the example shown in Figure 9.13, because there are six inputs, the rate of update will be approximately eight times per second (50 fields per second ÷ 6 ≈ 8).

Inclusion of alarm inputs further enhances the display and/or recording ability. For example, the unit can be programmed so that inputs which are not in an alarm condition are not recorded as frequently as those which are. Looking again at Figure 9.13, let us suppose that inputs 1 and 3 have an alarm activation, indicating that there is movement in those

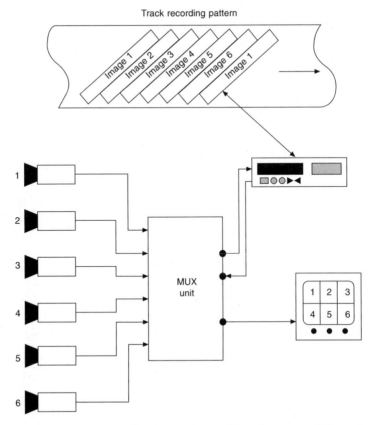

Track recording pattern

Figure 9.13 *Improved recording format is possible where a multiplexer is employed*

areas. The output to the VCR could be modified to follow a pattern of 1, 3, 2, 1, 3, 4, 1, 3, 5, 1, 3, 6, 1, 3, 2, etc. If an intruder is moving around the premises causing further alarm activations, the recording pattern can be altered accordingly, giving a crude form of tracking.

Alarm inputs may be PIRs, etc., however some multiplexers have in-built *video motion detection* (VMD) circuits which enable the camera images to be used as a detection medium. VMD will be discussed later in this chapter.

An important consideration when recording multiplexed signals is the relationship between the time-lapse period and the number of cameras in the system. This factor was discussed in Chapter 8 (Figure 8.13). In many multiplexers the engineer set-up menu includes an option to inform the multiplexer of the mode in which the VCR is operating, allowing the MUX to adjust its output to the VCR accordingly.

Stating the obvious, keeping the time-lapse period short results in more information being recorded, and as a general rule the 24-hour mode tends to produce the optimum results, this being the best compromise between tape duration and information loss. However, when specifying a system, the engineer needs to take a number of points into consideration with regard to this matter which include the number of cameras in the system, the level of risk (and thus, perhaps, the amount of information that needs to be recorded), the availability of personnel to exchange tapes and whether alarm inputs are to be employed. For example, a system may have fifteen cameras, however it might be that every weekend the tapes will have to run for at least 60 hours (Friday evening until Monday morning). In this event the VCR and MUX would have to be set to operate in the 72-hour mode, but this would mean that the dwell time is 0.5 seconds (see Table 8.1), meaning that with fifteen cameras the period between each individual camera update will be $15 \times 0.5 = 7.5$ seconds.

In some situations this lengthy period might not be considered to be a problem, but in most cases this would be unacceptable. One possible solution would be to install two smaller MUX units with provision for at least eight inputs, divide the system between them, and employ two VCRs. Alternatively, the layout of the site might mean that the use of alarm inputs to prompt a more regular recording of activated zones would be sufficient.

Not all multiplexers have the ability to accommodate two VCRs recording and replaying simultaneously. The extra processing and memory required to provide this feature increases the cost of the unit, but in some cases the customer is not prepared to pay such an amount for multiplexing equipment, or perhaps the system simply does not warrant it. Hence we have what are known as *simplex* and *duplex* MUX units.

A simplex unit has just one multiplexer inside (Figure 9.14), therefore its capabilities are limited to recording full-screen images whilst viewing live pictures in a number of screen layouts. When the operator wishes to replay the tape through the simplex unit, because the VCR is now providing a series of up to sixteen images, it is not possible for the unit to carry on processing the sixteen live inputs, and hence live monitoring is lost. Note that the unit is still able to offer the same screen layout options for replayed video as it does for live inputs.

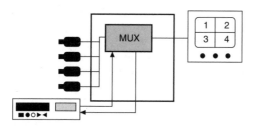

Figure 9.14 *Principle of a simplex MUX*

The duplex unit has two multiplexer arrangements inside (Figure 9.15) and thus one may be used to handle the live information whilst the other takes care of the VCR requirements. Therefore a duplex MUX is capable of displaying live images in a range of screen layouts and recording full screen images on the VCR whilst allowing a second VCR to replay a MUX recorded tape. The replayed tape images appear on a separate monitor, but they can be displayed in the usual range of screen layouts.

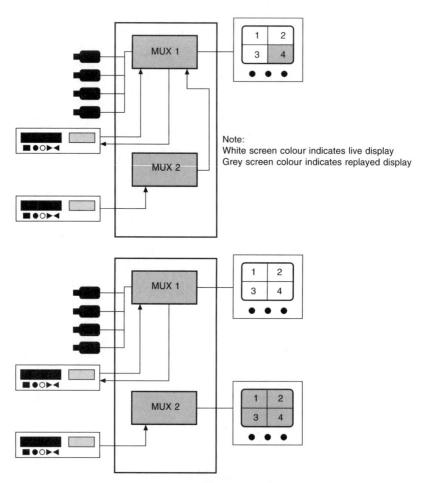

Figure 9.15 *When used with two monitors, a duplex MUX can continue normal operations whilst a recording is being viewed*

Another type of multiplexer known as *triplex* effectively has three multiplexers in-built (Figure 9.16). In this system the sixteen inputs are divided into two groups of eight. The unit does everything that the duplex can do, however, because the inputs are separated, the operator has the choice of dividing these between the cameras and a replay VCR. In this mode it is possible to view up to eight live images and eight recorded images simultaneously on the same monitor screen. The operator still has all of the usual options of picture enlargement or PIP. Alternatively, two monitors may be used to display sixteen live and sixteen recorded images in various screen layouts.

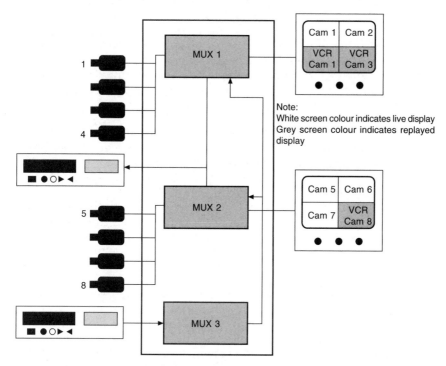

Figure 9.16 *A triplex MUX can display both live and recorded images on one screen*

It is not uncommon for a MUX unit to incorporate telemetry controllers, however this subject will covered in Chapter 10.

On-screen information is essential for identifying the date, time and location of video evidence, as well as assisting the operator in identifying an area quickly. The MUX usually has an *on-screen display* (OSD) facility which is set up during installation, in some cases using a laptop to speed up the insertion of characters.

Video motion detection (VMD)

Many CCTV installations rely on intruder alarm technology detectors such as passive infra-red, infra-red beam, microwave, etc. to activate the alarm inputs, however an alternative to this is to use the images coming from the video cameras as a means of intruder detection.

The principle of the VMD is to store a sample frame from the camera input and then compare subsequent frames to the sample, looking for changes in picture detail. Naturally it cannot look for a change in all of the picture information before triggering an alarm, otherwise the intruder would have to fill every part of the screen. Instead, the VMD divides the screen area into detection zones, and a change in one or more of these can trigger an alarm. By using zones the VMD can be given a degree of intelligence. For example, if used in an outdoor location, a sudden darkening of the entire scene caused by a cloud passing the sun can be ignored by the VMD. Similarly, where one zone is equivalent to only a very small area in the field of view, the unit can be programmed such that an activation of just one zone will also be ignored, as in all probability the would-be intruder is more likely to be a bird or other small creature.

The unit is designed to 'look' for changes in the contrast level in each detection zone, and the sensitivity may be adjusted by altering the amount of contrast change required to initiate an alarm.

Analogue VMD units have been available for many years, but their sensitivity is limited, making them prone to false alarms due to sudden changes in lighting level, movement of small animals, etc. For this reason analogue VMD units are better suited to indoor applications where the lighting can be controlled, as can the movement of small mammals!

Digital VMD units take the analogue signal and immediately pass it into an A/D converter. The reference picture is placed into a frame store so that each subsequent frame can be compared with this image. Digital units are capable of breaking the screen up into many thousands of detection zones, giving them a great deal of sensitivity, and the operator is able to control this sensitivity using two parameters; i.e. the amount of grey scale change and the number of zones over which this change takes place. To make the sensitivity adjustment simple for the operator to use, the unit often has some form of sliding scale on the OSD which is calibrated using arbitrary numbers.

The operator is normally able to set the detection area(s) for each camera using an array of rectangles generated by the OSD. This is illustrated in Figure 9.17. Note that these detection areas are not to be confused with the much smaller detection zones used by the VMD microprocessor for image analysis. Also note that the letters and numbers in the illustration are for the purposes of reference only, and would not appear on an actual screen.

In this illustration, let us suppose that there is legitimate movement in front of the building, however the operator is concerned about intruders moving along the flat roof area. The rectangles between points D2 to D10 (and possibly C2 to C10) could be made active, thus causing an alarm to be generated when there is any movement in this area.

VMD units are available as separate stand-alone items, some of these being multichannel to accommodate a number of cameras. However, some MUX units incorporate VMD as standard, making them an attractive choice of CCTV control equipment in small- to medium-sized systems, especially if telemetry is also included.

VMD can also be found in some cameras that have digital processing,

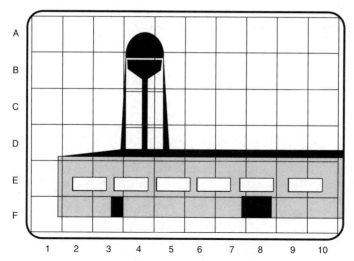

Figure 9.17 *A video motion detector divides the image into a series of zones. The operator (or engineer) decides which zones are to be active*

the alarm condition being present on a pair of switch contacts which can be connected to a MUX and/or VCR alarm input.

An important point with VMD is that the camera must be reasonably stable. If it is prone to movement in high winds, etc., the movement of the image can result in false alarms. Some VMD processors have in-built compensation for this effect, but nevertheless every system has its limitations, and a secure mount is recommended.

10 Telemetry control

Without some form of remote control, larger CCTV installations would be of limited use. The operator needs not only to be able to adjust the angle, zoom and focus of cameras, but also to perform other 'housekeeping' tasks such as washing and wiping of the front glass on external housings, control of lights, etc. Some of these commands are quite simple. Take, for example, the wash command; it is simply an on/off situation. However, other control requirements are more difficult to send. There is little to be gained from simply 'telling' the pan motor to 'pan'. Perhaps if the motor could answer back it might ask, 'Which way? For how long? And how fast?'.

Operators of fully functional cameras have come to expect a lot of their systems, and to some extent are attempting to emulate the actions of a broadcast camera operator, but from a distance. The number of commands needed to provide such complex control is substantial, and requires sophisticated telemetry to enable adequate communication. A list of the main commands is given in Table 10.1. Where the command includes speed, this refers to controllers that have a dynamic (or ballistic) joystick where the further the stick is pressed, the faster the motor moves. Thus, for example, an instruction may not just be 'Pan left' but rather 'Pan left at this speed'.

Table 10.1

Command	Number of instructions
Camera address (i.e. number)	1
Pan left + speed	2
Pan right + speed	2
Tilt up + speed	2
Tilt down + speed	2
Zoom in	1
Zoom out	1
Focus far	1
Focus near	1
Iris open	1
Iris close	1
Wash on/off	2
Wipe on/off	2
Lights on/off	2
Move to pre-set position n	Dependent on the number of pre-sets

From the table we see that there are no fewer then twenty-one commands for a fully functional camera, plus an additional number for the pre-set positions. In this chapter we shall look at ways of communicating this information to the various cameras in a system.

Hard wired control

Some of the earliest remote controlled CCTV systems relied on a direct power connection between the control room and each PTZ unit. The principle is illustrated in Figure 10.1 where switch S_1 performs the motor on/off function and S_2, which is a double pole changeover type switch, the motor direction. There are two major problems with this method. First of all, to control a fully functional camera position having PTZ plus focus, iris and wash/wipe facilities, a fourteen core cable would be required in addition to the co-axial video link. And secondly, for cable lengths of any distance, voltage drop along the cable is a major problem.

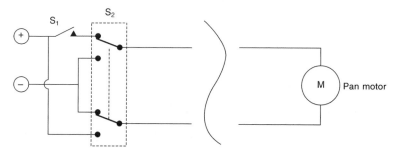

Figure 10.1 *Control of a motor using direct power coupling*

An improvement on this design is shown in Figure 10.2 where the problem of voltage drop along the multicore is largely overcome by providing power to the motors locally at each camera location. Control is effected by switching low-current relays via the multicore. For example, closing S_4 at the controller causes relay RL4 in the site driver to energize, switching on the tilt motor. Because of the position of RL3 (de-energized) the motor will move the housing in an upward direction. Closing S_3 causes RL3 to energize, and the housing moves downwards.

Apart from greatly reducing the problem of voltage drop, another advantage of this method is that, because the negative side of the control signals are common along one conductor (cable No. 5 in the multicore), less cores are required. Compared to the arrangement in Figure 10.1, which required fourteen cable cores, this circuit would require just eight cores to provide the same number of functions.

Despite the improvements in the arrangement in Figure 10.2, the system was far from ideal and was phased out with the development of other

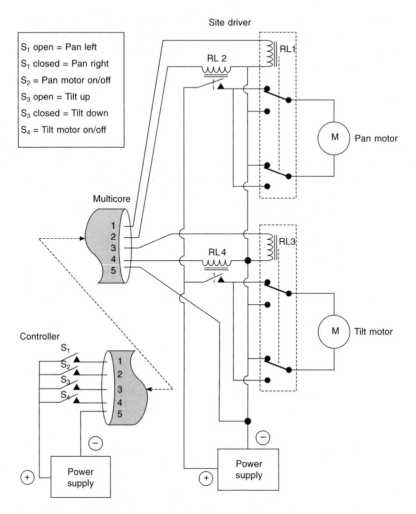

Figure 10.2 *Control of motors using indirect power coupling*

telemetry control methods. Nonetheless, Figure 10.2 serves to show us more clearly what it is that we are trying to achieve in a telemetry control system, which is to send commands simultaneously down a single conductor and thus replace the eight (or possibly more) conductors with just two, and to do this in such a way that voltage drop is so negligible that the command signals may be sent over a few kilometres if need be. Another point to note from Figure 10.2 is the relay arrangement in the site driver which is basically the same in modern telemetry receiver units; it is only the method of controlling them which has altered.

Control data transmission

The principle of remote control using data protocols is illustrated in Figure 10.3. Each command is encrypted into a data format and sent along a two-wire link to a receiver. The receiver contains a decoder chip which interprets the commands and operates the appropriate relay(s) via the relay driver chip. The relay driver performs the function of switches S_1–S_4 in Figure 10.2, energizing the power switching relays.

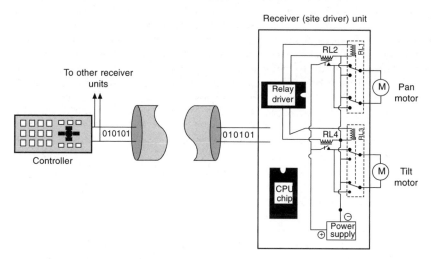

Figure 10.3 *Control of motors using a data link*

There are two ways that the data links may be connected to the receiver units. The first is like that illustrated in Figure 10.3 where the controller uses individual outputs to each receiver. The other way is to place the control data onto all of the lines simultaneously, enabling receivers to be connected individually to the controller and/or daisy-chained. This is illustrated in Figure 10.4.

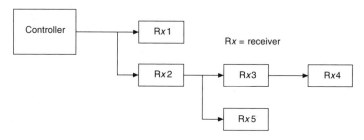

Figure 10.4 *Simultaneous data transmission*

Where a daisy-chain design is used, the encoder includes an address in the command. For example, if the operator selects camera 5 to pan left, then the encrypted data is effectively saying, 'Camera 5, pan left'. Note that the first part of the command contains an address, 'Camera 5'. Thus, although the signal is picked up by all of the receivers, only the one which has been assigned as camera 5 responds. The receivers are assigned their addresses during commissioning. Note that a controller designed for individual output transmission cannot be connected daisy-chain fashion because it will not be sending any address data.

It is most common for the co-axial cable to carry both the telemetry data and the composite video signal. This makes a lot of sense as it reduces the number of cables required in a system. Some telemetry units, however, use a separate co-axial cable, whilst others employ a twisted pair conductor. This is especially useful where lengthy cable runs are involved. Where fibre-optic cable is employed, co-axial-fed telemetry is preferable because the data and composite video signals are converted from one transmission medium to the other – and back again – at the same time.

Whichever transmission medium is used, some means of keeping the video and data signals separate must be employed, otherwise the entire system will break down as data would be displayed on the monitors as noise, and the telemetry receivers would become confused trying to decode a video signal. The two common methods of multiplexing data and video are *frequency division multiplexing* (FDM) and *time division multiplexing* (TDM).

Frequency division multiplexing is illustrated in Figure 10.5. The data is modulated onto a carrier signal in the order of 8–12 MHz, this frequency being well above that of the upper limits of the video signal which, for PAL, is typically 5.5 MHz (4.2 MHz NTSC). Each telemetry receiver has a demodulator circuit that removes the data from the carrier. The decoder can then process the data to derive the commands.

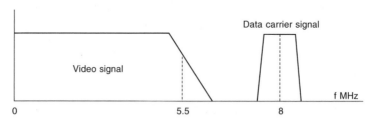

Figure 10.5 *Signal spectrum for frequency division multiplexing*

Time division multiplexing is a take-off of the Teletext system used in the UK broadcast television service where data is transmitted during the field flyback blanking interval, during which time the electron beam in the CRT is cut off whilst the scanning circuits adjust themselves to begin scanning the following field from the top of the screen. When viewed on an oscilloscope, the signal appears similar to that shown in Figure 10.6. As with FDM, the telemetry receivers each have a decoder circuit which picks out the data transmission and deciphers the commands.

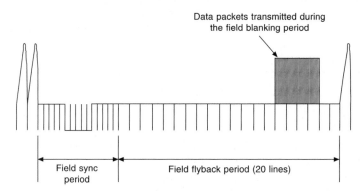

Figure 10.6 *Time division multiplexing. The data is sent at a different time to the video information*

The TDM signal is at a frequency somewhere in the region of 4.5 MHz, and thus we see that in the case of both TDM and FDM, it is essential that the bandwidth of the system is up to specification. Any faults in the cabling or termination that would introduce a high frequency filtering effect will not only remove the high resolution components of the picture, but they may also filter out the telemetry data. Such faults can be intermittent, or may only affect certain camera locations.

Pan/tilt (P/T) control

The pan and tilt unit comprises of two motors and a number of gears to convert the motor speed into torque. The motors may be 24 V d.c., 24 V a.c. or 230 V a.c. Whilst a.c. motors are generally more efficient and often produce greater torque than their equivalent size d.c. counterparts, speed control of an a.c. motor is somewhat more complex than for d.c. motors. Thus, single speed 230 V a.c. motors are ideal where it is anticipated that high winds are likely to exert a heavy load on the camera assembly and a high torque drive mechanism is required to overcome this. However, where dynamic joystick control is to be incorporated in the system, d.c. P/T units will allow multi-speed (where the speed alters in incremental steps) or variable speed operation. It is usual for the motor to be coupled to the gears via clutch assemblies that will slip in the event of the mechanism jamming, thus protecting the motors from stalling and burning out.

For simplicity the circuits in Figures 10.2 and 10.3 show d.c. motors. Where a.c. motors are connected to the driver circuit the arrangement is similar, however simply reversing of the polarity of the a.c. supply to the motor will not cause it to reverse! To achieve this, the relay changeover contacts must reverse the connections to the motor field windings. a.c. motor theory is not something that the CCTV engineer needs to become too involved with, however, it is important when installing or replacing P/T units to ensure that they are compatible with the drive voltage on the site driver. Applying 230V across a 24V d.c. motor is likely to have disastrous results! Some site drivers have the facility to select the type of drive voltage (see later in the chapter).

A P/T unit contains at least four limit switches. These are a form of cut-out which are adjusted to set the maximum points of deflection in both the horizontal and vertical directions. Without these the motors could simply drive the unit in circles, causing the interconnecting cables between the housing and the receiver to become twisted around the mounting until they break, or until the housing becomes jammed. During installation the engineer adjusts the limit switch positions to suit the particular location, but in most cases the unit is designed such that it will not pan through more then 355° before stopping.

Limit switches are satisfactory if the camera is only going to be moved occasionally, however with permanently manned systems the need became evident for a facility whereby a number of pre-determined positions could be set for each fully functional camera location. For these pre-sets to be effective it is not only necessary to fix the pan and tilt positions, the zoom and focus settings for that position must also be fixed. Clearly mechanical limit switches are not able to offer this amount of control, and some other means had to be devised.

The most common solution is to place variable resistors inside the pan/tilt unit and the zoom lens assembly (this was discussed in Chapter 4; see Figure 4.19). As the motors move each of the pan, tilt, zoom and focus mechanisms, the associated potentiometer rotates producing a d.c. feedback voltage which can be monitored by the control circuit. During programming, the operator moves the P/T unit to the desired position, adjusts the zoom and focus, and enters these into a memory store, allocating a pre-set number. At this instant the control unit measures the d.c. feedback from each potentiometer, passes this to an A/D converter, and stores the digital values in memory. During operation, whenever the pre-set number is selected, the control unit checks the position of the potentiometers, and moves the four motors until the feedback voltage from each potentiometer is equal to the value stored in memory.

With this control method the pre-sets and limit positions are not set mechanically, but in the PTZ controller. Thus there is, in theory, no limit to the number of possible pre-set positions. Depending on the controller, as few as five and as many as one hundred pre-set positions can be programmed. A large number of positions is not a lot of use to a CCTV operator because it is not feasible to expect him/her to remember every one. Consider a ten camera system where each camera has one hundred pre-set positions programmed; who could remember one thousand pre-set position numbers? However, many control systems have an *automated patrol* facility whereby, in the absence of any activity or perhaps at times when the system is unmanned, the operator can leave the cameras moving through a set pattern of positions. It should be pointed out that where this facility is used extensively, the wear and tear on the P/T unit gears and clutches can take its toll.

Another use of multiple pre-sets is in conjunction with alarm signals (see Chapter 9). Upon receipt of a particular alarm signal input, the controller can often be programmed to move one or more cameras to a given position and prioritize these video signals in the recording process.

Receiver unit

A typical telemetry receiver unit is shown in Figure 10.7. In this illustration we can identify many of the features we have discussed so far in this chapter.

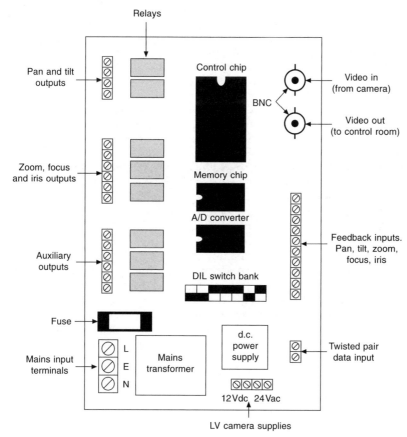

Figure 10.7 *Typical receiver unit*

Where the data is multiplexed with the video signal on one co-axial cable, it is necessary for the camera signal to loop through the receiver in order that the data can be extracted (bear in mind that the video signal is passing from the camera to the control room, whereas the data is going the other way). Some receivers may have the option of a twisted pair telemetry input, and this brings us to the next point, the DIL switches. These are used to customize the receiver to the system and location, providing such options as co-axial or twisted pair data input, 4 wire or 3 wire lens wiring, 5 V or 12 V lens operation, PT motor drive voltage, auxiliary output functions, etc. The correct setting of these switches during installation is of utmost importance as the unit will not function correctly (if at all) if any of these are in the wrong position for the type of installation. Manufacturers' instructions must be carefully adhered to.

For the driver in Figure 10.7, the P/T and lens outputs are effectively those we looked at in Figure 10.2, however the auxiliary outputs are somewhat different. Because these may be used for switching either mains voltage or low voltage devices, the terminals are simply taken to a set of clean relay contacts on the PCB. The installer can therefore connect the required power for the device through these switch contacts. The DIL switches are used to assign each output to a particular task (e.g. wash, wipe, lights, etc.) so that when, for example, the operator presses the button labelled 'lights' on the keyboard, the auxiliary output assigned to the lights changes states. If, when 'lights' is selected, the washer starts, it is possible that a DIL is incorrectly set.

The control chip performs all housekeeping functions in the receiver as well as data signal decoding, output switching, etc. The memory chip stores the pre-set levels which come from the potentiometers via the A/D converter chip.

With all telemetry-controlled systems, the protocols used between the controller and site drivers vary between manufacturers, and it is important that equipment is not mixed within a system unless it is known for certain to be compatible. Where equipment is incompatible, in most instances the telemetry simply will not function.

The receiver requires a local 230 V a.c. supply, which must be earthed. All cables between the receiver unit and the P/T and camera must be made to be flexible, and for protection are normally fed through a Copex flexible conduit. Note that to conform with IEE regulations on cable segregation, any cables carrying mains voltages must not be passed via the same conduit as co-axial and any other extra-low-voltage (ELV) cables unless the insulation of the ELV cable is rated to withstand mains supply voltages.

Dome systems

In recent years pre-assembled domes containing a P/T unit, site driver and power supply have grown in popularity. In some cases a camera is included as a part of the assembly, however this can be somewhat limiting as the installer then has no choice of camera specification, and domes are available where a camera and fully functional lens of the installer's choice can be fitted. Internal and external versions are available.

There are, perhaps, a number of reasons for the popularity of the dome. Very often they are preferred by the customer because they are overt, and yet covert. That is, people can clearly see that the premises are monitored by CCTV, but they never actually know when they are being observed. Aesthetically domes often look less out of place than traditional PT and site driver assemblies. Installers have less work because they are ready-assembled. But perhaps one feature above all of these is the availability of high speed domes that are capable of 360° continuous rotation.

The high speed function enables the PT unit to move the camera at rates in the order of 300° per second, with a corresponding response from the zoom and focus servos. The inclusion of multiple pre-sets offers rapid response to operator or alarm-activated requests. The speed control is made possible by the inclusion of sophisticated servos on the site drivers controlling either d.c. stepper motors or, in some instances, a.c. synchronous motors using a variable high frequency supply voltage. (Note: altering the frequency of the a.c. supply to a synchronous motor changes its speed.)

The 360° rotation is made possible by the use of slip rings to make all of the electrical connections, including the video signal, between the camera and the site driver. This principle is illustrated in Figure 10.8.

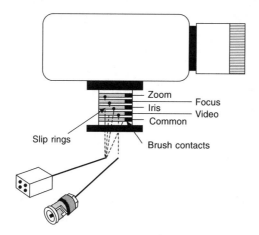

Figure 10.8 *Principle of using slip rings to couple a rotating camera to fixed cables*

Data communications

It is clear from what has been discussed so far that computer technology plays a significant role in CCTV, and therefore it is a natural progression to use this technology to integrate the system, enabling communication and thus control between the different parts. For example, in Chapter 9 we saw why it is necessary for a multiplexer to 'know' the operating mode of the time-lapse VCR. Similarly, the operator may wish to control the VCR from the telemetry keyboard rather than have to move across the desk and interrupt the monitoring process, perhaps at an inopportune moment. Indeed, in the case of a remote monitored system the operator may be several (hundred) miles away, wishing to move cameras to verify an alarm activation. These complex controls involve microprocessor chips communicating with each other, perhaps over a telephone line.

Using the telephone network to transmit digital information requires special equipment because the narrow bandwidth of the system will not effectively pass high frequency TTL-style 5V pulses. The data must be converted into two audible tones; one to indicate logic 0 and another for logic 1. This conversion is performed by a piece of equipment known as a *MOdulator/DEModulator*; or *MODEM*.

To enable equipment of different industries and manufacture to communicate, some means of standardization of signal level, polarity and frequency is necessary. In addition to this, the configuration of connectors between equipment must be the same. Common standard interfaces are *RS232*, *RS422*, *RS485* and *RS425* (RS = Recommended Standard). RS232 and RS422 ports are common on CCTV equipment, enabling the kind of control we have just been considering, and when a MODEM is included in the installation the system can be controlled from anywhere in the world with an apparent instantaneous response. Figure 10.9 shows an example of a remote monitored system.

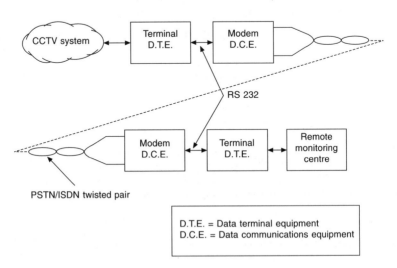

Figure 10.9 *Two-way communication via the telephone system and RS232 interface*

Introduced in 1962, the RS232 is a very common interface and is used extensively to link computer-based equipment. In most cases the connector known as the *D Connector* is used; the pin configuration for this is shown in Figure 10.10.

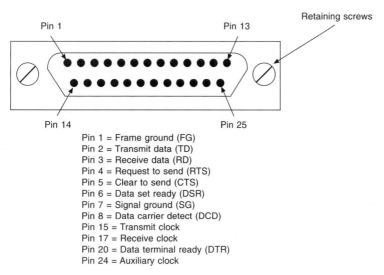

Pin 1 = Frame ground (FG)
Pin 2 = Transmit data (TD)
Pin 3 = Receive data (RD)
Pin 4 = Request to send (RTS)
Pin 5 = Clear to send (CTS)
Pin 6 = Data set ready (DSR)
Pin 7 = Signal ground (SG)
Pin 8 = Data carrier detect (DCD)
Pin 15 = Transmit clock
Pin 17 = Receive clock
Pin 20 = Data terminal ready (DTR)
Pin 24 = Auxiliary clock

Figure 10.10 *RS 232, 25-pin D type (DB25) connector*

Referring to Figures 10.9 and 10.10: *frame ground* (pin 1) is a protective earth which protects the sensitive microchips from damage which would occur if static were allowed to build up around equipment cases. It also serves as a screen, preventing RFI and EMI from corrupting the data. *Transmit data* (pin 2) is the main data link from DTE to DCE. *Receive data* (pin 3) is the main data link from DCE to DTE. *Request to send* (pin 4); when the DTE is ready to send data it takes this pin to logic 0, prompting the DCE to activate its carrier and translate the data signals into audio tones. *Clear to send* (pin 5); in response to a logic 0 on pin 4, the DCE takes pin 5 to logic 0 as soon as it is ready to transmit. In other words, it is telling the DTE that it is ready. *Data set ready* (pin 6); when the DCE is active it takes this pin to logic 0 to let the DTE know that it is connected to a 'live' DCE. *Signal ground* (pin 7) is a common negative to which all signals are referred. *Data terminal ready* (pin 20); this is the compliment to the pin 6 action. The clock signals (pins 15, 17 and 24) maintain correct timing/synchronization between devices for the purposes of transmitting and receiving data.

This activity between pins 4 and 5 is known as *handshaking*, the term describing the co-operation between devices that are exchanging data. This protocol is necessary because it is not possible for equipment to send and receive at the same time. A typical handshake sequence would be; DTE asserts RTS – slight delay whilst DCE starts up – DCE responds with a reply on CTS – DTE begins transmission of data.

The voltage levels for RS232 are much higher than for TTL logic circuits; logic 0 is between +3V and +25V. Logic 1 is between –3V and –25V. The main limiting factor with regard to RS232 is the relatively short cable length, which is specified as having a maximum of 15m. The main reason for this short length is the amount of capacitance in the cable which, as we saw in Chapter 2 (Figure 2.2), integrates the square pulses and corrupts the data signal. Another limiting factor is the low baud rate (the speed at which data is transmitted, expressed in bits per second or bp/s). The maximum specified speed for RS232 is 20kbp/s. In any data transfer system it is essential that the speed of both the transmitter and receiver are set to match, otherwise the receiver will not clock the signals in and communication will not take place. Thus, any system that uses an RS232 link will be restricted to this very slow data rate.

Improvements on the RS232 are standards such as RS422 and RS485 which make use of low impedance differential signals along twisted pair cable. Much longer transmission distances are possible (in the order of km), and the twisted pair feature reduces the effects of induced noise. Special line amplifiers/drivers are required to launch and receive the differential signals. The principle is illustrated in Figure 10.11, whilst the principles of twisted pair transmission were considered in Chapter 2.

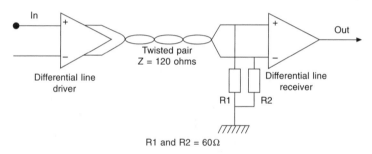

Figure 10.11 Illustration of RS422/485 transmission. R1/R2 form a 120ohm termination resistance across the line; Note the reference to earth (see text)

Introduced in 1983, RS485 is designed to support up to 32 devices on one twisted pair, although modified versions are able to support up to 256 devices. Devices are connected in parallel across the twisted pair in a daisy chain. In a CCTV application, the master device may be a telemetry controller and the other 31 devices the site drivers. Where the system is to be administered by a PC, the RS485 network may be connected to the PC via either an RS232 (COM) port or USB port. In this case a special line driver would be used to interface to the RS485 network. An illustration of a PC-administered system is given in Figure 10.12.

RS485 is described as a two wire (single twisted pair) system. Whilst this is true, the line drivers also rely on a ground connection to derive the signal voltage and, bearing in mind what was discussed in Chapter 2 regarding ground potential differences (Figure 2.11), problems may arise

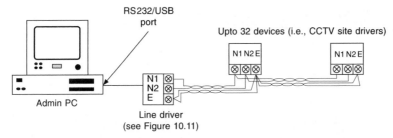

Figure 10.12 *The line driver converts the RS 232 or USB output to RS 485. Devices are then daisy-chained across one pair, the second pair serving as a ground wire*

where the potential at each end of this ground connection is different. In order to provide a reliable ground connection between devices, many manufacturers of RS485-based equipment specify double twisted pair cable, where the second pair are connected together to the ground terminals. The doubling up of conductors ensures a low electrical resistance, providing a much more reliable ground connection than electrical earth.

11 Ancillary equipment

Up to this point we have examined each of the primary components in a CCTV system, looking at their operating principles, their function, variations in technology, setting up and adjustment methods and have identified typical fault symptoms and causes. In this chapter we shall deal with those components in a CCTV system which, although at times may appear mundane, nevertheless play an essential role.

Camera mountings

CCTV cameras are both expensive and delicate and in many cases need to be protected from either the elements, vandals, thieves, or a combination of these threats. A range of protective mountings is available and the choice for any given application may be determined by such factors as the degree of protection required, size of camera, aesthetic requirements, mounting location and whether it is to be a covert or overt installation.

The simplest form of camera mount is a wall bracket and, although these do not offer protection against any threat, in indoor locations where the threat is slight, brackets offer an effective and inexpensive means of securing a camera. All cameras have a standard mounting, which somewhat simplifies the choice of bracket and the only points left to consider are the length and weight of the camera. For obvious reasons weight is an important factor, but it is not only the load-bearing ability of the bracket that must be considered, the surface to which the bracket is to be fixed must also be taken into account. For example, where an internal camera is to be fixed to a thin plasterboard surface, it may be advisable to employ a toggle or gravity bolt fixing, however not all internal brackets have mounting holes large enough to accommodate such fixing devices. The length of the camera must be taken into consideration when choosing a bracket to ensure that there is enough clearance behind, not only to allow free movement when setting the camera angle but also to provide sufficient room to allow for the cabling.

Some brackets, both internal and external, incorporate a cable management system where the video and power cables pass through the bracket. This is an important feature where cables are prone to vandalism or malicious attack.

When selecting a suitable housing for a camera the engineer should consider such points as internal or external use, the size of camera, the method of fitting and removing the cover(s), wash/wipe and heater requirements, overt or covert design, the degree of risk of attack (i.e.

should an anti-vandal type be used?) and whether there any ergonomic requirements. The traditional housing design incorporates an elongated shell with an option for P/T mounting or a wall-mounting bracket, perhaps incorporating integral cable management. The metal casing should be protected from corrosion by galvanization, anodizing or coating with a weatherproof paint. There will be a footplate inside the housing onto which the camera will be fixed and, in the case of housings intended for mains voltage operated cameras, power terminations at the rear of the assembly. When used in cooler climates, external units should have a thermostatically controlled heater to prevent misting of the front glass and the lens. These heaters usually take the form of a 15–20 W wirewound resistor connected in series with a thermistor to the mains supply voltage. For anti-vandal versions the front glass will be shatterproof.

The shell will have some means of opening to allow camera installation and future maintenance and for this there are a number of design trends. For larger housings, the top cover is generally held in place by clips and lifts off for access, allowing ample room to work on large camera/lens assemblies. One problem that may be encountered is what to do with the housing top once it has been removed. If working from a hydraulic platform there should be room to place it on the floor, but if the engineer is only required to perform a simple operation which may be accessed via a ladder, then grappling with a large housing cover may become something of an issue. In some cases the manufacturer provides for this eventuality by fixing a steel wire between the cover and the housing bottom, allowing the top to hang from the assembly when removed.

Smaller housing designs have a variety of access methods but some of these may prove problematic for certain installations. For example, in some cases the camera is fixed to a footplate which is then inserted into the rear of the housing. In theory the engineer should be able to swing the housing around to give room for this operation, but this is not always possible. Furthermore, once installed, it is very difficult for the engineer to then perform adjustments to the lens and back focus. Other designs have the top cover slide on and off which, again, is not always a simple operation in some situations. For most situations the best form of housing cover is where the top is either hinged, or is lifted off and allowed to hang from a secure cable. For higher security situations where the camera might be accessed by unauthorized persons, securing the cover using anti-vandal screws is a viable option.

Another design feature is the provision of a sun visor. Direct sunlight on the lens may cause the iris to close down, resulting in a very dark image, or it can cause multiple reflections within the lens that produce undesirable light streaks or halo effects on the picture. Similarly, when sunlight falls directly onto the front glass, unwanted halos or bright patches may appear on the picture. To eliminate these problems, external housings should incorporate some form of sun visor. This is generally formed into the top cover and provides shielding to both the top and sides of the front glass.

Another factor that may determine the choice of external housing is whether or not a wiper is required, as not all housings are designed to accommodate this. The wiper and associated motor are often specified by the manufacturer as an optional item, allowing the installer to use these only where it is felt necessary and therefore to reduce the installation cost. When considering these costs it is important to remember that it is not only the wiper hardware that must be included but also the cost of providing telemetry to control the motor. In the case of a fully functional camera this is not a problem because telemetry will already be present, however for fixed cameras where there is no need for telemetry the added cost of a wiper plus telemetry will raise the cost of that camera installation considerably, begging the question, does that particular camera really need a wipe facility?

A wash facility may be installed at camera locations where there is excessive dust or dirt, however careful consideration must be given to this. It will be necessary to accommodate a reservoir somewhere close to the camera in a place where it will not be tampered with. In the example shown in Figure 11.1 the reservoir is housed in the base of the camera column, but this will not be possible on a wall-mounted camera installation. Wash reservoirs designed for location at the camera head are available, but in many cases it may prove very difficult to replenish them. In the case of wall-mounted installations, some installers have attempted to locate the reservoir on the roof of the building, however because it is above the outlet nozzle the water is prone to siphon away. In the majority

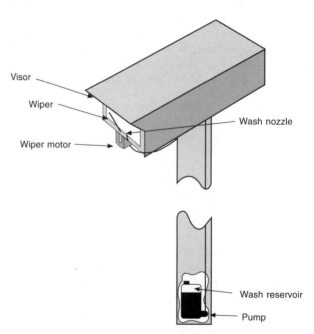

Figure 11.1 *External housing incorporating common features such as wash and wipe and sun visor*

of cases a wash facility is not essential because a well-maintained wiper will be able to cope with light deposits of dust and dirt, assisted often by the action of the rain.

Although the traditional form of housing is still very popular, there is an increasing move towards dome housings owing to their ability to permit rapid 360° panning movement (this was discussed in Chapter 10) and the fact that they are much more pleasing aesthetically. Another advantage of the dome housing when used externally is the fact that it negates all of the problems of wind drag which, as we shall see in a moment, affect housings mounted onto P/T units. Perhaps one drawback with the external dome housing when compared with a traditional design is that, at the time of writing, no-one has come up with an effective design for a wash/wipe mechanism other than a mop on a long pole! In particularly dirty environments this should be given serious consideration because, where the camera is not easily accessible, the lack of a wipe facility can mean that the pictures very quickly become obscured by splashes of dirt on the dome.

Dome housings are particularly useful where it is desirable not to reveal the direction in which the camera is pointing. By coating the dome with chrome or aluminium, or by using a smoked cover, the camera can be concealed. The drawback of using such dome covers is that the light input is attenuated, by as much as two F-stops in the case of a coated cover and as much as one F-stop in the case of smoked covers. A further drawback is that the curvature of the dome cover will inevitably introduce a degree of optical distortion, and in some cases this can be quite noticeable. When choosing a dome the issues of light attenuation and optical distortion should be considered.

Although some manufacturers of camera housings simply state the intended applications for each of their units, the majority use Standard BS EN 60529: 1992 which is the correct method of specifying any form of enclosure within the electrical industry. The degree of protection afforded by an enclosure is indicated by a rating known as an *index of protection* (IP). The IP codes are summarized in Table 11.1. In the code, the first digit indicates the level of protection against ingression by solid objects, whilst the second digit indicates the level of protection against liquids. Where an 'X' appears in place of the first or second digit, this indicates that there is no guarantee of any protection in the corresponding area. An additional letter may be placed at the end of the IP number in cases where it is necessary to indicate a level of protection of persons that is higher than that afforded by the first digit.

As can be seen, the codes are intended to include a wide range of protection ratings ranging from minute particle ingression to whole body ingression, and from full immersion in water to no moisture protection whatsoever. From the point of view of CCTV this may appear somewhat extreme, however it must be borne in mind that these ratings apply to any containment intended for electrical installations, including high voltage.

Table 11.1 *Outline of IP (Index of Protection) codes*

IP number	First digit (touch and solid objects)	Second digit (liquids)
0	No Protection	No Protection
1	Protection against contact by large part of body or objects >50 mm diameter	Vertical dripping water shall not impair equipment operation
2	Protection against contact by Standard Finger and objects >12 mm diameter	Dripping water shall not impair equipment operation when housing is tilted to 15° from vertical
3	Protection against solid objects >2.5 mm thick	Spray or rain falling 60° from vertical shall not impair equipment operation
4	Protection against solid objects >1 mm thick	Spray or rain falling from any direction shall not impair equipment operation
5	Protection against dust ingress in quantities capable of interfering with equipment operation	Low pressure water jets from any direction shall not impair equipment operation
6	Total protection against dust ingress	High pressure water jets from any direction shall not impair equipment operation
7	–	Immersion of housing shall not permit water ingression (within specified time and pressure)
8	–	Indefinite immersion of housing shall not permit water ingression

Additional Letter: A = Protection against contact by a large part of the body.
B = Protection against contact by a Standard Finger.
C = Protection against contact by a tool.
D = Protection against contact by a wire.

Example

A camera housing has a rating of IP50. In this case the housing would offer a high level of protection against dirt and dust, but absolutely none against moisture. Such a housing would be suited to indoor use only.

Example

A camera housing has a rating of IP66. In this case the housing would offer a high level of protection against dirt, dust and moisture. Such a housing would be highly suited to outdoor use.

Example

An electrical equipment housing has a rating of IP4X. In this case the housing would offer a reasonable level of protection against small objects, but gives no guarantee regarding moisture ingression. Such a housing would be suited to indoor use only, and even then only in a clean and secure environment.

Example

An electrical equipment housing has a rating of IPXXA. In this case the housing would offer protection against accidental human contact, but gives no guarantee regarding moisture ingression and does not protect against dust, dirt and deliberate ingress by persons. Such a housing would be suited to indoor use only, and even then only in a clean and secure environment.

Towers and columns

Mounting a CCTV camera on top of a tower is common practice, however there are a number of things to take into consideration such as positioning, possible planning permissions, installation of supply and signal cables to the site, the physical installation of the tower, cable management, protection against attack, installation of site drivers and other ancillary devices and access for servicing. Let's look at each of these in turn.

Positioning of a CCTV camera tower can be very important and the specifier who looks at the problem purely from the point of view of obtaining the best field of view may find him/herself coming unstuck. For example, companies that have installed cameras directly in front of private dwellings may quickly find themselves having to disconnect them when the owner of that dwelling takes out a court order on the grounds of it infringing his/her human rights. It may also be that the location of the tower is determined by the location of existing underground cable ducts, the cost of excavating for new cables being prohibitive. In areas where building development is still taking place, the specifier must try and take into account the erection of structures that may impair the camera once it has been installed; it would not be the first time that a lamp post or hoarding has been erected directly in front of a CCTV camera!

Town councils are very particular about what can and cannot be erected in their centres, and special planning rules may apply; for example, the style of the tower may have to blend with that of the street lighting, or the housing may have to be of a dome design and not a pan/tilt head.

The laying of underground cables is always expensive, so if a cost-effective means of laying the power and signal cables out to a camera site can be found it is always worth considering, even though it may not be the best location from a field of view perspective. The client has to decide if a marginal improvement in camera performance is worth a considerable increase in installation cost.

Tower structures require a solid anchor and should be installed by skilled civil engineers. Manufacturers will provide guideline instructions on such things as the minimum depth and area of the foundation, but knowing the correct mix and the minimum curing time of the concrete is something that only qualified persons will know, not to mention that digging holes in built-up areas often unearths such things as high voltage cables, sewers, gas and water mains, etc.

CCTV camera towers are generally of two designs: the solid column structure and the lattice tower (Figure 11.2). The lattice tower is by far the strongest structure because its low surface area offers less wind resistance and the triangular lattice produces a very rigid construction. However, an open lattice means that the cables must pass largely unprotected up through the centre of the tower, a feature that is not very desirable for most installations. Some protection can be afforded by using steel conduit, but this will not prevail against a determined attack. Solid columns are, by comparison, far more suited to the task because they offer considerable protection of the vertical cables. With regard to their strength and rigidity, a hexagonal solid column will be more stable than a circular design which means that there should be much less of a tendency for the column to wobble in high winds. This added stability can be of real advantage in high columns where the camera is fitted with a high magnification lens.

Physical attack against CCTV camera installations is becoming more commonplace as those who would wish to indulge in a life of crime find CCTV increasingly cramping their style. What these people are rapidly learning is that once a camera is 'taken out', it may be some time before the owners have found a budget to have it repaired. This said, it is up to the specifiers and installers to do their utmost to protect cameras, and mounting them atop a high tower is one effective method of achieving this, provided that the access cover at the base of the tower is secure! Manufacturers have for a long time employed anti-vandal bolts or other methods of deterring would-be attackers, however in recent times a number of access cover designs have proven to be woefully inadequate against a large crowbar, and once a fire has been lit inside the tower there is usually little left of the fibre-optic cables above ground afterwards. Such damage is costly and time-consuming to put right, which is precisely what the criminal fraternity like. Therefore, when selecting a column for situations where such attack is likely (housing estates, town centres, etc.) look carefully at the design of any low-level access covers and be convinced that it will hold out against sustained attack.

With respect to attack, also be aware of the monkeys who are capable of climbing columns. If a person is able to get up to the camera head, then they can very quickly inflict extensive damage and put the camera out of action. To cater for this eventuality, manufacturers offer a range of optional anti-climb devices which generally take the form a series of spikes mounted around two thirds up the tower. Beware when fitting these; when working from a hydraulic platform these spikes are quite likely to take out the eye of the installer whilst he is securing the fixing bolts. Eye protection is advised.

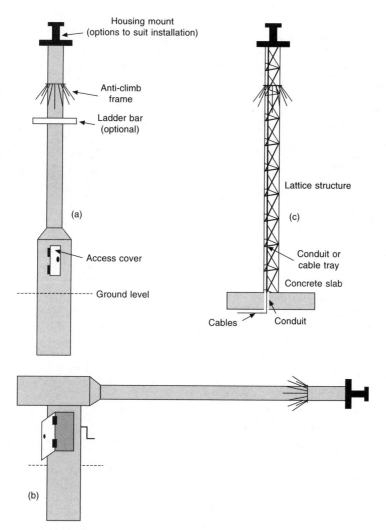

Figure 11.2 *Typical camera towers and columns.* (a) *Fixed column, may be cylindrical or hexagonal.* (b) *Wind down column.* (c) *Lattice tower structure. These may also have a wind down mechanism*

Remember that for fully functional cameras it will be necessary to house a site driver somewhere atop of a tower. Many designs have optional brackets or other mounting devices to accommodate these items, but make sure that the tower you are having installed has such facilities – preferably before you install it!

It is one thing to install a tower that offers a high degree of protection against attack, but the service engineer must be able to access it at a later date. In the case of lower towers having only a fixed camera, ladder access may be adequate, but this does mean that a ladder bar should be fitted to the tower before it is erected. These bars usually drop down over the tower and are then secured. The bar offers a solid point against which a ladder can rest and be secured, and a well-designed bar will have flanges at each end to prevent the ladder from sliding off.

For higher towers with more complex installations on top, access will either have to be via a hydraulic platform, or a wind-down tower may be installed. There are a number of designs of winding mechanism available, depending on the weight of the tower. When installing such towers, take into consideration the direction in which it must wind down; for example, having it fall across a motorway carriageway might not be the best idea!

Pan/tilt units

Earlier in this chapter it has been pointed out that a motorized dome housing has many advantages over the more traditional pan/tilt unit and camera housing assembly. Nevertheless, the older style camera housing still has some advantages over dome technology; for example, dome housings do not easily accommodate large lenses, cleaning can be problematic, a dome assembly does not accommodate lighting units, and motorized dome assemblies, at the time of writing, still tend to be more expensive than an equivalent P/T and housing assembly. There are still many occasions where these advantages tip the choice of assembly in favour of a camera housing which, where the camera needs to be moved, necessitates the use of a P/T unit.

Where it has been decided to use a traditional P/T unit and camera housing, before selecting the unit there are a number of points to consider such as loading, wind drag, supply voltage, maximum drive speed and is the assembly to carry lighting?

Loading refers to the physical weight that the pan/tilt unit is to carry and will include the combined weight of the housing, camera, lens, lighting units and anything else that is on the assembly. A pan/tilt unit with an excessive load will initially fail to meet operational expectations, its movement being sluggish and possibly having a tendency to overrun when the operator expects it to stop. In the long term the excess load will cause wear of the gears and possibly motors, resulting in premature failure of the unit. A further problem that may be encountered with excess loading is that the unit may have insufficient power to lift the assembly up when it has been tilted downwards beyond a certain point.

Each pan/tilt unit has a maximum load rating which is typically between 12 kg and 50 kg, although with the reduction in size and weight of cameras and lenses during recent years the requirement for heavier duty units is becoming less. When selecting a unit the specifier should first of all calculate the total weight of the proposed assembly and then add another 2 kg allowance for cable drag and wind resistance. In environments where snow or ice are likely to build up on the housing, a further 3 kg should be added to the total weight calculation. Having arrived at a final figure for the maximum possible load, a unit with a rating that exceeds this figure by at least 15% should be selected. Another consideration with regard to loading is future developments. If it is anticipated that further equipment may be added to the assembly at a later date (for example, a pair of lamp units), it is advisable to include the weight of this equipment in the initial calculation to save having to replace the pan/tilt unit with a higher specification when the system is upgraded. Where infra-red lighting is a requirement, one possible method of reducing the load on the pan/tilt unit is to use LED lamp units rather than tungsten halogen types (see Chapter 3).

In open areas the problem of wind drag can be quite serious. An underrated pan/tilt unit will not be able to function well in strong winds, and it is not uncommon to have badly specified assemblies that simply spin around like a weathercock in strong winds because the forces acting on the housing overcome the torque in the gear train. In some cases this action can break the teeth off the drive gears, however, better quality pan/tilt units may incorporate some from of clutch assembly which will allow them to slip without damage. Having said this, a correctly rated and installed pan/tilt unit should function perfectly well in strong winds, although the units may require more frequent servicing in the form of lubrication and greasing than units that operate in less hostile conditions.

Some pan tilt units have the housing mounted on top whereas others have it mounted to one side (Figure 11.3). In general, top-mounted units tend to have a lower load capacity than an equivalent rated side-mount unit because of the difference in the centre of gravity of the load with respect to the drive mechanism. This point is illustrated in Figure 11.4 where it can be seen that, because of the leverage effect of the housing on the drive shaft, the amount of energy required to lift the assembly back from a tilted position is much greater for a top-mount pan/tilt than it is for a side-mount. This does not mean to say that side-mount units are necessarily better, because a top-mount design should always be able to perform to its design specifications, it is just a fact of physics that a side-mount unit will be able to handle its load with a lesser amount of energy than its top-mount equivalent.

Top-mount units come into their own when the assembly is required to have one or two lamp units fitted. Although it is possible to hang a lamp unit from the underside of a side-mount assembly, it is far easier to do this with top-mount units – especially when two lamps are required because in this case they may be mounted below and to either side of the camera housing, producing a balancing effect on both the assembly and the pan/tilt gearbox.

Returning once more to the issue of wind drag, the effects of wind on top- and side-mount units can be somewhat different. The pan/tilt unit in a side-mount assembly offers a degree of shielding to the housing from side winds, whereas for a top-mount unit the housing is exposed in all directions. Furthermore, because of the leverage effect of the housing

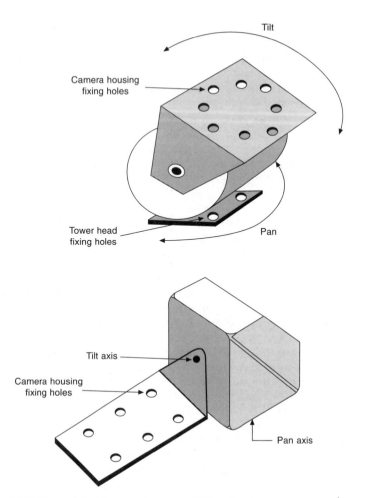

Figure 11.3 *Top- and side-mount pan and tilt units*

on a top-mount unit, the wind forces acting on the pan/tilt gears are far greater than for side-mount designs.

Pan/tilt motors are usually rated at 24 V a.c. or 230/110 V a.c., although d.c. units are available, including 12 V d.c. for internal applications. The decision whether to opt for a low or high voltage device will be dependent largely upon the operating voltage of the rest of the system. For example, if everything else in the camera assembly is rated at 24 V a.c., there seems little point in employing a high voltage pan/tilt unit as this would negate one of the main advantages of having a low voltage system, i.e. simplified installation requirements with regard to Electrical Installation Codes of Practice.

The methods of power connection to pan/tilt units can differ between manufacturers, however the wiring configuration given in Figure 11.5 is

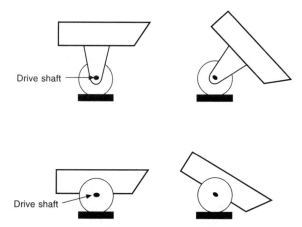

Figure 11.4 *A side-mount unit does not have the problems of leverage associated with top-mount units*

one that is shared between a number of major manufacturers. Before purchasing a unit for an application, make certain that the connection arrangement is suited to the site driver with which it will be expected to function.

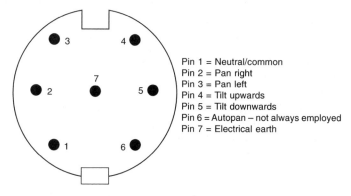

Pin 1 = Neutral/common
Pin 2 = Pan right
Pin 3 = Pan left
Pin 4 = Tilt upwards
Pin 5 = Tilt downwards
Pin 6 = Autopan – not always employed
Pin 7 = Electrical earth

Figure 11.5 *Common pan/tilt connection arrangement using an Amphenol plug and socket connector*

Cable management for fully functional camera assemblies is very important because a poorly installed connection between the moving housing and the fixed site driver can result in restricted movement, additional loading, water ingress and failure of the assembly due to broken connections. For a sound installation the cables should be contained within a flexible conduit and fixed at both ends using appropriate moisture-resistant glands. All cable entries should be at the bottom of both the housing and the side driver containment to minimize the chance of moisture ingression. The cable should be long enough to permit free movement of the assembly through all of its required field of view and should neither restrict nor be restricted by the movement of the housing. Having a long drop of cable between the site driver and the housing is the key to unrestricted movement and limited loading effects.

A particular point to look out for is where the housing assembly is fixed at the end of a boom arm which is itself secured to a solid structure – usually a building. In this case the cable should be secured by some form of tie wrap along the boom before entering the housing, allowing enough slack at the housing end to permit free movement without the flexible conduit rubbing on the boom. Such a rubbing action will result in wear of the conduit and, subsequently, the cables inside.

The drive speed for a pan/tilt unit is quoted in degrees per second, and this can vary considerably between different units. Panning requires less energy than tilting, so for any given unit the panning speed is usually much higher than the tilting speed. When considering quoted speeds, bear in mind that these are generally quoted assuming a near-to-maximum load condition, however this speed performance may alter if the load figure deviates either side of the maximum stated load condition.

To prevent a pan/tilt unit from overrunning in either the horizontal or vertical directions, limit switches may be employed. For a d.c. motor circuit this principle was discussed in Chapter 4 with regard to the zoom lens motor and is the same for the pan and tilt motors in a P/T unit. When the pan/tilt unit reaches the limit position, the switch opens and power to the motor is cut. As can be seen from Figure 11.6, diodes across the switches enable the motor to power-up when the polarity of the supply is reversed. For a.c. motors the principle is somewhat different because it is not possible to reverse the motor by simply reversing the voltage polarity. In this case the limit switches are connected to the site driver which will cut power to the motor. Motor reversal is then usually performed by having two sets of windings in the motor. Limit switch adjustment generally involves some method of releasing microswitches and sliding them to the desired positions before securing them once again. A minimum of four switches is required to set limits for left, right, up and down movement. Limit switch adjustment is important if the housing is to be prevented, for example, from hitting a wall or from tilting downwards to a point from which the motor has insufficient torque to lift it back up.

Pan/tilt units require routine maintenance if reliable performance is to be assured. This largely takes the form of lubrication or greasing of the gears, but in some cases may involve the cleaning away of old grease that has become thick due to ageing effects or contamination from dirt or metal particles from worn gears. During maintenance, gears should be inspected for signs of wear and replacements fitted as necessary. It should be pointed out that any servicing that requires the unit to be dismantled would normally be undertaken in a workshop rather than at the camera head.

Motors are prone to overheating when the movement of the unit becomes

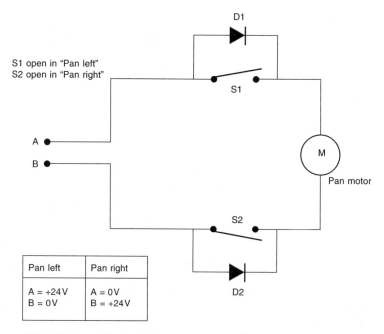

S1 open in "Pan left"
S2 open in "Pan right"

D1

S1

A

B

M

Pan motor

S2

D2

Pan left	Pan right
A = +24V	A = 0V
B = 0V	B = +24V

Figure 11.6 *Limit switch circuit for a pan motor. The same arrangement would be used for the tilt motor*

restricted, which in turn may be caused by faulty gears or overloading of the unit. A motor that has overheated will often have short circuit turns in its windings which will result in a reduction of torque, causing the unit to become sluggish. In extreme cases a motor may cease to function altogether, resulting in the loss of either the pan or tilt function. Where a motor is found to be defective, it is worth investigating the possible causes for its failure rather than simply installing a replacement.

Other servicing points would include a visual inspection of all cables, conduits, mounting brackets, etc. for signs of wear/corrosion. Also check that limit switches are secure and are still functioning.

Monitor brackets

In many respects the same rules that apply to the selection of camera brackets also apply to monitor bracket selection, however it must be kept in mind that a monitor is generally much heavier than an internal camera installation. There are a number of swivel mount bracket designs available specifically for monitor use and it is advisable to employ these rather than adapt something else, if only to avoid litigation in the event of any mishap. But of course, it is still up to the installer to ensure that the bracket chosen is rated to carry a load in excess of the expected monitor weight.

The installer must also verify that the surface to which the bracket is to be fixed is capable of retaining the proposed fixings. Where there is any doubt, additional means of support must be applied – monitors are generally sited where people circulate, and one simply cannot take the risk of a unit falling onto a person.

Power supplies

It is usually a simple thing to connect all of the equipment in the control room to the 230/110 V mains supply. However, this is not always as easy for cameras and other remote equipment because it may involve a lot of expensive civil work to install the cables. Alternatives to mains-operated cameras are 12 V d.c. and 24 V a.c. versions. These use appropriate low voltage power supplies which may be installed either in the control room or at suitable locations around the site. Extra Low Voltage (ELV) cables are installed alongside the co-axial signal cables to carry the power.

A variety of 12 V and 24 V power supply units are available offering different current ratings, typically between 1 A and 4 A. As with any power supply, the required rating is determined by the load, and care must be taken not to overrun a power supply as it will very quickly fail. The issues surrounding power supply rating for cameras were discussed in Chapter 6.

An a.c. power supply unit is primarily a mains-to-24V step-down transformer with a rating of at least 1 A. For higher current ratings a larger transformer may be used, however this can lead to problems with voltage regulation. When a transformer is operating with little or no load, the secondary voltage often rises above that stated; the output voltage falling progressively as the load current is increased. It is asking a lot of a transformer to provide a constant 24V across a load current range between 0 A to 4 A, and because of this some larger a.c. power supplies incorporate a number of separate 1 A rated transformers. Alternatively a transformer with a number of secondary outputs may be used.

A d.c. power supply is more complex because it requires rectifier, filtering and regulation circuits (see Figure 11.7). The regulator has the task of maintaining a constant 12V d.c. output irrespective of load current.

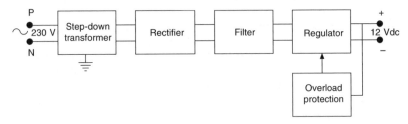

Figure 11.7 *Block diagram of a d.c. power supply*

However, it will have a maximum current rating, usually between 1A and 4A. Overload protection is essential if damage is to be prevented in cases where the rating is exceeded, or an accidental short circuit occurs across the line. A fuse is the simplest form of protection, however many regulator ICs incorporate an overload protection circuit which switches the output voltage to 0V until the overload condition is removed.

Power supplies are generally constructed within metal housings to prevent external RFI getting onto the supply lines, and also to contain any EMI coming from the power supply. This screening only functions effectively if the earth connection to the casing is properly made.

The main advantage of using ELV is the fact that cable installation is very much simplified and avoids the more involved inspection and testing required for 230/110V installations, which include visual inspection of all mechanical protection and housings, insulation resistance tests, earth loop impedance tests, and polarity checks. In essence, mains installations must be carried out by a 'competent person', which does not simply mean someone who thinks they know what they are doing, but someone who has proven their competence; in other words, a qualified electrician. By contrast, in the UK, 12/24V cables only have to comply with IEE regulations regarding segregation and mechanical protection, and they must be tested for earth leakage and insulation resistance integrity prior to connection into the system.

The main problem associated with low voltage supplies is that of voltage drop, especially in longer cable runs. For any given conductor, if the cross-sectional area is doubled, the area through which electrons pass is doubled, so the resistance is halved. Conversely, doubling the length of the conductor will double the resistance. This relationship is expressed in the formula

$$R \propto \frac{L}{A}$$

where the symbol $\propto$ means 'is proportional to'. This relationship is illustrated in Figure 11.8.

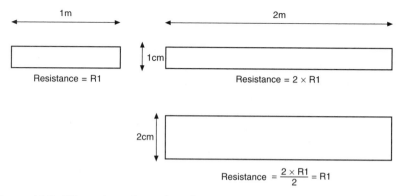

Figure 11.8 *Effect of conductor length and area on resistance*

All cable contains resistance, and although this is very small in a short length, because the resistance increases with conductor length, for longer cable runs the resistance can amount to a few ohms. It should also be remembered that a power supply requires two cables for positive and negative or, in the case of an a.c. supply, send and return. Therefore the resistance becomes double. The equivalent circuit for a power supply and load showing the cable resistance is given in Figure 11.9.

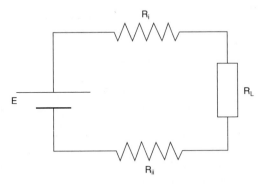

Figure 11.9 *Cable resistance in a circuit, represented by R_i and R_{ii}*

For d.c. and 50/60 Hz a.c. supplies the cable can be considered to have a purely resistive effect, and thus voltage drop can be considered from the point of view of Ohm's Law. For the circuit in Figure 11.9, the voltage drop would be found from $V = I \times (R_i + R_{ii})$, where the current can be considered to be the rated current for the equipment constituting the load. For example, if the load is a colour camera for which the manufacturer has specified a current of 300 mA, then the voltage drop would be taken to be $V = 300 \times 10^{-3} \times (R_i + R_{ii})$.

Cable resistance is usually quoted in Ω/m or Ω/km, although in some cases a manufacturer might quote actual voltage drop figures, in which case you might see something like; 80 mV/A/m at 22°C. Note that the resistance of copper increases with temperature, and this is why the temperature at which the measurement was taken must be stated. If this cable were made to function at 30°C, then the resistance would rise slightly.

The resistance can vary considerably between different types of cable, and a manufacturer's technical information or support line should be consulted where voltage drop needs to be calculated during the system planning stage.

Consider the following example. The camera in the system illustrated in Figure 11.10 is quoted as having a current rating of 250 mA and a minimum operating voltage of 9 V d.c. The resistance of the cable is quoted as being 0.015 Ω/m at 20°C. Calculate the voltage drop in the cable, and determine whether or not the camera would be able to operate satisfactorily.

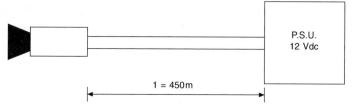

Figure 11.10

Solution

Total cable length = 2 × 450 m = 900 m
(remember there are two conductors, + and −).

Total cable resistance at 20°C = 900 × 0.015 = 13.5 Ω

Voltage drop = $I \times R_{cable}$ = 250 × 10⁻³ × 13.5 = 3.375 V

Voltage at camera = $V_{psu} - V_{cable}$ = 12 − 3.375 = 8.625 V

Thus it can be seen that the camera would not function correctly, if at all. One possible method of overcoming this problem would be to use a higher gauge cable, remembering that increasing the cross-sectional area reduces the resistance. Where a multicore cable is being used with spare cores available, doubling-up the cores can cure the problem. In the case of the above example, doubling the cores would reduce the cable resistance to 6.75 Ω, and therefore the voltage drop would be 250 × 10⁻³ × 6.75 = 1.7 V. This gives 12 − 1.7 = 10.3 V at the camera, which is within its operating voltage range.

It is sometimes stated that the voltage drop for a.c. is 'less than for d.c.', and that this is why a.c. power supplies are better. Well, it is true that a.c. supplies are better because the voltage drop *appears* to be less, yet in fact the 50/60 Hz alternating current is subject to just the same resistance, and hence power loss, as a d.c. current along the same cable. The reasons why voltage drop figures appear to be less for a.c. powered cameras are: (1) the current consumption of the camera is less because of the higher operating voltage (24 V); (2) the 24 V is actually the RMS figure, and the true peak value is 24 × 1.414 = 33.9 V. Summarizing, the voltage drop for a.c. power supplies is less of a problem because the reduction in current causes a reduction in voltage drop, and a voltage drop of, say, 3 V equates to an RMS loss of only 3 × 0.707 = 2.12 V.

12 Commissioning and maintenance

Commissioning

System commissioning is vitally important. This is the point in the installation where every part of the system is tested against the original specifications to ensure that they are met in every way. It is where the system may be proven to be meeting any Operational Requirement (OR) that is in place (in terms of such things as live and recorded image resolution, camera fields of view, zoom capability, ability to perform under differing lighting conditions, etc.). It is where the quality of the installation workmanship is proven. It is where the safety of the system is proven (in particular, does it conform to IEE 16th Edition of the Wiring Regulations – BS7671?). It is where test results are recorded for future reference and, when commissioning is properly carried out, it is where the installation company can hand the system over to the client with confidence.

To begin with, a visual inspection of all parts of the system should be carried out. In particular the connections to fully functional cameras should be checked for freedom of movement and, in the case of external cameras, integrity of weatherproof seals. Also check the position of termination switches and that cables are clearly tagged and identified.

Programming and setting up of equipment should be checked to ensure that the system will meet the requirements of the OR or, where this does not exist, that it will meet the customer's requirements and needs. The inspection should include the programming of multiplexers, matrix switchers, operator levels of authority (restricted access), PTZ limit switches, dome pre-sets, VCR time-lapse mode, alarm input response(s), VMD zones and sensitivity.

The correct operation of all equipment must be confirmed, not forgetting peripheral items such as lights, VCR replay facility, alarm detectors, video printers, bulk erasers, etc.

It should go without saying that the results of all of these tests and inspections are documented and filed for future reference. The installing company should also notify relevant authorities such as the local council (where planning permission was originally required for external equipment installation), police, Inspectorate body, etc.

Measuring resolution

The subject of resolution has been discussed on a number of occasions in this book, but how can this actually be measured in a way that is meaningful to all concerned? Or to put this another way, how can the commissioning engineer actually prove that the system is performing to the design specifications or Operational Requirement? Resolution is affected by many factors, and one cannot make assumptions about the quality of the picture, even when the system has been built using high-specification equipment throughout. Changing lighting and weather conditions can have a dramatic effect on system performance, as can other changes in the environment in which the cameras are operating. For example, in a town centre system when the Christmas illuminations are turned on, the dramatic change in the colour temperature can cause iris settings to alter which in turn may cause changes in the depth of field and focussing, not to mention the fact that some cameras may be blinded almost completely.

Various methods have been devised for testing the picture performance of a system, perhaps the simplest of these being the use of an approved test card. The card is positioned in front of the camera, which is adjusted so that the image fills the entire monitor screen. In this condition each set of markings on the card corresponds to a particular TVL picture resolution, which is normally specified in the instructions that come with the test card. Note that the monitor should be adjusted for best picture before any observations are made.

To test the system performance under site conditions the test card should be held or fixed in front of each camera in turn, and the camera adjusted so that the image of the card fills the monitor screen. The maximum TVL resolution is determined from the smallest set of markings that can be resolved on the displayed card. It is not uncommon for the measured resolution figure to be lower than that quoted for the camera or monitor. This may be due to such factors as lighting conditions, length of cable runs, or the quality of other components in the system. For example, a high quality camera fitted with a poor quality lens will have its performance impaired.

An important point to note from the test procedure described above is that it applies to a situation where a stationary image is filling the height of the screen. But how does this relate to an image of a person filling only, say, 25% of the screen height, and moving at a speed? This is a much more subjective measurement and has been the cause of some debate. In the UK, the Police Scientific Development Branch (PSDB) have carried out research into the issue of image size and picture resolution, and from this research a set of guidelines have been devised. These have been adopted by inspectorate bodies such as NACOSS and the SSAIB.

The PSDB have formulated the following classifications of CCTV system use, these are *Monitoring, Detection, Recognition* and *Identification.*

Monitoring is defined as an image that allows the observer to see the location, speed and direction of a person in the field of view. This will usually be a wide angle view. For monitoring purposes the image of a person will be not less than *5% of the screen height.*

Detection should allow the observer to locate a person with a high degree of certainty having been prompted to do so by a guard, police, alarm system or other means. For detection purposes the image of a person will be not less than *10% of the screen height.*

For *recognition*, the picture quality must be adequate to permit an observer to say with a high degree of certainty that the person on the monitor is the same one they have seen before. In this case the image of a person will be not less than *50% of the screen height.*

Identification is the highest resolution image of a person and must contain sufficient detail to enable the operator to see the person clearly enough to be able to describe them, or to identify them again. Such an image is only possible from a close-up or zoom shot, the disadvantage of this being that you cannot see or record any activity other than that by the person being monitored. For identification purposes the image of a person will be not less than *120% of the screen height.*

These image sizes are illustrated in Figure 12.1. Note that for each classification it has been assumed that all parts of the system are adjusted and functioning correctly, and that the height of the person is 1.6 m. It might also be necessary to test the performance under different lighting conditions.

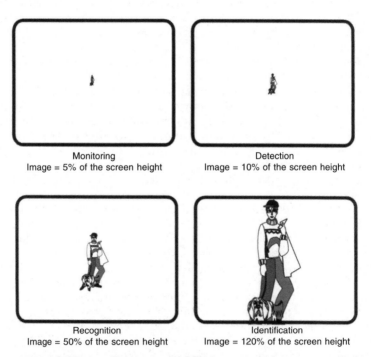

| Monitoring | Detection |
| Image = 5% of the screen height | Image = 10% of the screen height |

| Recognition | Identification |
| Image = 50% of the screen height | Image = 120% of the screen height |

Figure 12.1 *PSDB classifications of CCTV images, with recommended minimum image size for each classification*

From these specified image sizes it is possible to draw up system specifications which include a TVL figure for a given image size. For example, the specification for a certain camera location could be that it will be used for recognition purposes, and that the image must have a resolution of at least 250 TVL. In other words, the image of a person filling 50% of the screen height must have a resolution of 250 TVL. For an engineer to test this during final commissioning using a test card, the camera will be adjusted so that the card fills 50% of the screen height. Under these viewing conditions, the 250 TVL markings on the card should be discernible.

An alternative to using a test card is to employ a test target known as a *Rotakin*, illustrated in Figure 12.2. This target stands 1.6 m tall when fixed to its frame and, in addition to the human head outlines, has a range of markings relating to TVL. The TVL figures for each marking are given in the table accompanying Figure 12.2. Note that these figures apply when the image height of the Rotakin fills the monitor screen. This condition is defined as 100% R.

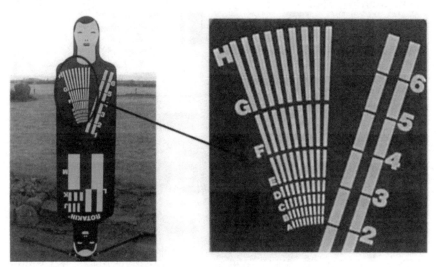

Marking	TVL figure for 100% R
A	500
B	450
C	400
D	350
E	300
F	250
G	200
H	150
J	100
K	80
L	40
M	20

Figure 12.2 *Rotakin standard test target. The higher resolution bars are highlighted in the close-up picture*

Up to this point we are still looking at a stationary, clear target, and we have yet to take into account a camouflaged moving target.

To meet the problem of camouflage the Rotakin comes with a combat style jacket which can be fitted when required. This is particularly useful when testing the system performance for picking out people other than black and white striped ones! In other words, in this mode the Rotakin is no longer being used to determine TVL resolution, but rather the ability of the system to display a useful image under difficult conditions. With the jacket fitted it is also possible to estimate the response time of the operator.

To simulate a moving target the stand on which the Rotakin is mounted has a 12 V motor which rotates the target at a rate of 25 rpm. This provides a representation of a person ' . . . moving quickly but stealthily', to quote the Rotakin manual.

System handover

Handover is one of the most important stages in a CCTV installation, and yet it is too frequently glossed over as something that is only of limited importance. It has been proven that where a well-presented handover has taken place there is much less chance of multiple site re-visits during the first few months of the system going into operation. Such visits are far more likely to occur when the owner/operator has little or no idea of how to operate and maintain the system.

Handover is the point where the engineer becomes a training officer, and as soon as he/she realises this, the whole issue of instructing the customer takes on a new importance. Have you ever attended a manufacturer's training course where the person delivering the training appears covered in dirt, wearing overalls that have been through a few filthy loft spaces, his hair completely unkempt, smelling of sweat and other unsavoury odours, and looking like he really doesn't want to stay to deliver the training because he is just too tired? One would hope not! Yet too often this is what the proud owner of a new, expensive CCTV system (or other security system) is presented with when the moment for handover arrives.

A well-presented handover begins like any other well-presented training session, with planning and preparation. The installer should know in advance when the system will be ready for handover, and should therefore plan ahead. It is important to know how many people will be involved in the use of the system and, where relevant, the level of authority of each of these people. The owner should be made aware of the need to have these people available to attend the handover training. Also let the owner know that the area must be 'controlled' during the handover; that is, interruptions should not occur, and it should be possible to demonstrate the operation of all equipment. For example, there is no point in trying to demonstrate VMD in a department store when it is full of customers. A mutually convenient day and time should be agreed, which may be done verbally, but it is much better if the arrangements are made in writing, therefore covering any 'misunderstandings'. Finally, when the engineer turns up for the handover session, he/she should appear well-presented and looking prepared. Some installing companies insist that before beginning a handover the installer washes, puts on a shirt and tie and generally makes themselves presentable. In the case of larger installations it is more than likely that handover will not take place directly following the fixing of the last cable clip and sweeping of the control room floor area, so the engineer will be travelling to the site, either directly from home or the office, and should do so suitably dressed.

The amount of preparation for handover will of course be governed by the size of the system. The handover of a town centre sized system cannot be compared to that of a two camera, one monitor and one VCR type of installation in a local petrol station. Nevertheless, the same principles can still be applied to both situations.

Before beginning the handover, make sure that all documents are available and correct. These documents should include such things as user manuals, handover agreement, maintenance agreements, contact numbers and addresses, copies of commissioning checklists, etc.

Upon meeting the owner and any other persons involved in the handover, establish by means of questioning how much they know or do not know about CCTV. In the majority of cases people know very little as it is relatively new technology, however where a system has been upgraded it might be that the installer is only required to explain the differences the upgrade may have made to the system operation and capability.

At the start of the handover, walk the owner around the system showing them the location of every item of equipment, making them aware of the area of view of each camera. Demonstrate the operation of the equipment, making sure that the customer regularly handles it for themselves during the handover. In fact, the owner should handle the equipment more than the engineer during this period.

Tape management, as outlined in Chapter 8, should be explained, as should the implications of the Data Protection Act 1998 (applicable in the UK). That is, that the owner of a CCTV system is legally responsible for the security of recorded material, and should any member of the public bring a formal complaint about recorded material being released into the public domain, either intentionally or otherwise, the CCTV system owner might well be brought to court. The days of passing CCTV footage to TV companies for the purposes of entertainment might well be at an end, because any member of the public upon seeing themselves 'starring' in such a programme, or even appearing incidentally, could complain that it is misuse of the system, and that it is in breach of their Human Rights.

In relation to maintenance, instruct the owner in the use of wash/wipe, de-misters, etc., as well as VCR head cleaning cassettes (Chapter 8). Inform them of the need to store tapes away from the magnetic fields which emanate from many items of electrical/electronic equipment. Also, where relevant, point out the health hazard associated with unshielded tape degaussers (bulk erasers); there is the possibility of these units upsetting the operation of heart pacemakers, and people who have one of these fitted should never operate this equipment.

Preventative maintenance

The BSIA Code of Practice for the Planning, Installation and Maintenance of Closed Circuit Television Systems; 109: Issue 2: October 1991 breaks preventative maintenance down into two levels. Level 1, which is basically a full system test, and Level 2 which is a full system test plus an inspection of all equipment associated with the installation.

A Level 1 visit must be made at least every twelve months, the first visit taking place within twelve months of the handover. The engineer should test the operation of every piece of equipment, including each wash/wipe facility, lights, PTZ, etc. The picture quality from each input should be examined, and careful attention paid to loss of quality due to such things as dirt on the housing windows or cobwebs. Also check the picture contrast, colour quality and noise level, noting any possible deterioration and logging it for further investigation.

Compare the system operation against the original OR. Make sure that fields of view are unaltered, housing stop positions are correct, etc. Also make sure that the field of view for each camera has not become obstructed by objects which were not present when the system was installed. For instance, the large tree which was a mere sapling a few years previous, or the new lamp post which the council thought to site directly in front of the camera. Although it is not the job of the engineer to cut down the tree (or dismantle the lamp post!), it is his/her responsibility to inform the owner of the system of environmental changes which mean that the system is no longer able to perform to the OR.

A Level 2 visit, as defined by the BSIA, does not have a fixed frequency, but is to be agreed between the owner and the installing company. On the other hand, the sort of checks that this visit involves should be made at least every two years, if not every year.

During a Level 2 visit, all of the system tests for a Level 1 visit are carried out. In addition, visual inspection of all equipment must be carried out. Camera housings, receiver units and P/T units must be opened and inspected for corroding of electrical terminals, water ingression and any other signs of wear or damage. P/T units should be greased, wiper blades replaced as necessary, heater performance verified, flexible cables checked for damage or wear, etc.

Camera towers or columns should be inspected for signs of damage or corrosion, as should wall mounting brackets. In particular, the fixing points of towers and brackets should be inspected for signs of corrosion, fatigue and loose or missing bolts.

All lighting should be tested, and where the lights are not easily accessible it is suggested that the lamps are replaced as a matter of course whilst access equipment is in place. This is probably more cost effective than having to return in the not-too-distant future to replace a defective lamp.

Any repair or replacement work that cannot be completed at the time of the maintenance visit should be recorded, and arrangements made for the work to be completed at the earliest opportunity. All maintenance work should be recorded and the document signed by both the engineer and the owner, or a representative of the owner. A copy of the record should be left for the owner, and the original returned to the company office where it should be stored in a secure place for future reference.

Where maintenance or servicing involves the temporary disconnection of equipment which will leave a part of the system inoperative, a temporary disconnection notice should be completed and signed by both the engineer and the owner, or other responsible person.

With particular reference to VCRs, as discussed in Chapter 8, because of the wear and tear on the mechanism in a time-lapse machine, a full service should be carried out every twelve months. This will involve the removal of the machine from the site for a period of time, and it may be necessary to install a machine on temporary loan. In this case the engineer must compare the features of the loan machine with the one that it is replacing, ensuring that either (a) the machine is capable of offering all of the features needed to maintain the system performance, or (b) the customer is made aware of any VCR operations that are not available.

At all times the engineer must be careful not to degrade the performance of any part of the system by replacing defective components with parts of a lower specification or parts that are incompatible. For example, if a camera is found to be defective, the replacement should be a model that is of equal if not better specification. Similarly, if the hard disk in a digital recording system fails, replacing it with a lower capacity unit will have a serious impact on the recording and archive period.

Corrective maintenance

Just as it is necessary to create accurate and legible preventative maintenance records, the same applies to any corrective work that is carried out on the system, either during routine visits, or in response to a breakdown call.

Copies of all corrective maintenance documents must be stored in a secure place in the system file at the company office. On the one hand this protects the company in the case of any redress from the owner, who may in the future find reason to accuse the company of failing to carry out certain work. On the other hand the information in these records can prove helpful in the event of future problems with the system.

Fault location

This subject has to a large extent already been dealt with, having considered the fault diagnosis and repair techniques pertinent to the equipment under discussion in each chapter. However, we will now look at fault diagnosis from a *system* point of view.

A *logical approach* to fault diagnosis is essential if servicing is to be both sound and cost effective. But what is logical fault diagnosis? Well, perhaps it is easier to begin by stating what it isn't; all too often engineers when faced with a problem fall into a state of panic and, throwing all theory knowledge aside, resort to replacing items of equipment at random until at last the problem goes away. Having personally observed both CCTV and intruder alarm trainees in this 'state', it has been interesting to note that in many cases not only is the theory thrown aside, but the test equipment remains safely stored in (unopened) cases. In some instances trainees have been seen to pull out and replace a complete cable run just to see if it is the cause of a problem, before having applied any form of test meter to the cable. This is *not* a logical approach to fault diagnosis!

To locate a fault efficiently, an engineer would usually begin by giving careful consideration to the fault symptom(s). Television can be a very informative piece of equipment in this respect because each symptom displayed on the screen very often points to the fault area, as long as the engineer can recognize the symptoms. From the fault symptom, the engineer should be able to deduce which parts of the system may be responsible, and which parts can be ruled out.

The next step in logical fault diagnosis very often is to fall back onto experience. Here the engineer's mind is working somewhat like a computer database, searching though archive files for any previous experiences of the same symptoms on identical equipment. This does not mean to say that the cause of the trouble will definitely turn out to be the same, but where the engineer is aware of a common problem in a certain item, or combination of equipment, it makes sense to begin by testing in this area.

Where experience alone does not produce a rapid diagnosis, the engineer must change gear and begin to search his/her mental 'database' for the appropriate CCTV and/or electronics theory. The skill and ability of an engineer can usually be determined from how well they can do this because, as much as it is unsatisfactory to throw the theory aside, it can be equally unhelpful to pull down so much theory that the engineer becomes totally confused. Having the ability to apply the correct theory at just the right moment is a skill in itself.

It is one thing to have the knowledge, yet this may not be a lot of use unless one has access to the test equipment to enable voltage and waveform measurements to be taken. A calibrated, quality multimeter is the bare minimum that an engineer should carry. With this the engineer can verify the presence and value of a.c. and d.c. voltages and currents, as well as test for open circuit, short circuit and resistance faults. *Remember that when measuring mains voltage potentials, only approved shrouded and fused test leads must be used.*

For testing co-axial cables the multimeter resistance ranges are of limited use, and therefore a *time domain reflectometer* is another very useful piece of test equipment for the service engineer, and can very quickly pay for its self by saving a lot of time and effort in trying to locate a fault along a length of co-axial cable. The TDR was discussed in Chapter 2 (Figure 2.25).

Because we are dealing with video signals it has to go without saying that the best way of testing the condition and level of these signals is to display them on an oscilloscope. And yet the CCTV industry is proving very reluctant to move in this direction for fault location. There are a number of reasons for this. First of all it is fair to say that lugging a scope around a site (possibly in the rain) is not the best thing for either the engineer or the scope. Secondly, a scope suitable for CCTV use will cost at least £400 brand new, and thus it is not viable to provide every engineer in a company of any size with such an item. But there is a third reason for not using oscilloscopes, and this is that many engineers are afraid of them and simply don't know how to operate one. This third reason is not a valid one for ignoring the value of an oscilloscope in locating certain difficult types of fault.

The truth is that the CCTV engineer does not have to be an expert at operating an oscilloscope, because he/she is not trying to display a wide range of signals. In practice the engineer usually wishes to display the same type of signal every time, this being one or two lines of a 1V pp CCIR television signal. Therefore, once the scope has been set to display this signal, it will never require anything more than possibly minor fine adjustment each time it is used for this purpose. Later in this chapter we shall look at some default settings for using an oscilloscope for CCTV applications.

It is often helpful to know the condition of a video signal, but because the scope is such an item to unpack from the vehicle, set up and find a suitable mains supply for, resorting to its use is often a last resort. To overcome this problem, a number of hand-held video signal level indicators have been developed. Compared to an oscilloscope these are far less expensive, cumbersome and delicate and are a worthwhile addition to any service engineer's test kit. An example of such an indicator was illustrated in Chapter 2 (Figure 2.24). This version comes with its own signal generator, which brings us to our next point.

Scoping or measuring video signals from cameras is not the best way of testing for some faults, and the engineer sometimes needs to know for sure that the signal being injected into a cable or item of equipment is a CCIR standard video signal. To this end, a small portable video signal generator is very useful for fault finding in CCTV systems. The simplest of these put out a black and white bar signal, whilst more sophisticated versions produce a selection of coloured and black and white patterns, perhaps the most useful of which is the standard colour bar display, or staircase when viewed on an oscilloscope.

Oscilloscope default settings

One TV line has a time duration of 64μs, and a peak-to-peak voltage of approximately 1 V (when terminated into 75 Ω). To display this waveform on an oscilloscope *the volts/div control must be set to around 0.2 V*, and *the timebase speed adjusted for around 10 μs/div*. If the signal level is correct, then a stable trace should be obtained with *the trigger control set to the 'Auto' or 'Normal' position*. These are the default settings, and once a scope has been adjusted to display a stable video signal waveform, if the controls are left in this position, then a stable trace should be displayed immediately a video signal is applied to the input.

The expected display for these settings when a grey scale video input is applied is illustrated in Figure 12.3.

Oscilloscopes differ between models and some offer features that the CCTV engineer will never use – these features result in a lot more controls on the front, making them more difficult to set up. (They are actually no more difficult to set, but the additional controls gives more opportunity for the unwary operator to become confused.) When choosing an oscilloscope for CCTV use, a basic dual beam model *with a minimum bandwidth of 20 MHz* is an ideal choice. The bandwidth of an oscilloscope is important as, among other things, it determines the triggering ability. Anything below 20 MHz will struggle to display a stable video waveform, and models with a bandwidth between 30–40 MHz are generally a good compromise between quality and price (for CCTV applications).

For those who do not regularly use an oscilloscope, the following procedure should produce a stable, single beam display on the majority of models (refer to Figure 12.3).

1. Switch on.
2. Adjust INTENSITY (brightness) control to mid position.
3. Set TRIGGER LEVEL control to AUTO (NORMAL) position.
4. Adjust X and Y POSITION controls for centre position.
5. Set channel 1 Y GAIN/AMPLITUDE control to the 0.2 V position (or nearest value on your scope).
6. Set Timebase control to 10μs/div.
7. Set TRIGGER SELECT switch to CH1 position.
8. Set trigger switches to a.c. and + positions.
9. Set INPUT COUPLING switches on channels 1 and 2 to a.c. position.
10. Connect scope to the equipment under test.
11. Adjust FOCUS and INTENSITY controls for best definition.

Provided that the signal under test is good, then a stable display should be obtained. If the display is jittering or moving horizontally across the screen, try adjusting the trigger control, perhaps switching it to the MANUAL position. If in doubt as to whether or not the scope is set correctly, try applying a known good video signal rather than the one under test. A correct display will confirm both that the scope is set up correctly, and that the signal under test is indeed incorrect.

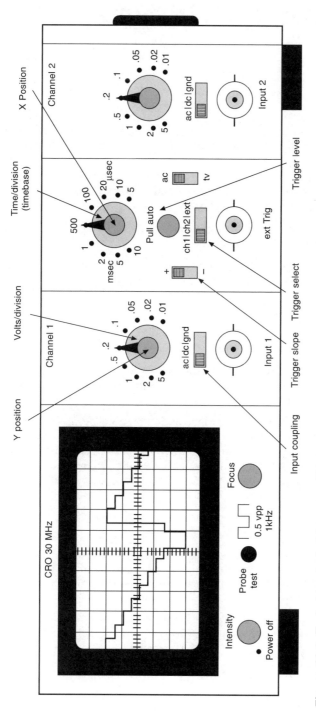

Figure 12.3 *Typical basic dual beam oscilloscope*

Glossary of CCTV terms

Some of the terms listed in this glossary may have more than one meaning, depending on the context in which each one is taken. Where this is the case, the definitions given here relate to closed circuit television.

Alarm activation A piece of equipment that is made to change its mode of operation by the activation of an alarm input. Typically a VCR, multiplexer or matrix switcher.

Algorithm A mathematical term used to describe a procedure for resolving a problem.

Amplitude Modulation (AM) A transmission method where the signal to be sent is added to a much higher frequency carrier signal in such a way that the carrier amplitude is made to change in sympathy with the wanted signal. Used to transmit audio and video signals. Also used in magnetic video tape recording.

Analogue A signal that is represented by changes in voltage level.

Aperture The size of the hole produced by the iris. The size of the aperture determines the amount of light that will fall onto the pick-up device.

Artefact In relation to digitized video signals, an artefact is any visible component in the picture display which is not a part of the original. This is rather like 'noise' in analogue displays, however where large amounts of compression of the video signal have taken place, many artefacts may appear as a result of both losses and incorrect attempts by the de-compression circuits to 'guess' at the picture content.

Aspect ratio The ratio of the horizontal and vertical monitor screen dimensions. For CCTV this is 4:3.

Aspherical lens A non-spherical lens that produces much less optical distortion than a conventional lens and, because of the way that the light travels through the glass, offers a higher light output for the same aperture setting.

Attenuation Term used to describe a reduction in signal amplitude as it passes through a system or medium.

Automatic Gain Control (AGC) Amplifier circuit that automatically changes its gain as the input signal level varies to maintain a constant output signal level.

Automatic Iris (AI)   Iris that is controlled by the signal level in the camera. Changes in light input level result in changes in signal amplitude which are in turn used to adjust the iris to compensate.

Automatic Level Control (ALC)   A circuit that maintains a constant output signal level despite large changes in input signal level (see also **AGC**). In CCTV such a circuit may be used to control the lens iris.

Back focus   Mechanical adjustment of the position of the image device in a camera. Used to set the distance between the back of the lens and the pick-up to 12.5 mm for a CS mount lens, or 17.5 mm for a C mount lens.

Back Light Compensation (BLC)   Feature in a camera that causes the iris circuit to ignore the bright areas of the image and to open up sufficiently to allow the darker areas to be visible – albeit at the expense of the light areas.

Back porch   Period lasting 5.9 µs following each horizontal sync pulse. It is at black level to ensure that the electron beam in the CRT is cut off for the duration of the line flyback period.

Balanced cable   A two wire method of signal transmission where the signal phases are such that unwanted interference signals are cancelled out at the receiving end.

Bandwidth A term that is used to define the range of frequencies between the upper and lower cut-off points of a transmission system (measured at the –3 dB points). In CCTV there is a direct relationship between bandwidth and picture resolution.

Baud   Unit of measuring the data rate in a digital system, usually in bits per second (bps).

BIT   Derived from the term B*inary* dig*IT*. This is a single piece of data at either logic 0 or logic 1.

Black level   In a video waveform, this refers to the voltage level that produces black level on the CRT or other display device. For a CCIR standard signal this is 0.3 V.

Blanking period   Times during both the horizontal and vertical scanning periods when the electron beam in the CRT is returning ('flying back') to the position for the next start of scan. During these periods the video signal waveform is held at the black level (0.3 V) to ensure that nothing is displayed on the screen. For a UK PAL transmission, the line or horizontal blanking period is 12 µs and the field or vertical blanking period is approximately 1 ms.

BNC   Co-axial cable connector commonly employed in CCTV installations. The term 'BNC' is derived from 'Bayonet–Neil–Concelman'.

Byte   Term used to define a group of 8 bits (binary digits) in a digital system. The term was derived because the earliest computers used only

8-bit words for communication, whereas modern processors commonly communicate using 32-bit words.

Cable equalizing   Equipment added to a co-axial cable transmission system for the sole purpose of correcting for high frequency losses in the cable.

Candela   The unit of luminous intensity. One candela is the amount of light that is radiated in all directions from a black body that has been heated to a temperature equal to that at which platinum changes from a solid to a liquid state.

CCD (Charge Coupled Device)   A solid-state device that is capable of storing small electrical charges. Originally intended for use as a digital store for computing applications, it has been adapted to store the output voltages from the photo diodes in a camera pick-up prior to them being passed on to the signal processing stages.

CCIR (Committée Consultatif Internationale des Radiocommuni-cationale)   The English translation means 'Consultative Committee for International Radio'. This is the European body that has been responsible for the setting of Standards for television systems in Europe.

CCTV (Closed Circuit Television)   A television system that is not broadcast to air and therefore its images can only be accessed by persons with a connection to that system.

Characteristic impedance   The impedance of a cable. This is a function of the inductive, capacitive and d.c. resistive properties of a cable and is usually quoted assuming a (theoretical) cable of infinite length. For CCTV applications, co-axial cable must have a characteristic impedance of 75Ω.

Charge   An accumulation of electrons in a device or area. Electrical charge is measured in coulombs and is equal to an accumulation of 6.289 $\times\ 10^{18}$ electrons.

Chroma burst   A sample of the colour subcarrier signal. It is transmitted during the back porch period and comprises of 10 cycles of the 4.43 MHz subcarrier for a PAL transmission, or up to 10 cycles of the 3.58 MHz subcarrier for NTSC transmissions. The burst signal serves as a form of sync signal for the colour decoding circuits in a television, monitor or VCR.

Chrominance   Term used to define the colour signal components in a television transmission.

C mount   Common screw thread developed for lenses used by the ciné industry but adopted by the CCTV industry. A C mount lens has a distance of 17.5 mm between the image device and the back of the lens.

Co-axial cable   An unbalanced cable comprising of a core surrounded by a braided or solid screen. The two conductors are separated by an insulating material that is designed to act as a capacitive dielectric. The total inductive, capacitive and d.c. resistive properties of the cable produce an opposition to a.c. currents that is known as the characteristic impedance. For CCTV applications, co-axial cable must have a characteristic impedance of 75 Ω.

Colour temperature   The type of light produced by a source. It is a scientific measure of the wavelengths of light, stated in degrees Kelvin (K).

Composite sync   A signal that contains both the horizontal and vertical sync pulses but no video signal components.

Composite video   Signal containing the luminance, chrominance, sync and colour burst components.

Compression   With respect to digitized video signals, this refers to the removal of binary data containing information relating to the signal that is considered, for one reason or another, to be redundant. Compression is required to overcome the need for the large amounts of digital storage capacity associated with digitized video signals.

CS mount   The most common lens mounting type used in CCTV. It has a distance of 12.5 mm between the image device and the back of the lens. A CS mount lens cannot be used with a C mount camera.

Dark current   Thermally induced currents in a camera pick-up device which produce an apparent signal output even in a total absence of incident light.

Data cable   Cable used for the transmission of digital signals. Typically twisted pair but may be co-axial.

dB (decibel)   Logarithmic unit used to define the ratio between two signal amplitudes. A change of 3 dB represents a doubling or halving of electrical power; a change of 6 dB represents a halving or doubling of electrical voltage.

Depth of field   The range (in distance) in front of the lens where objects remain in focus. This decreases when either the focal length or the aperture size is increased (F-number decreased).

Digital signal   A voltage signal used to represent the binary values of 0 and 1.

Direct drive (DD)   Term used to describe a CCTV camera lens having an electro-mechanical iris that is controlled via a changing d.c. voltage derived in the camera.

Distribution amplifier   A device containing a single input and a number of amplifiers which provide separate (isolated) outputs. Used for sending a single video signal to a number of pieces of equipment without affecting the 1 V pp level.

DOS (Disk Operating System)   Software used by the majority of computers to enable communications between the CPU and hardware devices such as hard disk, printer, etc.

Duplex   When used with respect to CCTV multiplexers (MUX), this term refers to a unit that is able to offer simultaneous recording and replay (note that for analogue systems, two VCRs must be available).

EI (Electronic Iris)   A circuit in a CCTV camera that varies the amount of time that the pick-up device is active during any field period. The 'exposure' time is reduced as the light input increases, thus emulating the action of a mechanical iris. This feature enhances the performance of a camera that has a fixed iris lens fitted.

EIA (Electronics Industry Association)   The body that has been responsible for the setting of Standards for television systems in the USA, Canada and Japan. Namely, the NTSC 525 line system.

Electromagnetic radiation   Electric field with an associated magnetic field travelling through free space at the speed of light in the form of waves. A wide range of frequencies, known as the electromagnetic spectrum, exist. Some of these are used for the purposes of radio signal transmission, others produce the visible light spectrum, whilst others are harmful to humans (e.g. X-rays, Y-rays and Gamma rays).

Electron beam   Stream of electrons emitted from the cathode of a cathode ray tube (CRT).

EMI (Electromagnetic Interference)   Electromagnetic signals that enter a system or item of equipment and corrupt the wanted signals. EMI may be naturally occurring (e.g. lighting, solar flares, static electric charge), or man-made (e.g. radio transmissions, electric motors, electrical switch gear).

Fast scan   A technique for transmitting CCTV signals digitally over the ISDN telephone network.

fc (foot candle)   Unit of light measurement, used primarily in North America. 1 foot candle (1 fc) is approximately equal to 10 lux.

Fibre-optic transmission   Signal transmission method that uses light pulses passing through a thin length of optically clear material. Capable of low-loss transmission over long distances and is impervious to the effects of RFI and EMI.

Field   This contains one half of the video information in a television frame. The CCIR Standard has 50 fields per second, each field containing $312^{1}/_{2}$ lines. The EIA Standard has 60 fields per second, each field containing 262.5 lines

Field of view   The area that may be viewed through a lens. It is determined by the relationship between the angle of view and the distance between the object and the lens.

FIT (Field Interline Transfer) chip   CCD image device that combines the technologies of the Interline Transfer and Frame Transfer chips, offering improved S/N ratio, low smear and good low light sensitivity.

FM (frequency modulation) A transmission method where the signal to be sent is added to a much higher frequency carrier signal in such a way that the carrier frequency is made to change in sympathy with the wanted signal amplitude. Used to transmit audio signals. Also used in magnetic video tape recording.

F-number Figure used to denote the size of aperture in a lens. It is determined by the ratio of the focal length to the effective diameter of the lens/iris aperture. A small F-number indicates a large aperture and a high light throughput.

Focal length The distance, measured in millimetres, from the secondary principal point in the lens to the final focal point (at the image device). A short focal length produces a wide angle of view.

Format With respect to CCTV lenses and cameras, this describes the size of the active area of the pick-up device, typically $^2/_3''$, $^1/_2''$, $^1/_3''$, or $^1/_4''$.

Frame One complete television picture made up from 625 (525 NTSC) line of information over two interlaced fields. The frame rate is 25 (30 NTSC) per second.

Frame store Commonly a digital memory device capable of storing the data relating to one complete digitized television frame.

Frequency Measurement of the number of times in one second that a cycle repeats itself. The unit of measurement is Hertz (Hz) or, in the USA, cycles.

Front porch Period lasting 1.4 µs prior to each horizontal sync pulse. It is at black level to ensure that the electron beam in the CRT is cut off for the duration of the line flyback period.

F-stop Aperture setting on a camera lens. Each stop position represents a doubling or halving of light throughput.

Galvanometer A device that can convert electrical energy into mechanical energy without the mechanical complexity of a d.c. motor. Used to control the iris veins in a DD lens.

Gamma correction Modification to the shape of a luminance signal in a camera made in order to correct for non-linearity in a CRT phosphor response. In many CCTV cameras this is adjustable to compensate for differing monitors or lighting conditions.

Gen lock Means of maintaining sync between cameras in a CCTV system. A master sync signal is taken from either one camera or from a master generator and is fed to the 'Gen Lock' input on each camera.

Ground loop transformer A 1:1 transformer capable of passing video signal frequencies. Placed in series with a co-axial cable to break the direct earth connection between camera and monitor formed by the cable screen.

Ground loop   Circulating earth current formed by the screen on a co-axial cable. Such currents can cause rolling shadows on the picture (known as a hum bar), poor synchronization, horizontal tearing of the picture, or loss of telemetry functions.

Hard disk   Data storage device employed in all computers. Uses a solid metal disk onto which data is stored using magnetic recording principles.

Hertz (Hz)   Cycles per second. The unit by which frequency is measured.

Hue   This term refers to the frequency of a light source, e.g. red, green blue, etc.

Hum bar   See **Ground loop**.

Illuminance   Measurement of light in lumens per square metre. The unit of measurement is the lux.

Illumination   Measurement of light coming from a secondary surface or source. The unit of measurement is the lux.

Imaging device   Device that is able to convert light energy into electrical energy. In modern CCTV cameras this will be a charge coupled device (**CCD**) chip.

Impedance (Z)   The opposition to current flow in an a.c. circuit, measured in ohms. It is the combined effect of the d.c. resistance and the inductive and/or capacitive reactances.

Infra-red cut filter   A filter that blocks the passage of infra-red light frequencies. Such filters are used in colour CCTV cameras to prevent the ingress of IR light that would otherwise result in incorrect colour signal production.

Infra-red (IR) light   Frequencies of light that are just below those of visible light (wavelengths between 700 nm to 10 mm). All CCD image chips are sensitive to these frequencies and in many cases this can be used to an advantage.

Infra-red pass filter   A filter that only allows infra-red light frequencies to pass through. Such filters are placed in front of white light sources in the manufacture of IR lighting units. Typical wavelengths for CCTV lighting units are 715 nm and 850 nm.

Infra-red spectrum   See **Infra-red (IR) light**.

IRE (Institute of Radio Engineers (of America))   A unit of measurement for a 1 V pp video signal. It divides the signal between sync tip and peak white into 140 equal levels. For example, 140 IRE = 1 V pp video signal, the 0.3 V sync pulse level would be 42 IRE, etc.

Interlaced scanning   Method of producing a television picture by scanning each frame in two parts; first the odd television lines and then the even lines. Used to reduce picture flicker in CRT display units.

Interline transfer chip Type of CCD image chip where the storage areas are adjacent to the photodiodes. This technique eliminates the vertical smearing problems associated with frame transfer chips, but the chip is less sensitive in terms of light input/signal output.

Internal sync Horizontal and vertical synchronizing pulses that are produced by the camera internally.

IP rating The Index of Protection rating for an enclosure; e.g. IP65. The first digit indicates the level of protection against ingression by solids, the second digit indicates the level of protection against ingression by liquids.

Iris Mechanism in a camera that governs the amount of light input.

ISDN (Integrated Services Digital Network) A high-speed telephone transmission system for digital signals. 64kB and 128kB speeds are available.

Kell factor Figure used when deriving the horizontal resolution for a television picture.

LAN (Local Area Network) Term used to describe a data communications network within a defined area, usually a single site.

LED (Light Emitting Diode) Gallium arsenide diode that emits light when a current passes through its PN junction.

Lens In CCTV, this term usually refers to a lens assembly which is an array of lenses with an iris mechanism. Its function is to gather light and focus it onto the pick-up device.

Light meter Hand-held measuring device comprising of a photo pick-up and a meter. The meter is calibrated to display the light level in units of lux.

Line fed The camera power is supplied via the co-axial video signal cable.

Line locked Synchronization pulses produced by each camera and are referenced to the a.c. mains frequency.

Luminance (Y) Monochrome or black and white content of a video signal.

Lux Unit of measurement of light.

Matrix switcher Equipment used to switch a number of cameras between one or more monitors.

Microwave transmission For CCTV, this is a video signal transmission method using microwave radio signalling, usually in the 3GHz to 10GHz band. Greater range than infra-red signal transmission.

Modal distortion   Signal distortion in fibre-optic cable caused by a multiple of light paths through the cable.

Modem   Term derived from its function, which is a *mod*ulator/*dem*odulator. Used to interface equipment having a digital output, and a conventional analogue telephone line.

Monochrome   A black and white television signal or system.

Multimode   Fibre-optic cable where the light is made to 'bounce' from side to side as it travels along. This cable type introduces modal distortion, however it is much less expensive than mono mode cable, where the light travels in a direct line along the cable length.

Multiplexing   Signal transmission method where two signals are transmitted on the same cable or carrier in such a way that they can be separated at the receiving end. The term also refers to equipment capable of processing video signals such that more than one image can be displayed on a screen, or recorded simultaneously (see **MUX**).

MUX   Abbreviation for a video multiplexer. A unit that processes video signals such that more than one image can be displayed on a screen, or recorded simultaneously.

NTSC (National Television Standards Committee)   Committee that set the colour television system standards for North America and Japan.

ND (Neutral Density) filter   A lens filter that affects all frequencies of light in the visible spectrum by the same amount, therefore causing an overall reduction in the light level entering the lens. It is used to simulate low light conditions, forcing the iris to open and giving the best conditions for lens focus adjustment.

ND spot filter   A graduated filter at the centre of a lens. It has minimal effect when the iris is wide open, however its effect increases as the iris closes. This type of filter prevents the aperture from becoming too small to control effectively under bright light conditions.

Noise   Electrical interference on the video signal. Usually manifest as grain (speckles) over the picture.

Optical fibre   A transparent material along which light can be transmitted.

Oscilloscope   Displays electronic signals in a graphical form, enabling them to be measured and analysed.

Overscan   The monitor display is adjusted such that the electron beam scans farther than the edges of the screen, resulting in a loss of some picture information around the edges.

PAL (Phase Alternate Line)   The most common system for the transmission of analogue colour television signals. The system maintains correct colour reproduction by cancelling out the effects of signal phase errors that occur during transmission.

Patchcord   A short length of flexible fibre-optic cable with a connector fitted to each end. Used to reconfigure a route between two pieces of equipment.

PSTN (Public Switched Telephone Network)   In the UK, the original low bandwidth telephone network provided by the Post Office and later British Telecom. Intended only for speech transmission, it is now used for the transmission of digital signals, however its low bandwidth makes it of little use for CCTV applications.

PCM (Pulse Code Modulation)   Signal modulation method whereby the width of a continuous stream of square wave pulses is made to change in sympathy with the modulating signal.

Photo diode   A diode in which the forward bias current is determined not only by the applied voltage but also by the light falling upon the PN junction.

Photo cell   A device in which its electrical resistance is determined by the light falling upon it.

PING command   Computer command executed in DOS. Used to confirm that an IP addressable item of equipment is connected to, and communicating with, the IT network.

Pixel   Term derived from *PIC*ture *El*ements. A pixel is a single element of picture information – the greater the number of pixels, the greater the picture resolution.

Primary colours   The three colours (frequencies) of light – red, green and blue – that are perceived by the human eye and are integrated by the brain to derive all the colours of the visible light spectrum.

Pulse and bar generator   An item of test equipment that produces a continuous black, white and grey video test signal.

Quad   Abbreviation for a unit that enables four camera signals to be displayed simultaneously on a monitor.

Raster   The blank white screen that results from the scanning action of the electron beam in a CRT before video information is applied.

Reflectance   A figure which represents the ratio of light falling onto and returning from a surface, expressed as a percentage.

Reflected light   Area illumination multiplied by reflectance.

Refraction   Effect on a ray of light whereby as it passes through different media its velocity alters, causing it to bend.

Resolution   In relation to the definition of a television picture, this is a measure of the smallest detail that may be discerned. The most common unit of measurement is TVL (television lines).

RS port   RS = Recommended Standard. Standard input/output connectors used for data communications. Common standards are RS232, RS422 and RS 485.

S/N (signal-to-noise) ratio   Measurement of the amount of noise in a signal, expressed in decibels (dB). For video signals, any figure less than 40 dB will result in unacceptable amounts of noise (grain) in the picture.

Scanning   Rapid horizontal and vertical deflection of the electron beam in a CRT to produce a light output from the entire screen area (see **raster**).

Scan coils   Inductive coils placed around the neck of a CRT. Currents passing through these coils produce electromagnetic fields which interact with the electron beam, causing it to deflect both vertically and horizontally.

SECAM   Sequential Couleur Avec Memoire (sequential colour with memory). Colour television broadcast system developed and used in France. It is not directly compatible with either PAL or NTSC systems.

Simplex   When used with respect to CCTV multiplexers (MUX), this term refers to a unit that can record or replay images, but not at the same time (unlike Duplex units).

Silicon intensified target (SIT)   Type of camera pick-up device developed for use in very low light conditions.

Slow scan   An early video signal transmission system that used the conventional PSTN telephone network. It employed analogue transmission and had a very slow refresh rate.

S-VHS (Super-Video Home System)   Analogue video recording format based on VHS, but offering much higher picture resolution (400 TVL as opposed to the 240 TVL for VHS). S-VHS recordings will not replay on conventional VHS machines.

Synchronizing pulses   Pulses added (at the camera) to the video signal. Used by the monitor to maintain correct scanning correlation between the camera and the monitor.

Telemetry   Signalling system used to control functions at a camera head such as pan, tilt, zoom, wash, etc. May be analogue, but is now more commonly a digital system that employs decoders (site drivers) at each camera installation.

Telephoto lens   Correct term for a zoom lens. These lenses have a long focal length giving them a high magnification but a narrow angle (field) of view.

Termination   With respect to CCTV, this term is frequently used to describe the 75 Ω termination impedance required at each end of a co-axial cable. Modern equipment employs automatic termination methods that detect the presence of a BNC connector at the socket, however for many years a termination switch would be found close to the video output socket on monitors or other signal processing equipment.

Timebase Corrector (TBC) An item of equipment that is used to align the timing of the sync pulses from all cameras in a system, thus preventing picture roll during camera switching. In most cases the TBC is incorporated inside the MUX.

Time-lapse VCR A video recorder (commonly S-VHS) that is capable of recording for very long periods on a standard 3-hour cassette by operating a continuous record/pause action.

Transducer Any device that converts one form of energy into another. For example, a CCD chip converts light energy into electrical energy, whereas, a CRT will do the opposite.

Triplex When used with respect to CCTV multiplexers (MUX), this term refers to a unit that is able to offer simultaneous live monitoring, recording and replay (note that for analogue systems, two VCRs must be available).

Twisted pair Type of cable having two wires that are twisted together, producing a balanced effect whereby electrical interference signals are cancelled out. Capable of much greater transmission distances than co-axial cable types. In some cases the cable may have an outer screen.

Underscan Switchable feature on a monitor that enables the entire picture to be seen.

Unshielded Twisted Pair (UTP) Twisted pair cable type having no outer screen (see **twisted pair**).

VHS (Video Home System) Analogue video recording format developed for the domestic market and later adapted for CCTV applications in the form of time-lapse recorders. It is a low-resolution format – 240 TVL for colour and 300 TVL for monochrome recordings.

Video Motion Detection (VMD) An alarm detection facility whereby the picture content from a camera is analysed to look for evidence of change (movement). Originally analogue, modern equipment employs digital analysis techniques.

Vacuum Tube Device such as a CRT, fluorescent display or camera pick-up tube. Uses thermionic electron emission to produce a current flow between a heated cathode and an anode.

Varifocal Lens having a manually adjustable focal length, giving a degree of choice over the field of view.

Vertical streaking Bright vertical lines produced in some types of CCD chip under certain conditions.

Video launch amplifier Amplifier used to correct for signal losses in exceptionally long lengths of cable. Can be tuned to give greater compensation at higher frequencies where the cable losses are most acute.

Video line corrector Equipment used to correct for uneven frequency losses in long cable runs. Similar in action to a video launch amplifier, however it may not have such a high gain.

Video signal See **composite video**.

Wavelet (compression) Method of compressing a digitized video signal in order to reduce the amount of data (file size) needed to restore each picture frame. Uses a mathematical algorithm known as wavelet transform.

Wavelength Measurement (in metres) of the propagation distance of one cycle of an electromagnetic wave. It is taken between any two adjacent points in a waveshape. Relates directly to the signal frequency.

White level Voltage level in a video signal that produces peak white. For a CCIR signal this is 1 V (0.7 V above the black level).

Y/C Term used to describe the separate luminance (Y) and chrominance (C) signals. An S-VHS signal connector uses Y/C signal transmission where the Y and C are passed along separate screened cores within the cable. This results in improved picture quality because the two signals are unable to interfere with each other.

Zoom lens See **telephoto lens**.

Index